ESSAYS ON THE POLITICAL ECONOMY
OF RURAL AFRICA

**California Series on
Social Choice and Political Economy**

Edited by Brian Barry, Robert H. Bates, and Samuel L. Popkin

ESSAYS ON THE POLITICAL ECONOMY OF RURAL AFRICA

ROBERT H. BATES

California Institute of Technology

UNIVERSITY OF CALIFORNIA PRESS

BERKELEY   LOS ANGELES   LONDON

University of California Press
Berkeley and Los Angeles

University of California Press, Ltd.
London, England

© Cambridge University Press 1983
First published 1983 by Cambridge University Press.
First paperback edition published 1987 by the University of
California Press.
Reprinted by permission of Cambridge University Press.

Library of Congress Cataloging-in-Publication Data
Bates, Robert H.
   Essays on the political economy of rural Africa.
   (California series on social choice and political
economy)
   Reprint. Originally published: Cambridge
[Cambridgeshire] ; New York : Cambridge University
Press, 1983. (African studies series ; no. 38)
With new pref.
   Bibliography: p.
   Includes index.
   1. Agriculture—Economic aspects—Africa.
2. Agriculture and state—Africa.   3. Peasantry—
Africa.   4. Africa—Economic conditions.
5. Africa—Rural conditions.   I. Title.   II. Series.
HD2117.B37   1987   330.96′0328′091734   86-25120
ISBN 0-520-06014-8 (pbk. : alk. paper)

Printed in the United States of America
1 2 3 4 5 6 7 8 9

Contents

To the Memory of Mary Dexter Bates

Acknowledgements

The chapters of this book represent the fruits of a project funded by the National Science Foundation (Grant No. Soc. 77-08573). I wish to thank the Foundation and the Division of Social Sciences of the California Institute of Technology for supporting this work.

I was ably assisted by the staff of the Millikan Library and the Munger Africana Library of the California Institute of Technology. Jill Irby typed and retyped drafts of this manuscript with skill and good humour; she kept the project – and the author – on course despite numerous disruptions. Kenneth McCue, Mariam Eichwold, and Leslie Madden provided research assistance.

Numerous people have read and criticized the papers that form this study. They include Thayer Scudder, Elizabeth Colson, Samuel Popkin, David Laitin, Gordon Tullock, Marc Ross, Charles Plott, John Ferejohn, Gary Miller, Bruce Cain, Gordon Appleby, Roger Noll, Gary Cox, Joshua Foreman, Richard Sklar, Michael Lofchie, Lance Davis, Douglass North, Philip Hoffman, Ronald Cohen, Eleanor Searle, George Dalton, William O. Jones, Bruce Johnston, Raymond Hopkins, David Grether, David Brokensha, Bernard Riley, Vernon Ruttan, Robert Keohane, David Abernethy, Barry Ames, Brian Barry, Carl Eicher, Elon Gilbert, Yujiro Hayami, Frances Hill, Goran Hyden, Marvin Miracle, Joe Oppenheimer, James Scott, Alan Sweezy, Judith Tendler, Stanley Greenburg, Margaret Levi, Ivor Wilks, Sara Berry, and several anonymous referees. I also wish to thank the editors of the African Studies Series of Cambridge University Press, and especially John Dunn, for their criticism and support. With so much assistance, the faults that remain are mine alone.

I wish to thank as well Naomi Schneider at the University of California Press for promoting the publication of a paperback edition of this work and to acknowledge the cooperation of Cambridge University Press, which had published the original, hardcover edition.

The Publisher acknowledges with thanks permission to reprint the following chapters: Chapter 1 from 'The Preservation of Order in Stateless Societies: A Reinterpretation of Evans-Pritchard's *The Nuer*' in *Frontiers of Economics, 1979* edited by Gordon Tullock (Center for Study of Public Choice, Virginia Polytechnic and State University, 1979); Chapter 3 from 'Pressure Groups, Public Policy and Agricultural Development' in *Agricultural Development in Africa: Issues of Public Policy* edited by Robert H. Bates and Michael F. Lofchie (© Praeger Publishers CBS Educational and Professional Publishing, a Division of CBS, Inc., 1980); Chapter 4 from 'The Commercialization of Agriculture and the Rise of Rural Protest in Black Africa' in *Food, Politics and Agricultural Development* edited by Raymond F. Hopkins, Donald J. Puchala and Ross B. Talbot (Westview Press, 1979).

Preface to the California edition

The essays in this volume represent a dialogue between theory and data. The theory is drawn from a branch of contemporary political economy which can be labeled the collective-choice school. The data are drawn from Africa. The book extends the methods of reasoning developed in collective choice from their original base—the advanced industrial democracies—to new territory: the literature on rural Africa. Such an extension challenges the power of this form of political economy. It also enriches it, for the central questions which motivate the contemporary study of political economy are often addressed with unique clarity in the scholarship on rural Africa.

The intellectual setting. During the late eighteenth and the nineteenth centuries, economics was not studied apart from politics; the two fields stood as one, with Adam Smith, Karl Marx, and John Stuart Mill writing not only about production, consumption, and exchange but also about tariff policy, monetary policy, class formation, and prison reform. Subsequently, of course, the fields diverged. To many economists, governments came to represent a "black box," while for political scientists, economics became an increasingly alien terrain.

In recent years, however, the gap between the fields has narrowed. Indeed, so frequent are the crossings between them that it is now necessary to group and classify works bearing the label "political economy." Such classification is perilous. But it is a necessary step here, particularly to distinguish the approach taken in these essays from other forms of political economy and to offer reasons for commending it above others.

The form of political economy which we call the collective-choice approach was largely developed by scholars in the United States and Europe.[1] Much of this approach represents an attempt to apply the methods of microeconomic reasoning to problems in democratic theory. Kenneth Arrow's foundational contribution, *Social Choice and Individual Values*, explores the logical possibility of rational individuals arriving at a coherent statement of the social welfare through the use of democratic procedures.[2] Anthony Downs's *An Economic Theory of Democracy* characterizes the outcome of competitive elections.[3] Duncan Black's *The Theory of Committees and Elections* analyzes majority rule in legislative settings,[4] while Mancur Olson's *The Logic of Collective Action* examines a fundamental problem of representation: why some interests but not others are able to organize in defense of their interests.[5]

While the literature which has grown up from these foundational works can be adequately surveyed only at book length,[6] it suffices here to emphasize some of its common elements. The individual constitutes the basic unit of analysis.[7] Individuals are assumed to maximize under constraints; they do so within well-defined institutional contexts; and equilibrium analysis is employed to explore the social states which result from maximizing behavior within institutional settings. Political institutions replace the market as the primary mechanism channeling individual preferences into social outcomes. The institutions analyzed tend to be those which characterize democratic societies. In this sense the literature is culture bound.[8] That is a limitation this book seeks to transcend.

A second variant of political economy also derives from the study of industrialized democracies, but it is more "macro" in orientation. The works of Tufte, Hibbs, Frey, and others explore the ways in which governments manage national economies in efforts to retain political power by satisfying the interests of key sectors within the domestic political economy.[9] In this second literature, parties, regimes, or labor movements replace individuals as the central political actors. And macro-level aggregates—unemployment, national incomes, money supply, or trade balances—replace preferences, prices, or markets as the key economic variables.

The work in this book draws upon the first stream of contemporary scholarship in political economy rather than the second. For purposes of the present study, the macro-level approach makes too strong a set of assumptions about both the political and economic properties of the societies under study to be readily transferable to an African setting. Parties of the left and organized labor, for example, commonly play a major role in these models; although characteristic of the polities of many industrialized democracies, such actors infrequently dominate the politics of Africa. The macro approaches, moreover, rest upon weakly established "micro foundations." This is true both of macroeconomic models, which structure the relations between policy choices and economic outcomes, and of the political models, which link economic outcomes to political preferences.[10] For these reasons, this work draws instead on the first variant of contemporary political economy, even while attempting to relax its most central limiting property: its assumption of democratic political forms.

Among North American and European intellectuals, there exists a third form of political economy which must be mentioned: the school of "public choice."[11] Practitioners of the public-choice school pioneered the study of the way in which rational individuals make choices within institutions other than markets. Like the students of collective choice, they too characterize the collective allocations which result from such decisions. Differentiating the public and collective-choice schools, however, are normative evaluations of the market. The followers of public choice believe that market allocations provide a standard by which to measure and critique the performance of other institutions; the followers of the collective-choice school are far less prone to take such a position.

The approach taken in this work seeks to retain the contributions to positive theory made by the public-choice school while discarding its normative apparatus. For the normative claims are weak, and they often lead to superficial political analysis.

The basic normative criterion of the public-choice school is "Pareto optimality." By this criterion, an allocation of resources elicits ethical approval when no alternative allocation would allow one person to be made better off while making no other person worse off. One of the fundamental theorems of contemporary economics is that perfectly functioning markets yield allocations which are Pareto optimal.[12] Because allocations reached through political institutions differ from those which would be reached in perfect markets, public-choice analysts often treat politics as a source of social costs; only insofar as political actions correct for market failures do they regard them as justified. As a result, rather than deeply investigating the origins and processes of political action, public-choice theorists too often simply call for less politics.[13]

The practitioners of the collective-choice approach to political economy identify with those who criticize the welfare position of the devotees of the market. For they too realize that the allocations resulting from market exchanges can only elicit ethical approval insofar as the initial endowments which people bring to these exchanges can themselves be justified. An increase in the welfare of a lord which leaves a peasant no worse off would be Pareto optimal. And voluntary exchanges can and have been made between peasants and lords. But the allocation of resources in such an unequal situation remains unjust. The case for the market is weakened even further when the conditions are specified which guarantee that market equilibria yield Pareto-optimal allocations; the conditions are *extremely* restrictive.[14] The likelihood of the market generating ethically desirable outcomes even in so flawed a sense as that associated with Pareto optimality is thus small.

The collective-choice approach draws upon the contributions of public choice to the positive analysis of non-market institutions. But it refuses to give uncritical approbation to market processes. In part because of this refusal, it recognizes that social and political institutions are, like markets, a common, central, and enduring feature of human life, and that they cannot be seriously studied by those who decry their existence or who treat them as unfortunate "distortions." As a consequence, the followers of collective choice are far more willing than their public-choice counterparts to investigate in depth the structure and operation of political institutions. They have studied regulatory agencies,[15] committee systems,[16] political parties,[17] labor movements,[18] and international organizations[19] in an effort to see how rational individuals behave in settings other than markets and how their behavior in political settings determines outcomes for society as a whole.

Contributions from Africa. In pursuing this agenda, the followers of the collective-choice school have often acted as if the advanced industrial democracies constituted the full population of relevant political experiences. While sometimes fulminating against "area specialists," they have often committed the very errors which they decry, immersing themselves within the details of the political practices of a particular political system while claiming the universality of their findings. By focusing on a literature drawn from a different region of the world, this book compels those who practice collective choice to test the power of their approach against new materials.

The extensions prove provocative and illuminating. Thus the theory of games offers insight into lineage politics among pre-colonial, tribal societies (chapter 1). Market-failure analysis helps to explain the politicization of rural markets and the rise of rural protest (chapter 4). The theory of rent seeking instructs the study of the formation of states in tribal societies (chapter 2) and the politics of post-independence policy making (chapter 5). And incidence analysis, developed to analyze budgetary allocations by the United States Congress, provides a means for accounting for the agricultural policies pursued by African governments.[20]

The materials from Africa provide new challenges to contemporary political economy. They raise fundamental issues and pose in stark form classic intellectual problems. For this reason, many may welcome this effort to extend the domain of contemporary political economy to incorporate materials drawn from the African continent.

1 An outstanding exception is, of course, Amartya K. Sen. See Amartya K. Sen, *Collective Choice and Social Welfare* (San Francisco: Holden-Day, 1970).

2 Kenneth J. Arrow, *Social Choice and Individual Values* (New York: John Wiley and Sons, 1963).

3 Anthony Downs, *An Economic Theory of Democracy* (New York: Harper and Row, 1957).

4 Duncan Black, *The Theory of Committees and Elections* (Cambridge: Cambridge University Press, 1958).

5 Mancur Olson, *The Logic of Collective Action* (Cambridge, Mass.: Harvard University Press, 1971).

6 See the reviews in William H. Riker and Peter C. Ordeshook, *An Introduction to Positive Political Theory* (Englewood Cliffs, N.J.: Prentice Hall, 1973); Norman Frohlich and Joe A. Oppenheimer, *Modern Political Economy* (Englewood Cliffs, N.J.: Prentice Hall, 1978); Brian Barry and Russell Hardin, eds., *Rational Man and Irrational Society?* (Beverly Hills, Calif.: Sage, 1982); and James Alt and K. Alec Chrystal, *Political Economics* (Berkeley and Los Angeles: University of California Press, 1983). See as well Dennis C. Mueller, *Public Choice* (Cambridge: Cambridge University Press, 1979) and Charles R. Plott, "Axiomatic Social Choice Theory: An Overview and Interpretation," *American Journal of Political Science*, 20 (August 1976): 511–96.

7 While the firm—on the supply side—and the household—on the demand side—are maintained as aggregates, attempts are now being made to disaggregate even these units to the level of individual behavior. See, for example, Oliver Williamson, *The Economic Institutions of Capitalism* (New York: The Free Press, 1985) and Gary Becker, *A Treatise on the Family* (Cambridge, Mass.: Harvard University Press, 1981).

8 Others would argue that the premise of individualism also leads to culture-bound analysis. My own field experience in several cultural groups in Africa suggests to me that the premise of individual maximization is not restrictive but rather does apply in African settings. See, for example, Robert H. Bates, *Rural Responses to Industrialization* (New Haven and London: Yale University Press, 1976). For a broader overview which argues that the cultural suppression of individual wants has not occurred in Africa, see Lloyd A. Fallers, "Are African Cultivators to Be Called 'Peasants'?" in *Economic Development and Social Change*, ed. George Dalton (Garden City, N.Y.: Natural History Press, 1971), pp. 169–77.

9 See, for example, Edward Tufte, *The Political Control of the Economy* (Princeton: Princeton University Press, 1978); David R. Cameron, "The Expansion of the Public Economy: A Comparative Analysis," *American Political Science Review*, 72 (1978): 1243–61; Douglas Hibbs, "Political Parties and Macroeconomic Policy," *American Political Science Review*, 71 (1977): 1467–87; B. S. Frey and F. Schneider, "An Econometric Model with an Endogenous Government Sector," *Public Choice*, 34 (1979): 29–43. See also Neil Beck, "Parties, Administrations and American Macroeconomic Outcomes," *American Political Science Review*, 76 (1982): 83–93 and Adam Przeworski, *Capitalism and Social Democracy* (Cambridge: Cambridge University Press, 1985). Much of this literature is competently reviewed in Alt and Chrystal, *Political Economics*.

10 Consult once again the excellent critique offered in Alt and Chrystal, *Political Economics*.

11 For a review, see Dennis Mueller, *Public Choice*. See also the contributions in the journal *Public Choice* and the numerous contributions to the literature by James Buchanan, Gordon Tullock, and their students. Perhaps the best of their works is James M. Buchanan and Gordon Tullock, *The Calculus of Consent* (Ann Arbor: University of Michigan Press, 1962).

12 See any proof of the fundamental theorem of welfare economics. An example would include Gerard Debreu, *Theory of Value* (New Haven and London: Yale University Press, 1959).

13 An example in the development field is Deepak Lal, *The Poverty of Development Economics*, Hobart Paperback 16 (London: The Institute of Economic Affairs, 1983).

14 See, once again, Debreu, *Theory of Value*.

15 See, for example, both the content of and the literature reviewed in Terry M. Moe, "Congressional Control of the Bureaucracy: An Assessment of the Positive Theory of 'Congressional Dominance,'" Paper Presented to the 1985 Annual Meeting of the American Political Science Association, New Orleans, August 27–September 1, 1985.

16 For example, Kenneth A. Shepsle, "Institutional Arrangements and Equilibrium in Multidimensional Voting Models," *American Journal of Political Science*, 23 (1979): 27–60.

17 See, for example, George Tsebelis, "Parties and Activists: A Comparative Study of Parties and Party Systems," Ph.D. Dissertation, Washington University, St. Louis, 1985.

18 Michael Wallerstein, "The Micro-foundations of Solidarity: Protectionist Policies, Welfare Policies, and Union Centralization," Paper Presented to the 1985 Annual Meeting of the American Political Science Association, New Orleans, August 27–September 1, 1985.

19 Robert Keohane, *After Hegemony* (Princeton: Princeton University Press, 1984) and Robert Axelrod, *The Evolution of Cooperation* (New York: Basic Books, 1984). See also Robert H. Bates and Da-Hsiang Donald Lien, "On the Operations of the International Coffee Agreement," *International Organization*, 39 (Summer 1985): 553–59.

20 Kenneth A. Shepsle and Barry R. Weingast, "Political Preferences for the Pork Barrel: A Generalization," *American Journal of Political Science*, 25 (1981): 96–111.

Introduction

Rural Africa is important in its own right. For scholars, it is important as well in that it poses problems which offer opportunities for intellectual progress.

Until recently, most observers behaved as if the urban and industrial areas were determining the fundamental character of the African continent. For some, the cities embodied and instilled new cultural values. For others, they propagated new forms of social organization. And, for most, the urban and industrial sectors contained the forces of change; the rural areas, the forces of inertia. Certainly, for political scientists, the cities represented the critical political arena; for it was in the towns of Africa that political movements were organized, voters mobilized, riots fomented, and coups set in motion.

Despite the rapid growth of the towns and the concomitant growth in expectations of rapid social change, the vast preponderance of Africa's population has remained in the rural areas. And, despite massive investments in industry and manufacturing, the vast bulk of Africa's economy has remained in agriculture. The agrarian population of Africa has, from time to time, won the attention it thus warrants; but such recognition has most generally come at moments of high drama, such as times of drought or of triumph by rural liberation movements.

Increasingly, however, less dramatic but more powerful forces have begun to compel a reassessment of the importance of rural Africa. Most fundamentally, a recognition has grown that the limits to Africa's capacity to undergo social change are determined in large part by the performance of its rural sector. It has been realized that the stagnation of many African economies, the decline of others, and the sporadic growth of still others result at least in part from economic forces which originate from the countryside.

This book joins with the work of others who are convinced of the central importance of Africa's rural populations. It seeks, moreover, to advance our understanding of Africa's problems of rural development; thus the last portion of this volume is devoted to an examination of the agricultural policies of African states. But the origins of this volume lie deeper than in its

1

concern with contemporary development problems. They lie as well in the realization that rural Africa poses fundamental problems not only for policy makers but also for fields of scholarship. And for no subject is this more true than for political science. The study of rural Africa raises questions which are both substantive and analytic in nature. Both kinds of questions are equally compelling. The essays in this volume attempt to answer them.

The substantive questions pertain to the events or phenomena that have attracted the attention of political analysts. The questions include:

What was the nature of political systems in pre-colonial Africa? What were the sources of order in societies without states? And under what circumstances did state systems form in the pre-colonial period?

Under colonialism, how did the colonial system distort the pattern of development in rural Africa? How did it operate to bias the allocation of economic resources? And how did economic change which took place in the colonial era spark the nationalist reaction which provoked the withdrawal of the colonial powers?

In the contemporary period, why do the states of Africa choose policies which lead to the impoverishment of farmers? What influences the selection of these policies? And how do certain governments remain in power when they adopt policies which are antithetical to the interests of most of their citizens?

The analytic questions raise issues which are far more general in nature. They pertain not so much to the events and phenomena subject to study as to the forms of scholarship which are brought to bear upon them. In this volume, these questions raise issues fundamental to the study of political economy. They include:

Under what circumstances do *economic* motivations lead to *political* action? Why would persons concerned with enhancing their incomes turn to politics?

Why do states intervene in markets? What determines the pattern of state intervention and the nature of the biases which states introduce into the allocation of economic resources?

What is the relation between individual motivations and collective outcomes? Why do decisions motivated by the social interest often lead to undesirable consequences? And how can self-interested decisions be orchestrated into socially beneficial forms?

In dealing with issues such as these, the book is organized into three sections. The first two essays focus on pre-colonial societies, the second two on the colonial period, and the last on rural societies in post-independence Africa. Each essay analyzes a problem which arises naturally in the context of the study of rural Africa. The first analyzes the origins of order in societies without states, and the second the relationship between economic activity and state formation in pre-colonial Africa. The third essay examines the commercialization of agriculture in colonial Africa and contrasts the fate of producers' interests in the western and eastern portions of the continent.

2

The fourth looks at the economic basis of rural political protest in the period of nationalist politics. The last essay examines the agricultural policies that have been adopted in post-independence Africa and attempts to account for them.

Part I

The pre-colonial period

1

The preservation of order in stateless societies: a reinterpretation of Evans-Pritchard's *The Nuer*

> These affairs are like a game in which everybody knows the rules and states of development: when one is expected to give way, when to be firm, when to yield at the last moment, and so forth.[1]

The study of stateless societies represents one of the fundamental contributions of anthropology to political analysis. Nowhere have these studies been more vigorously pursued than in Africa. And among them, Evans-Pritchard's *The Nuer* stands as a foundational work.

In examining Evans-Pritchard's analysis, we shall, as have so many others, focus on the question: What are the sources of order in societies without states? In exploring his answers to this question, we shall underscore and exploit the parallelism between Evans-Pritchard's analysis and what is known as the prisoners' dilemma.

The Nuer are a pastoralist people. While they do cultivate gardens, they principally engage in rearing and herding cattle. Cattle form the basis of the Nuer economy. As Evans-Pritchard puts it, the Nuer 'not only depend on cattle for many of life's necessities but they have the herdsman's outlook on the world. Cattle are their dearest possession.'[2] Cattle are the main property among the Nuer, and the joint family – the father, his sons, and their wives – is the elementary property-holding unit. Each family seeks to care for, nurture, and increase its cattle holdings. Evans-Pritchard reports that they expend great effort in this endeavor and succeed remarkably well.

> It has been remarked that the Nuer might be called parasites of the cow, but it might be said with equal force that the cow is a parasite of the Nuer, whose lives are spent ensuring its welfare. They build byres, kindle fires, and clean kraals for its comfort; move from villages, to camps, from camp to camp and from camps back to villages for its health; defy wild beasts for its protection; and fashion ornaments for its adornment.[3]
> ... I have merely given in this section a few examples to illustrate a general conclusion.... that Nuer cattle husbandry could not in any important particular be improved in their present ecological relations.[4]

Among the Nuer, breeding and raising cattle is thus one means of increasing one's property. Another means, at least in theory, would be theft.

7

Each property owner could make himself better off by stealing the cattle of others. And every indication is that the Nuer are tempted to do so. They certainly do pillage the cattle holdings of neighboring tribes; thus, the last sentence of our first quotation from Evans-Pritchard reads in full: 'Cattle are their dearest possession *and* [the Nuer] gladly risk their lives to . . . pillage those of their neighbours.'[5] The strength of their desire to steal is further suggested by Evans-Pritchard when he recounts: 'As my Nuer servant once said to me: "You can trust a Nuer with any amount of money, pounds and pounds and pounds, and go away for years and return and he will not have stolen it; but a single cow – that is a different matter." '[6]

The puzzle, from Evans-Pritchard's point of view, was that, despite the potential for theft and disorder, the Nuer in fact tended to live in relative harmony. In so far as the Nuer raided cattle, they tended to raid the cattle of others; raids within the tribe were relatively rare.[7] Somehow the Nuer appear to have avoided the potentially harmful effects arising from the pursuit of self-interest. And they appear to have done so even while lacking those formal institutions so common in Western societies which specialize in preserving the peace and forestalling violence: the courts, the police, and so on.

Evans-Pritchard devoted much of his effort to determining how the Nuer, in the absence of such institutions, none the less achieved social order. In discussing Evans-Pritchard's analysis of the problem of social order, we can credibly abstract his account in a number of forms. Gluckman's treatment, which we will discuss below, highlights the role of interested parties and cross-cutting cleavages – a notion of conflict regulation that is familiar to political scientists of the sociological persuasion.[8] In this essay, we will highlight the structure of conflict in a way that is more relevant to those interested in political economy: we will portray it in the form of a two-person, non-cooperative, variable-sum game, traditionally known as the prisoners' dilemma.[9]

All that has been said thus far suggests that such an abstraction does little violence to Evans-Pritchard's analysis. What is required is that we conceive of the situation of two property-holding units, each of which desires to increase the number of its cattle, and the incentives which face them. Call the units families I and II, and assume that both hold ten cattle. Each family can choose between two alternatives: using force to gain more cattle or remaining passive and non-violent. Each knows that the other family faces a similar choice. And each knows what the results of their choice will be.

Both families know that should both abjure the use of force, each will continue to enjoy the possession of ten cattle. But both also know that raiding is profitable. Should family I raid family II's herd whilst family II failed to resist, it could appropriate eight of family II's cattle, we shall assume; similarly, should family II raid family I and family I not forcibly resist, family II could gain eight cattle at family I's expense. Both also know that in the face of a raid from each other, there are gains to those who resist, even though they may pay a price in physical suffering. For purposes of argument, assume that wounds, the breakdown of herding during the course of battle, and property damage result in losses equivalent to six cattle. In any case, this outcome is to be preferred to not using force to protect one's herds, for then eight cattle are lost to the predatory party.

The situation is summarized in Figure 1. The choices for family I are listed on the left: F designates the choice of force and F̄ designates the renunciation of force. The choices for family II are similar and are listed at the top of the table. The entries refer to the outcomes for the paired choices of families I and II, the value of the outcomes being expressed in terms of numbers of cattle, and the value to family I being listed first and the value to family II being listed second.[10]

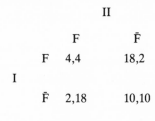

Figure 1.1

The nature of the dilemma is clear. It is rational for each family to choose to use force; as can be seen from Figure 1.1, each does best employing force *no matter what* the choice of the other. Moreover, it is also clear that the use of force is a stable social outcome and the only stable outcome. When both families use force, then the situation is in equilibrium, for it is in neither family's interest to renounce it. Were family I unilaterally to abjure the use of force, for example, then its holdings would drop from four cattle to two and the same is true of family II. Moreover, no other choice is in equilibrium; in all other cases, one or the other family does better by unilaterally altering its choice of strategy. The equilibrium outcome is thus unique.

What is peculiar and compelling, however, is the nature of this outcome. Under it, *both families are worse off*. Had they renounced the use of force, they would each have had ten cattle but they now get only four. Individual rationality thus leads to a socially irrational outcome, an outcome under which all persons suffer. Put another way, all would be better off living peacefully, but none can afford to live that way. The structure of the prisoners' dilemma thus captures the fragility of social order, and does so in a particularly compelling form.

In analyzing the origins of order in decentralized societies, Evans-Pritchard pursued two lines of inquiry and we shall analyze both. One was to look at the role of mechanisms for conflict resolution and dispute settlement; these mechanisms, in effect, were employed by the Nuer to curtail the natural tendencies set in motion by the incentive structure characteristic of the prisoners' dilemma. The second was to conjecture concerning more basic and fundamental institutions – ones that did not control socially dangerous behavior but operated at a deeper level and altered, in effect, the very structure of incentives which so threatened the cohesion of Nuer society.

Compensation
In analyzing how the Nuer attain social order in the face of incentives which promote self-seeking behavior which is socially debilitating, Evans-Pritchard placed strong emphasis upon the role of compensation. In this section, we examine how such a convention might work.

Assume that a system of compensation is available, and observe the consequences for the incentives which face a party contemplating the use of force. Say that family I is contemplating raiding the herds of family II. Family I now knows that family II gets to choose not only between the use of force and non-violence but also between those two alternatives and a third: having its cattle returned while exacting two cattle as compensation. Let F̄C stand for this option of no-force-with-compensation. The decisional problem now reads as in Figure 1.2:

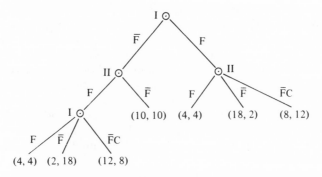

Figure 1.2

Family I now must confront the possibility that, if it attacks, family II will exact compensation; in that case, family I will be less well off than if it did not attack (it will have eight cattle instead of ten), and the incentives to attack are weakened. Moreover, family II is better off exacting compensation than it is resisting by force (it gets twelve cattle instead of four); and, if it knows that family I will also seek compensation if attacked, it has little incentive itself to raid the herds of family I. The rule of compensation thus reduces the incentives for violence. Both families will find it in their interests to live peacefully and enjoy their ten cattle.[11]

Procedures for compensation thus alter the incentives faced by the two parties and do so in such a way that it is no longer in their interests to choose the use of violence. And thus it is that Evans-Pritchard perceptively delineates that area within which compensation is paid from that area within which vengeance is taken. The former he regards as a political community, which he terms 'a tribe'. Within it exist institutions which reduce the incentives for violence, thus making possible higher levels of political order.[12]

Arbitration
Equally central to Evans-Pritchard's analysis of the attainment of social order is his stress on the role of arbitration; I refer, of course, to his discussion of the leopard-skin chief. In the political analyses inspired by Evans-Pritchard's work, few subjects have provoked as much attention as his discussion of this figure. And among the principal controversies have been debates concerning his source of influence.

Some, such as Greuel, have argued that the influence of the chief arises from his capacity to coerce;[13] Haight partially subscribes to this position, arguing that in those areas 'where members of the leopard-skin chief lineage were also members of the dominant lineage', and in those situations when a leopard-skin chief was also a 'senior kinsman', the leopard-skin chief had the power to compel the settlement of disputes.[14] While both Greuel and Haight may be right in pointing to coercion as a sufficient condition for the influence of the leopard-skin chief, it is clear in Evans-Pritchard's account that the capacity to coerce is not a necessary condition for chiefly powers. Moreover, it is also clear that Greuel, Haight and others who stress the power to coerce are simply missing the compelling quality of the Nuer case: the striking absence of the Weberian attribute of 'stateness'. The evidence for this is far too strong to be ignored, and Evans-Pritchard could not have made the point more clearly:

> I have never seen Nuer treat a chief with more respect than they treat other people or speak of them as persons of much importance. They regard them as agents through whom disputes of a certain kind can be effaced . . . and I have often heard remarks such as this: 'We took hold of them and gave them leopard skins and made them our chiefs.'[15]

> Likewise [the chief] has no means of compelling the people to pay or to accept blood-cattle. He has no powerful kinsmen or the backing of a populous community to support him. He is simply a mediator in a specific social situation.[16]

Others have explored the normative, as opposed to the physical, element of the influence of the leopard-skin chief. Opposing the components of legitimacy and power in their explorations of chiefly authority, scholars such as Burton and Beidelman emphasize the significance of the moral basis of political suasion. They stress in particular the capacity of the leopard-skin chief to evoke the primacy of moral considerations in private choice, thereby eliciting a social consciousness on the part of private individuals.[17] The discussion of the role of morality in social conflict is of obvious importance and will receive attention in later stages of this analysis. But just as invoking the capacity for coercion 'short circuits' Evans-Pritchard's analysis and thereby discounts its value, so invoking the capacity for virtuous behavior aborts recognition of what must be regarded as a major effort at investigating the possibility for socially coherent behavior by self-interested individuals.

Evans-Pritchard investigates an alternative path; this alternative requires neither value consensus at the level of individual motivation nor central coordination at the level of choice making. Rather, it offers the alternative of decentralized, non-cooperative behavior – a situation in which social institutions, such as the chief, serve to orchestrate individual, self-interested behavior into socially coherent outcomes. Social coherence comes neither from the organic immersion of individual preferences into an ethical order nor from the Hobbesian alternative of coerced compliance; rather, it is achieved as an emergent property of decentralized decision making.

Evans-Pritchard emphasizes that the role of the leopard-skin chief is to serve as a communication link between conflicting parties. By his account, it would appear that the offended party communicates two basic messages: (1) either we receive compensation or we exact vengeance, and (2) an idea of an adequate level of compensation. The offending party naturally responds by communicating his assessment of adequate compensation. And subsequent interchanges appear largely to represent bargaining sessions in which the level of compensation is negotiated.

Figure 1.2 suggests why this should be so. Say family I has used violence and family II has yet to undertake reprisals. The two families are at a point in which the distribution of payoffs is 18,2. Through the leopard-skin chief, family II offers family I a choice of two alternatives: revenge with payoffs 4,4, or restitution and some form of compensation, ideally (from its point of view) with payoffs of 8,12. The threat of forceful revenge will be a credible one as family II can gain thereby, while family I loses the equivalent of 14 cattle. So long as the message – pay up or suffer the consequences – is transmitted in a credible fashion (and care is taken to ensure that it is)[18] violence is not really at issue. What is at issue is the final level of compensation: i.e., how far family II can improve its position and to what extent family I can hold on to its ill-gotten gains. By communicating family II's unambivalent intention to inflict harm, and by serving as a go-between in the bargaining over compensation, the leopard-skin chief facilitates this bargaining and contributes to the peaceful resolution of the dispute.[19]

SOCIAL AND CULTURAL FOUNDATIONS FOR PEACE

Compensation and arbitration are thus central mechanisms for the preservation of order among the Nuer, according to Evans-Pritchard. And yet we must wonder how these mechanisms are maintained. Especially in the absence of formal institutions capable of apprehending evaders of the law, we would expect persons to refuse to abide by these mechanisms of dispute settlement. But they do not appear to do so. As Evans-Pritchard makes clear, the Nuer in fact willingly employ these mechanisms and, by and large, they tend to submit to whatever outcomes the mechanisms may dictate; and it is only the fact that the Nuer willingly do so, he argues, that makes these mechanisms work.[20] Considerations such as these lead us to seek more fundamental factors which may be at work – factors that would transform the payoff matrix being viewed by the Nuer in such a way that the incentives to use force are substantially altered and the compelling power of the prisoners' dilemma is weakened.

Deterrence
Evans-Pritchard repeatedly emphasizes the role of threats of violence in securing social peace. The very readiness of the Nuer to use violence, he argues, is a reason why it is not employed. By his account, the Nuer appreciate the role of deterrence and know that they must unambiguously and forcefully communicate their willingness to fight in order to prevent predation and the general social turmoil which then results. As he states: 'It is the knowledge that a Nuer is brave and will stand up against aggression and enforce his rights by club and spear that ensures respect for person and property.'[21] This point achieves further importance in Evans-Pritchard's delimitation of zones of peace and violence in Nuer society. It is precisely in those zones in which a man can recruit kin support to engage in battle and thus credibly threaten reprisal, he contends, that disputes are most likely to be settled peacefully.[22]

In recasting Evans-Pritchard's account into a choice-making framework, we can interpret it in two ways. One is to view his argument as contending that threats represent an informational strategy aimed at modifying an opponent's perception of one's probable behavior. In essence, threats transform the payoff matrix; they remove the off-diagonal cells by communicating that these payoffs will occur with probability zero. The new payoff matrix appears as in Figure 1.3:

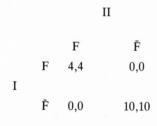

Figure 1.3

Given this perception of the payoffs to alternative behaviors, both parties, behaving rationally, will choose the option of non-violence.

The pre-colonial period

Evans-Pritchard's account can be interpreted in another fashion. Once again, the payoff matrix is altered and again in a way that removes the structure of incentives which generates socially harmful choice making by rational individuals. The existence of threats can be held to generate an expansion of the set of strategies to include not only the use or abnegation of force but also the *contingent* use of force, i.e. the use of force only as a form of reprisal. When the parties to potential disputes can elect this option – and here we label it alternative R – then the payoff matrix would appear as in Figure 1.4:

II

		F	R	F̄
	F	4,4	4,4	18,2
I	R	4,4	10,10	10,10
	F̄	2,18	10,10	10,10

Figure 1.4

By contrast with Figure 1.1, the use of force here does *not* represent a dominant strategy; it does not represent a choice which is unconditionally best, i.e. best no matter what the choice of the other family. Moreover, the choice of the strategy of reprisal, R, by both parties is stable; were each family to choose to use force only if force were employed by the other family, then neither would have an incentive unilaterally to alter its behavior. In the face of credible deterrent threats, it is thus possible for both parties, behaving rationally, to choose not to use force, and for this state of affairs – peace within the feud – to persist.

Cross-cutting ties

It was Gluckman who coined the phrase 'peace in the feud'. In a noted review essay thus entitled, Gluckman reappraised Evans-Pritchard's classic in the light of subsequent anthropological research.[23] He based his analysis primarily upon Elizabeth Colson's studies of the Plateau Tonga, in which she stressed the multiple interests that bind together members of small-scale societies.[24] These ties, he argued after Colson, appear to provide means of inflicting penalties that weaken the incentives to cause harm to others; they also appear to weaken the incentives for forceful retribution and to strengthen the incentives for compensation. In effect, they represent social institutions which alter the incentives which structure the choices made by conflicting members of society.

Rules of exogamy and dispersed residence represent two such social institutions. In Colson's essay on the Plateau Tonga, for example, she emphasized the role women played in mediating a dispute between two

14

clans. A murder had been committed and the parties to the dispute were on the verge of violent conflict. Because of exogamous rules of marriage, however, the daughters and sisters of the members of one clan were to be found as the wives of members of the other. The lobbying effort of the women promoted a peaceful resolution of the conflict; the pressures they exerted forestalled the threat of violence.[25]

Gluckman conjectures that dispersed residence promotes similar behavior among the Nuer. Members of a given family do not cluster in a unique village; they tend to be widely dispersed. When an injury is inflicted by one family upon another, the dispute is likely to divide the residents of villages. But in so far as the residents of a village cannot cooperate, their interests suffer. Acting as residents of common villages, members of opposing families may therefore champion a quick and peaceful settlement of the conflict.[26]

Gluckman's argument concerning cross-cutting ties – be they ties of marriage or of common residence – thus implies that certain social institutions impose costs upon those who would choose to utilize the option of force in situations of conflict of interest. In discussing the effect of exogamous marriage, for example, Gluckman notes:

> When a man has got a wife from another group, he has an interest in being friends with that group . . . It's not just sentiment. A woman remains attached to her own kin, and if her husband quarrels with them she can make life pretty unpleasant for him . . . A man's brother-in-law is maternal uncle to his children, and by custom is required to assist them in many critical situations. He can bless his nephew, and his curse is believed to be among the worst, if not the worst, a Nuer can receive, for, unlike the father, a maternal uncle may curse a youth's cattle, as well as his crops and fishing and hunting, if he is disobedient or refuses a request or in some other way offends him. The curse may also prevent the nephew from begetting male children. So for the welfare of his family, and the prosperity of his children, each man is led by his interests . . . to seek to be on good terms with his wife's kin.[27]

Similarly, given family dispersion, the decision to use violence leads to the loss of aid in herding, billeting, food acquisition and preparation, and access to water – resources that are distributed by neighborhood groups which, given the nature of Nuer institutions, recruit their members from a variety of families.

The consequence of such social institutions, in effect, is to alter the nature of the payoff matrix in such a way as to reduce the incentives to employ violence and thereby to make any level of compensation a relatively attractive alternative. Should the interests at stake be particularly strong, the payoff matrix will be transformed so that it no longer poses a prisoners' dilemma. Say, for example, that the losses experienced by the force-employing party in terms of those 'other interests' (be they conjugal or residential in nature) are worth the equivalent of nine cattle; then, as shown in Figure 1.5, the renunciation of force is a dominant strategy, and equilibrium exists $(\bar{F},\bar{F})$, and it is a social optimum.

II

	F	F̄
F	−5,−5	9,2
F̄	2,9	10,10

I

Figure 1.5

If the 'other interests' are not particularly strong, the parties to the dispute may well remain in a prisoners' dilemma situation; this is illustrated in Figure 1.6, where the user of force experiences a loss in his other interests equivalent to the value of one cow.

II

	F	F̄
F	3,3	17,2
F̄	2,17	10,10

I

Figure 1.6

None the less, because of the weakened incentive to use force, lower levels of compensation are required to alter the incentives to aggress, and the control of disputes is thus more easily obtained. Thus, as shown in Figure 1.7, applying a rule of restitution – merely that the appropriate cattle must be returned in full – makes the renunciation of force (with restitution) a preferred strategy for parties who have been aggressed upon.

II

	F	F̄	F̄R
F	4,4	17,2	9,10
F̄	2,17	10,10	10,10
F̄R	10,9	10,10	10,10

I

Figure 1.7

The figure helps to point out that when force is costly in terms of its effect on other interests, it is easier to devise a mechanism of compensation which will incorporate incentives for the preservation of peace. And this appears to be the core of the cross-cutting ties argument.

Religious beliefs

There is a last factor that has been used to explain the existence of social cohesion among the Nuer and this is their religion.

Nuer religion has been studied by Evans-Pritchard himself, by Beidelman and by Burton.[28] Insight into the religious values of the Nuer comes from studying their theories of misfortune; and these, it would appear, share common traits with the beliefs of other African societies. Personal misfortune, it is held, can result from ill-feeling, which in turn can be caused by being harmed. Thus, if one person has injured another, but not in a way that generates formal compensation and restitution, the offender is still liable to be punished; for as Gluckman states, 'bad feeling is charged with mystical danger'.[29]

One way of inflicting misfortune among the Nuer is through the curse. Evans-Pritchard discussed the role of the curse in the following terms:

> The curse is undoubtedly a powerful sanction of conduct, largely because it is not thought necessary that a wronged man should utter it aloud for misfortune to follow. He has only to think it. Such an unspoken curse Nuer call a *biit loac*, a curse of the heart. Indeed, it would seem that he need not expressly formulate a curse in his mind at all, a mere feeling of resentment arising from a genuine grievance being sufficient to cause injury to the person who occasioned it.[30]

The incentives for forceful appropriation are thus reduced, for the material gains are made at the cost of generating anger, which in turn can lead to one's death, illness, or misfortune. As Gluckman states: 'The beliefs exert . . . pressure on men and women to observe the social virtues . . . The beliefs support the moral order of the community.'[31]

A variant of this belief is the conviction that private acts can have public consequences. The occurrence of collective misfortunes, for example, provokes inquiries into unresolved private grievances and undisclosed misdemeanors. Drought, plague, or a series of lesser disasters may suggest the existence of an uncompensated injury; and the beliefs covering collective misfortune thus help to vest more securely personal property rights. For example, Evans-Pritchard reports: 'To kill a man and not to confess to the killing is a heinous offense in Nuer eyes because it puts the kin on both sides in jeopardy.'[32] An unpropitiated ghost, in Nuer beliefs, is extremely dangerous.[33] As Burton states, 'Those recently deceased are . . . thought to hold the same feelings toward the living as was the case when they were alive . . . While normally a number of months elapse between burial and the mortuary ceremony, it is understandable why the Nuer should

17

think of the power of the deceased to seek vengeance ... to be especially strong in the interim.'[34]

The obvious correlative of such beliefs is that care should be taken to insure that persons are not injured (lest they die with a grievance in their hearts) and that transgressions and injuries should be reported and dealt with (presumably prior to the victim's demise). Failing such measures, the collectivity is liable to calamitous misfortune.

While Burton and others stress the difference between the religious beliefs of different African societies and the variations in their impact upon social behavior, sufficient commonalities none the less remain among their theories of misfortune to suggest a common core. Goldschmidt's study of the Sebei represents a case in point. Goldschimdt reports that a clan, upon the death of *one* of its members, held an inquiry into the behavior of *all* of its members. It sought to determine recent transgressions that could have engendered sufficient resentment to provoke a death. Cases of possible theft, arson, adultery, and such were examined. 'They listed no fewer than seven possible sources of the evil influences that were invading them', Goldschmidt contends; 'a wide range in circumstances ... could ... operate as a source of death'.[35] Inquiries were made, he reports, and the grievances were settled; the social and moral order was thereby restored.

Thus, the beliefs of the Nuer, and of other societies, may be such as to alter the perceived gains to be made from forceful appropriation. They provide incentives to curtail those who may seek to take advantage of the absence of strong institutions and capabilities for enforcement that characterize these small-scale societies. It should be noted that these beliefs are of particular importance in societies like the Nuer where the costs of enforcement are high. Cattle are held in dispersed locations and are highly mobile, so a theft may be difficult to detect and proof of theft difficult to adduce. Moreover, lacking explicit and specialized institutions for law enforcement, it is difficult to collect compensation or to impose arbitration without voluntary consent. The result is that the system of controls over forceful appropriation is a fragile one; and, lacking a supportive structure of belief, it may fail to prevent persons from reverting to their non-preferred state: one in which all revert to force and exist at a level of well-being below that which is socially possible (four cattle equivalents as opposed to ten, in our example).[36]

CONCLUSION

While Evans-Pritchard's banner has been appropriated by the champions of several schools of scholarship, it has been captured by none. For the very source of the intellectual power of his work is the tension embodied in the problem which he defined. As recently argued by Evans, the problem of social order is precisely that: a problem. It can be characterized but not resolved.[37]

18

The problem of social order stands as a classic one, and it has been posed in many forms. In political science, it is sometimes cast as a tension between private interests and the public good, between rights and obligations, or between the individual and the collectivity. In economics, it has been cast as a research agenda: under what circumstances can maximizing behavior by self-regarding agents lead to allocational decisions that are consistent with a social optimum? Only in sociology, ironically, has the problem perhaps been slighted, and that for reasons which may be instructive.

Sociological theories tend to emphasize two major sources of order. One is morality, the other is coercion. In the Durkheimian tradition, some sociologists stress the role of moral sanctions and normative constraints. Others, such as those of a Marxian persuasion, stress the role of coercive sanctions or external restraints. The one emphasizes legitimacy and the other force. Still others, such as those in the Weberian tradition, emphasize authority which, being legitimate coercion, is but a mixture of both.

What is striking about these major strands of social theory is how blunt a set of instruments they offer when brought to bear upon the ethnography of the Nuer. Their inadequacy is affirmed by Beidelman, for example, who stands among the most distinguished of those now writing on the Nuer; in at least one major article Beidelman ends by calling for a fundamental modification in the schemata of Weber's thought.[38] Upon reflection, it should be clear why the sociological tradition works so poorly in the medium of the Nuer.

Where there is moral order, there can be no tension between the private interest and the social welfare. Where the public order has coercive sanctions at its command, then socially harmful choices can be penalized and reasonable people will not elect them. In the very concepts which it employs, political sociology is thus insensitive to the fundamental problem which motivated, and is motivated by, the Nuer. It works poorly because it minimizes the possibility of the very problem that inspired Evans-Pritchard's work.

It is damning, but true: the problem with political sociology is that it is too sociological. In affirming the primacy of society, it gives little reason to ask if it is possible for organized behavior to be orchestrated out of the decisions of individuals. Further signalling its inability to deal with the problem is the vigorous assertion of such methodological postulates as the 'independent validity of social facts' or the rigorous separation of 'levels of analysis'. An intellectual posture characterized by a conviction that social life is not problematic simply offers little encouragement to those who wish to examine the nexus between private choice and collective behavior. And yet the problem of social order requires precisely such an examination.

What of a discipline founded on the contrasting postulate of radical individualism? Economics, of course, is such a discipline. But classically it too provides little that would motivate an exploration of Evans-Pritchard's problem. Atomistic, maximizing individuals are the central agents in

19

economic analysis, and the market is the principal social institution. According to traditional theory, the market aggregates individual choices into socially desirable allocations. Through the disembodied operation of the pricing mechanism, individuals who seek to maximize find it in their interests to make decisions which sustain the use of resources in socially desirable ways. So, in its traditional form, economics, too, has elided the tensions that constitute the fertile paradox central to Evans-Pritchard's thought.

In its more contemporary forms, however, economic reasoning has altered in critical respects. Radical individualism remains intact as a basic premise; what is now in doubt is the capacity of individuals to secure their own best interests, much less outcomes which maximize the well-being of society. The prisoners' dilemma was expressly contrived by 'dissident' economists to exhibit the shortcomings of individual rationality. It was designed to capture the way in which behavior based upon self-interest can be self-defeating and to demonstrate how individual rationality can lead to outcomes which no individual would desire.

The contribution of Evans-Pritchard is to indicate the way in which social institutions and cultural values can help to resolve this paradox. He demonstrates the way in which institutions can coordinate individual choices so that they lead to outcomes which are not pernicious but which enhance the welfare of all members of society. Without fundamentally contradicting the premise of individual choice and self-interested behavior, Evans-Pritchard thus examined the ways in which social institutions can help to resolve some of the most powerful dilemmas to which they can give rise.

2

The centralization of African societies

It [is] a principal theme of this book that a man who wants to secure and maintain a following must be able to offer his followers some material advantage.[1]

The analysis of the origins of order in decentralized societies is perhaps the most famous contribution of African studies to the study of politics. Yet recent scholarship has argued that too much emphasis has been placed upon decentralized systems. On the one hand, their occurrence appears to be relatively infrequent; on the other, even in so far as decentralized societies do exist, they can arguably be regarded as transitory – as societies which once were centralized or which are in the early stages of a movement toward more centralized political forms.[2]

This essay examines various hypotheses concerning the economic basis for political centralization. For among the most frequently posited motives for the formation of states is the desire to achieve economic objectives – ones that presumably could not be achieved under decentralized political systems, such as those described by Evans-Pritchard.

By political centralization is meant the surrender of voluntarism as a basic principle of social action. Under a centralized system, individual members of society are no longer decisive; they cannot veto collective decisions and unanimity is not required. Instead, socially binding actions are taken by a sub-set of society's members, and individuals can be compelled to comply with decisions taken by these agents. As empirical marks of centralized systems, we can note the existence of a bureaucracy, an army, or a central political figure, such as a chief or monarch. The presence of such political attributes suggests a heightened capacity for coercion and the existence of political figures capable of making socially binding choices.

A key purpose of this chapter is to formulate, characterize and expound arguments concerning the economic basis for state formation. Many of these arguments have been left implicit in the literature; most are partial. An important objective of this essay is therefore to make the arguments explicit and fully to elaborate them. A second objective is to assess their credibility. Concerning this second task, a few comments are in order.

21

To evaluate the arguments concerning state formation, I employ the materials compiled in the Human Relations Area Files. These files consist of an annotated compendium of historic and ethnographic reports concerning a sample of thirty-six African societies.[3] The data are the richest available, but they are seriously flawed. The number of cases is small. The data were collected for one purpose and are being used for another; as a consequence, information is frequently missing. And, most galling, the principle of selection is unknown; there is no statement as to why one society is included and another is not, save for the fact that the one has attracted a greater amount of scholarly investigation. The nature and magnitude of the bias in the sample set of cases therefore cannot be estimated.

In the face of such difficulties, I have decided that the appropriate stance is one of modesty. I have used the data but I have approached their analysis as a 'five-finger exercise' – something that must be done but which can at best be small in scale and can never be decisive. I have therefore subjected the data to simple cross-tabulations, employing controls where numbers permit. While, for purposes of interpretation, I do assess the significance of the associations evidenced in these cross-tabulations, it must be stressed that the sampling procedures employed render significance tests relatively meaningless. The quality of the data renders them suggestive at best. Throughout this paper, I strive to respect that limitation.

A last prefatory comment is in order. Correlational analysis, rather than causal inference, is the highest level of data analysis to which this effort can aspire. One reason becomes obvious when the full range of hypotheses is examined: there are many possible economic 'causes' of political centralization. And, given the small number of observations, it is difficult to isolate the effects of single variables, as would be required for causal analysis. Even more important, it is clear that in the case of most of the hypotheses, causal effects run in both directions. In the face of reciprocal causation, and the modest quality of the data, we can observe at best correlations among the variables.

THE 'SMITHIAN' MODEL

One of the basic arguments linking political centralization with economic reward rests upon the desire of people to benefit from the gains in welfare which can be reaped from markets. In essence, the argument is Ricardian. Rather than attempting to be self-sufficient, different portions of society, it is held, can do better by specializing in the production of those goods in which, by dint of their resource endowments, they hold a comparative advantage, and by exchanging a portion of those goods for those made by persons with different resource endowments. In the context of this argument, the contribution of the state is to provide order and peace and thereby to render production and exchange possible for members of society. The origins of the state, then, lie in the welfare gains that can be reaped through the promotion of markets.

This argument, of course, has been advanced in fields other than African history. Indeed, its most notable development has been in the history of Europe. In a large variety of guises, the basic argument is repeatedly advanced: that the growth of the market leads to the emergence of centralized political forms.[4]

While thus echoing the works of other scholars, ethnographers and historians in Africa differ from them in important respects. They give particular emphasis to the role of trade; indeed, some have gone so far as to posit a distinctive African state system – one based on the extraction of the gains to be made from commerce.[5] Moreover, they develop distinctive themes in their treatment of this basic thesis, in part simply because they deal with a distinctive subject matter. In particular, to a greater extent than their 'European' counterparts, they contrast the efficiency of trade under decentralized political systems with that under more centralized systems, and seek thereby to demonstrate the superiority, and thus the desirability, of the latter.

Decentralized systems

Perhaps the best analysis of the economic strengths and weaknesses of decentralized lineage systems is offered by Colson. Colson illustrates how trade was abetted by the lineage system of one decentralized group, the Tonga of Northern Rhodesia (now Zambia). Lineages were dispersed and 'did not share a common residence'.[6] A person wishing to make exchanges 'could travel safely for considerable distances provided he exercised caution' by moving along 'the chain of kinship'.[7] In trading relations, the lineage system fortified property rights and provided security for exchanges: 'In the event that a claim was not met, the lineage had the obligation to take vengeance.'[8] The institution of the feud, characteristic of lineage-system societies, was used to provide security for those engaged in market exchanges:

> Those who wished a further safeguard could initiate a 'bond friendship' with prominent men along the route or at the place of destination. The man who accepted such a pact agreed to guarantee a friend's person and property while he remained within the neighborhood. An attack upon either was considered an attack upon the host who could then summon kinsmen and supporters to retaliate against the offender.[9]

Lewis finds a similar system was at work among the Somali; as he reports:

> To reach the coast in safety a caravan had to have protection on its journey among many different and often hostile clans. This was achieved by an institutionalized form of safe-conduct. The leaders of the caravan ... entered into a relationship of protection with those amongst whom he passed on his way to the coast ... Attacks on a protected caravan are attacks on the patron and his lineage whose honor and 'name' ... can only be upheld by prompt retaliatory action.[10]

A system of lineage relations could thus be used to support trade. But it apparently failed to do so efficiently. Colson indicates, for example, that the

23

The pre-colonial period

Tonga never really reaped the gains associated with economic specialization; they failed to specialize either by region or by craft and instead continued to adhere to the 'ideal of self-sufficiency'.[11] Moreover, the literature from other decentralized societies strongly suggests that, even were the system of lineage relations able to generate significant benefits, the costs of obtaining them in this manner appeared to be high. As noted in the last chapter, decentralized means of protecting economic rights rest in large part on the ability and readiness of persons to employ force. Each party must invest in means of protection. And, once provided, each must demonstrate his willingness and ability to inflict retribution. Order, in essence, is a by-product of the institutionalized feud. Decentralization is thus a costly system.

The centralized alternative

Indeed, the literature strongly suggests that more centralized systems are formed in order to avoid the turmoil of feuding. Ethnographers note that the societies now called the Alur actually *imported* chiefs from neighboring people in order to form a more centralized political community. They did so because, with the feud, they 'did not have any formal means of bringing hostilities to an end'[12]; the centralized system of chieftaincies was useful, for it 'introduced new techniques of peacemaking, arbitration, and conflict management' and provided a wider and more effective system of law and order.[13] Similar findings are reported for the Sukuma, the Anuak, the Tio, the kingdoms of Ruanda and Burundi, and for the societies of southeastern Nigeria.[14]

Nigeria, indeed, provides some of the most interesting insights into the relationship between exchange, feuds, and the organization of coercion. Northrup, Dike, Ottenberg and others have analyzed the spread of the Aro, a group which organized trade in southeastern Nigeria and provided as well a system of internal justice and military protection.[15] Quoting from interviews with Ibibio headmen, Northrup describes how villagers would meet to decide whether or not to call for the Aro to settle in their area: 'At this meeting the advantages of a permanent Aro settlement (wealth, disposal of criminals and other undesirables, exotic goods and "medicines", access to the Oracle) would have been weighed against the disadvantages. (The words ... meaning greedy and "tricky" occur with astonishing frequency in conversations about the Aro.)'[16] The Aro were themselves traders; they provided protection for trade; and they provided the 'Oracle' – a judicial system for resolving disputes without taking recourse to feuds. These advantages led to their rapid expansion, Northrup and others note, as local communities called them in.[17]

So, to secure the prosperity associated with trade, decentralized societies do contract for the services of more centralized systems. In addition, the evidence suggests that traders themselves preferred to transact with centralized groups. The basis for this preference is revealed in the accounts of early traders; as discussed by Goody, these accounts suggest that strangers 'passing through the country were called upon to pay duty to divisional chiefs. This payment was a kind of protection money and, provided the charges were not exorbitant, traders usually preferred to travel in relative security through such kingdoms rather than run the risk of being raided in the country of their chiefless neighbours.'[18]

Testing the argument
There is thus an arguable relationship between the existence of gains from trade and the formation of centralized coercive organizations, capable of enforcing property rights and securing exchange relations. This argument can best be summarized in the form of Figure 2.1.

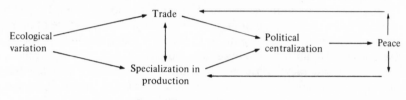

Figure 2.1

In an effort to test the 'Smithian' arguments, I use a variety of indicators of centralization. I have also collected information on a variety of factors relating to ecological variation, specialization, trade, and conflict.

As has been stressed since the time of Fortes and Evans-Pritchard, it is extraordinarily difficult to form a coherent typology of African political systems.[19] In particular, the concept of centralization is sufficiently fuzzy to engender caution in all those who seek to array these systems along that dimension. As a consequence, rather than try to generate any summary measure of centralization or to construct a unitary typology, I have chosen to employ a variety of measures of centralization and to examine the behavior of the societies with respect to each.

The first distinguishes among the following: (i) societies governed by a decentralized system of kinship, (ii) those in which there is a central monarch, and (iii) those in which there are chiefs (but no central monarch). Groups representative of (i) are the Tonga, Luo, Dorobo, and Nuer; examples of (ii) are the Mossi, Asante, Ganda, Bemba and Nupe; examples of (iii) are the Yao, Chagga, and Mende. The second indicator of centralization is the existence of a central bureaucracy. The third is the presence of any form of national army. The last is the existence of a national army which is recruited and commanded by a central military figure.

The 'Smithian' arguments suggest that the existence of potential gains from specialization and trade motivates the formation of a political framework capable of securing these gains. But causality can run in the other

25

direction as well; indeed, as has already been seen in the accounts drawn from the ethnographies, a centralized political system itself attracts traders. In the face of such reciprocal causation, the best that can be hoped for are correlations between the various measures of political centralization and the variety of key factors cited in the 'Smithian' arguments.

The first such factor is ecological variation. I asked my coders[20] to indicate whether the society had an internally diverse ecology, whether it abutted an ecological divide (e.g., living in the savannah but adjoining the forest), or whether it lacked proximity to any significant form of ecological variation. As seen in Table 1, two of the four measures of centralization – those having to do with political structure and the existence of a central bureaucracy – correlated with the factor of ecological diversity; the existence of a national or centralized army did not.

The second element in the argument is the existence of trade. I asked my coders to look for evidence of organized exchange: the presence of market centers or caravans or of long-distance trade. As seen in Table 2, societies which possess organized market centers more frequently had monarchs and a central bureaucracy; those in which there were trading caravans more frequently had monarchs and a central bureaucracy and slightly more frequently possessed a national army as well; and those which engaged in long-distance trade far more frequently were ruled by chiefs and monarchs and more frequently possessed a centralized bureaucracy. Trade and political centralization thus appear to go together, although the correlation is more characteristic of 'civilian' measures of centralization (the possession of chiefs and monarchs and a central bureaucracy) than it is of 'military measures' (the possession of a national army or of an army under a central command).[21]

The last element in the argument is the level of conflict. In the context of this analysis, the most relevant form of conflict is the feud. If centralization is adopted as a more efficient means of securing the benefits of economic exchange, then measures of centralization should correlate inversely with the presence of feuds. As seen in Table 3, political centralization has decisive impacts upon the level of feuding; societies with central monarchs and centralized bureaucracies far less frequently are subject to the costs of feuding.

Before undertaking further analysis, I wish to recall the parallels between these results and other historical materials. That long-distance trade is related to the development of states; that there is an intimate link between the presence of organized market places and the rise of centralized political forces; that the termination of feuding and the preservation of peace and order correspond with the rise of monarchs – these findings out of Africa resonate strongly with those from Western history, particularly from the medieval period. While the distinctive features of African culture and history must be stressed, what is striking at this juncture is the degree to which these findings underscore the generality of the African experience.

Augmenting the Smithian argument
The basic strategy of what is being termed the Smithian argument is to
relate institutional reform to gains in efficiency. Institutional reform – such
as the development of the capacity to maintain peace in the market – makes
higher levels of well-being possible – in this case, by facilitating trade. As
everyone could be better off under the new institution, the argument
contends, there are strong incentives for people to organize it. One way or
the other, it is argued, people will secure an institution under which they all
stand to gain.

Ironically, the basic problem with the argument is that it is insufficiently
motivated. As the gains in efficiency from the innovation of new institutions
are available to everyone, it is in no one's particular interest to provide
them. In essence, the gains which the new institution provide constitute a
public good. As all can enjoy these gains, each does better letting someone
else bear the costs of supplying them. To secure the provision of new
institutions the logic of free-riding must be overcome. In this section, we
examine one way in which this may be accomplished: by conferring an
over-riding private interest in the provision of new institutional arrangements. In particular, we determine whether a major portion of the gains
from trade were privately appropriable so that persons would be motivated
to lobby for the institutional reforms which would make them possible.[22]

One circumstance under which major private benefits would arise from
establishing the political foundations for peaceful trade would be if there
were but a small number of economic agents, each of whom dominated a
significant proportion of the market. The benefits to each would then
possibly outweigh the costs of providing those services which support the
operations of the market. While we cannot test this argument directly, we
none the less can test corollaries of it.

We would expect there to be, for example, a relatively small number of
relatively large-scale economic agents where economic activity is characterized by large investments. Particularly in societies where capital markets
are poorly formed, large investments would involve the interests of only a
few: those who for whatever reason were richly endowed. In Table 4 we see
that societies in pre-colonial Africa in which there took place large
investments of private capital, the political systems more frequently
possessed central monarchs. To a very slight degree, they more frequently
possessed centralized bureaucracies and national armies as well; they less
frequently were characterized by centralized command over the military,
however. Had these data been drawn from a random sample, it should be
noted, then none of the relationships would be statistically significant.[23]

Further data are contained in Table 2. A major lesson contained in these
data is that political centralization is related not just to trade but to
long-distance trade (*vide* the data on caravans and on whether trade was
with proximate or distant sources). The contention that long-distance trade
is a basis for state formation has, of course, long been made by certain

27

African scholars.[24] What is relevant here is that the pattern is what would be expected if efficiency gains must be privately appropriable in order to motivate the development of political institutions. This assertion rests on several grounds.

A key reason for the patterns in Table 2 may well be that the capital requirements imposed by long-distance trade meant that only a few could participate in it. By comparison with local trade, long-distance trade involved goods of high value; only such goods could withstand the transport costs. For security purposes, the goods had to be bulked and large numbers of carriers and defenders hired. Moreover, a wages fund had to be created in order to maintain the enterprise over the period of travel. As Roberts states:

> A large ivory caravan – and for self-defence it might number several hundred (some ran into thousands) – could not carry food for a long journey such as that between Tabora and the Coast (which usually took ten weeks). Instead, it carried goods with which to buy food. Furthermore, all caravans had to pay tolls at various points along a trade route and had to be supplied with an acceptable medium of payment.[25]

The initial outlays were thus large by comparison with local trade of cheaper goods, which, perforce, were marketed over shorter distances. Lastly, by comparison with local trade, the returns from long-distance trade were long postponed. As noted by Vansina, seasonality in the production of the goods involved often necessitated the protracted holding of expensive inventories.[26] Moreover, large amounts of capital were tied up in goods in transit; the 'turn around time' of long-distance transactions often involved many months.

The higher value of the items exchanged, the greater investment in transport, security, and a wages fund, and the larger amounts of capital tied up in inventories, all insured that, by contrast with local marketing, only the wealthy could engage in long-distance trade. As Dickson notes for West Africa:

> Trading was the prerogative of royalty, nobles and rich men. The reason for this may have been mainly economic . . . for trading at distant places in those times of general insecurity required . . . a heavy outlay as only wealthy persons could afford. . . . The poorer sections of the population were . . . effectively excluded from large-scale long-distance trade although there was no law expressly forbidding their participation in it.[27]

The relative concentration of benefits would help to explain why private interest would more readily translate into demands for public services in support of this industry, and therefore why long-distance trade would tend to relate to political centralization.[28]

Capital requirements thus constitute one factor leading to the concentration of benefits from trade. Another is the apparently inherent expansionary behavior of the markets themselves. Markets tend to exhibit increasing returns to scale. In part, the returns to scale derive from the fixed costs associated with entering a market: the cost of setting up business, unloading, and exhibiting wares, for example. They also arise from other forms of fixed costs – such as the provision of police protection, shelters for traders, protected warehouses. They result as well from the decline in search costs for consummating exchanges as the number of traders increases; buyers and sellers can be more certain of making a transaction the larger the number of agents engaged in trade. For all these reasons, all else being equal, it may be cheaper to transact in larger markets.

There are thus incentives for markets to expand. Other factors remaining equal, the number of markets would then decline. The consequence is that the incentives to lobby by trade groups strengthens, for the benefits associated with trading tend to be concentrated. Another consequence is that the occasions for political intervention become more frequent; market centers would tend to engage in oligopolistic rivalry as expansion leads to concentration and competition. The demands for state intervention, either to advance the interests of a particular market or to restrict rivalries between them, thus increase.

The expansion in the size of markets, their decline in number, the resultant pattern of competition and conflict between trading centers, and the mobilization of political power in support of trading interests – these patterns, which are derivable from the economics of market places, are widely recognized themes in the historical literature on Africa. Bonner, for example, notes the rise to prominence of Delagoa Bay as a trading center and the resultant conflicts in southern Africa which this engendered. As he states, 'the volume of trade handled by Delagoa Bay expanded substantially from the middle of the eighteenth century, and this promoted an escalation of conflict throughout the hinterland'.[29] Bonner concludes that, while the chief beneficiaries of the growth of trade in Delagoa Bay were the Tembe, 'there are grounds for believing that each of [the other local] kingdoms owed their early development . . . to competition for trade'.[30] Stevenson, writing of Dahomey, notes that: 'In the latter half of the nineteenth century there . . . emerged [a] major contest for . . . domination in the trading zone, which in the Dahomey instance led to the reduction of the number of competing units.'[31] Northrup, too, attributes increasing political concentration among the trading states of coastal Nigeria in part to the growth and expansion of business conducted by individual trading centers.[32] Consolidation was further abetted, he notes, by 'the natural desire of European captains to be able to gather an entire cargo from a single port rather than taking on partial cargoes at each of several smaller ports' and to the competition among the trading states to which this gave rise.[33] 'As the trade . . . expanded', he concludes, 'the coastal communities underwent gradual but decisive territorial growth [and] political centralization.'[34] The wars and rivalries associated with the desire to secure the dominance of particular trade centers or trading routes are too frequently noted and too familiar to require further documentation.

These arguments thus allow us better to comprehend the relation between the existence of market centers and the development of centralized political structures demonstrated in Table 2. They also lead us to expect further relationships in the data. They lead us to expect, for example, that the greater the movement toward political centralization, the greater the tendency for societies to protect trade routes and marketing centers. While the lack of information in the data sources renders the number of cases excessively small, the data do tend to support this contention: only central monarchs provided protection to markets and trade routes, they suggest, and those societies with national bureaucracies and armies tended to provide it more frequently than did others. Moreover, contributors to the literature suggest that centralized states can secure the triumph of particular markets or promote peace among competing ones. We should therefore expect political centralization to be associated with fewer instances of market rivalry. Again, missing information bedevils the data; but what few data there are (eight to twelve observations) suggest that market rivalries are more frequently found in societies which lack chiefs or monarchs, a centralized bureaucracy, or a national army.

There is, of course, a last reason for private interest to be linked to the political promotion of trade: the fact that the *rulers* can secure their incomes from the taxation of commerce. In an important recent essay, Robin Law argues that, while West African societies were based on agriculture, West African polities derived the bulk of their incomes not from agriculture but from trade.[35] This position has also been argued, though in less detail, by Coquéry-Vidrovitch.[36] Should rulers derive the bulk of their revenues from trade, then they would, of course, have strong incentives to employ their political power to promote it. Linked by the factor of taxation, states and markets should therefore grow together.

The data only partially support this argument. I asked my coders to indicate for each society all the 'significant' sources of public revenue. The most frequently mentioned sources of revenue were agricultural: the ruler's own estates or gardens, his own cattle, or tribute, much of which was made up of agricultural products. Forced labor and confiscation were the next most frequently mentioned. Then came trade, with market fees representing the least frequently mentioned source of public revenues.

With centralization, trade did in fact become a more frequently noted source of state income: market fees and trade were more frequently cited as a significant source of public revenues. With centralization, states tax other things as well, however. Other sources of state income were more frequently mentioned in the data files, none of these sources deriving from markets or trade. The increasing use of trade and markets as a source of public revenue may thus reflect not any systematic preference for the taxation of trade but simply the increasing ability of more centralized polities to levy taxes.

While the data thus suggest that agriculture remains a significant source of public revenues, they do in one respect support the thrust of Law's analysis: that with centralization goes an increased use of trade as a source of public income. This is sufficient to suggest a self-interested basis for providing political support for commerce. The growth of the market and the rise of states may go together simply because of the increase in public revenues which the market can provide and the incentives which are thus supplied for public officials to protect and promote commerce.

The fiscal link between trade and state formation arises in another fashion. In so far as states derive their monies from taxes on markets, it is politically undesirable to have *proximate* markets which are under *separate* jurisdictions. For, when such markets exist, traders can switch to the market which is less heavily taxed; and the states, in search of revenue-yielding commerce, have incentives to lower taxes. Under such circumstances, the states acquire fewer funds. They can attempt to negotiate a common tariff policy; but, given the advantages which accrue to the state with lower tariffs, such agreements would be unstable. Or they can consolidate their jurisdictions through either negotiation or conquest and then impose a single – and presumably higher – level of taxes. Mechanisms of taxation can thus link the existence of markets to the expansion of states. These dynamics apparently underlie much of the 'port politics' of West Africa. Akinjogbin, for example, stresses their importance in accounting for the rise of Dahomey.[37] And scholars of later periods stress their significance in accounting for the tendency of the colonial flags to follow colonial commerce in the period of imperialist expansion in West Africa.[38]

Production

Thus far I have tended to concentrate on the market portion of the Smithian argument. Significant arguments also arise with respect to the relationship between production and political organization. To these we now turn.

Marxist analysis emphasizes, of course, the centrality of the role of production in determining political relations. Moreover, in explaining the rise of the state, it gives primary emphasis to the role of capital. One need not be a Marxist, however, to argue that capital formation and political centralization go together. Major investments, for example, entail high present costs; the returns often accrue only after the passage of time. The acquisition of skills, moreover, represents a human investment – one that also pays off only after the passage of time. Prior to investing in physical goods or human skills, therefore, people must be certain of their future returns. On these grounds alone we should therefore expect to find greater levels of capital formation in more highly organized political systems – ones which offer greater prospects of peace and order – than in systems which lack central agencies of coercion. Those forming capital would promote centralization, in other words, in order to secure returns from their investments.

The argument echoes that advanced by some historians of American industrialization. Kolko, for example, argues that a reason for the abandonment of decentralized markets and the development of central regulatory agencies by the United States government in the Progressive Era was that investors sought profits from new capital-intensive technologies – those centering on the steel and rail industries – and that their decisions required a stable and favorable planning horizon, one that could be established by the mandating of set charges and prices.[39] A similar argument is advanced by scholars of developing societies. Guillermo O'Donnell, for example, relates the growth of bureaucratic power in Latin American countries to the need by investors for a stable economic environment prior to their commitment to the formation of fixed capital for heavy domestic industries.[40]

With respect to the African data, we have already noted the relationships portrayed in Table 4. I also collected data on the degree to which people held large inventories. This I used as a measure – albeit a very awkward one – of investment. And I collected data as well on the extent to which the societies contained craft specialists. As seen in Table 5, both measures strongly associate with the civilian indices of centralization. It should be noted that they do so even when controlling for the importance of trade; the relation is thus not merely a corollary of our previous findings.[41]

There is additional evidence for the relation between the need for economic stability and the rise of centralized states. Historical studies suggest that those whose interests were tied to production and trade sometimes took a distinctive position in debates over public policy. In particular, they appear on occasion to have formed a pressure group opposing the pursuit of war. Thus Wilks notes the formation of a 'political party' in Asante which stood for 'peace, trade and open roads' and opposed the continuation of warfare by the Asante military elite as it threatened these objectives.[42] A similar lobby existed in Oyo; its activities apparently played an important role in the split between Alafin and the Oyo Mesi that so characterized the politics of that kingdom.[43] Conflicts between commercial interests and an aristocracy which lived off warfare also constituted a major political divide among the Wolof of Senegal and helped to promote the rise of Islamic sectarian movements in that and other savannah societies in pre-colonial West Africa.[44]

Economic interests thus appear to have favored peaceful, stable and predictable relations – ones that would allow them better to reap the rewards of their outlays. In so far as politically centralized states could provide a more stable economic environment, then these interests allied with the forces of centralization. But in so far as centralized agencies – such as military forces – threatened their prosperity, then these interests withdrew their support from that element of the centralized polity. While a central army may provide protection for investments and trade, it can also be employed in political adventures – something that threatens the interests of those who need the certainty of an uninterrupted flow of positive returns before they can enrich themselves by investing.

This argument, which is largely derived from narrative sources, helps to explain a strongly anomalous pattern in the data: the relatively weak performance of military as opposed to civilian indices of centralization. This contrast in the behavior of the civilian and military measures of centralization has hitherto been disconcerting. But, upon reflection, it is what would be expected were capital formation and inter-temporal stability primary objectives of major social interests.

DEMOGRAPHY, LAND, AND CROWDING: PROPERTY RIGHTS ARGUMENTS

The essence of the Smithian model is that state power facilitates the attainment of economic gains and that it does so by securing property rights over returns from productive investments or from transactions in the market place. There is a second strand in the literature which also stresses property rights; but it looks less at trade and production than at people and natural resources.

The argument begins by noting the relationship between soil quality and state formation. When societies were located in areas of soils of uniform quality, the literature suggests, states did not form. When they were located in particularly fertile soils, however, states may have formed. Colson, for example, notes the disparity in soil qualities in East and Central Africa and comments: 'The soils elsewhere in sub-Saharan Africa favoured shifting cultivation with . . . a dispersal of population. Exceptions were found in the intra-lacustrian region bordering on Lake Victoria with its rich volcanic soils . . . and in the flood plains of the Upper Zambezi, where soil fertility was renewed by the annual flood.'[45] It was in the intra-lacustrian area and the Zambezi valley, Colson notes, that centralized states were formed.

In one of the major essays on the politics of pre-colonial African societies, Gluckman examines the dynamics of state formation. Gluckman explains the failure of states to form throughout much of southern Africa in terms of the relatively uniform productivity of the land and in terms of its abundance. Thus, he argues, when 'rising numbers place . . . a steadily increasing pressure on the resources of [a] tribe's territory [then] sections of the tribe . . . moved away to [other] lands and to independence'.[46] It was only when good lands became relatively scarce, he claims, that the process of state formation began, and in particular, that the region witnessed the rise of the Zulu nation. Gluckman's argument concerning the Zulu – who engaged in one of the most rapid and explosive instances of political organization in recorded history – has received strong support from more recent scholars, such as Bonner and Omer-Cooper.[47]

The literature thus suggests that we should expect greater degrees of political centralization in areas of comparatively fertile soils. The data in Table 6 lend modest support to this conjecture.

In linking the quality of natural resources to state formation, scholars tend to invoke a second major factor: population density. Particularly favorable natural endowments tend to attract greater numbers of people. And as the density of population increases, it is held, the occasions multiply in which the behavior of one person influences the productive activity of another. This is particularly true with respect to land usage. The greater the number of claimants for land and the greater its relative scarcity, then the greater the extent to which one person's use of this resource precludes another's. There is thus an incentive to render land a well-defined commodity: one that is amenable to compensation for its utilization. And the agency that enforces the rights which define commodities is, of course, the state. This argument is central to Engels' interpretation of the rise of 'primitive' states; ironically, it is also central to the new institutional economics as developed by such neo-classical economists as Demsetz, North, Thomas, and Davis.[48]

The critical role of population density in political change has been most thoroughly investigated in non-African settings. Carneiro, for example, has developed the concept 'environmental circumspection', which refers to the property of distinctive locational advantage which, he argues, induces a high density of population with an attendant rise of land scarcity, conflict, and the formation of political systems.[49] And students of medieval history, such as Postan and Le Roy Ladurie, have related changes in population to changes in the extent and depth of the market, to changes in the distribution of income (via alterations in relative factor prices), and to changes in the institutional framework of agrarian societies, including their political relations.[50]

While lacking the centrality achieved in other fields, such demographic hypotheses have been vigorously debated in the African literature as well. Stevenson and Vengroff, for example, have argued the general proposition that high population densities were associated with the formation of states.[51] The case has been most carefully and persuasively advanced in particular case studies, however; so too has the contention that resource scarcity and the need for mechanisms of conflict resolution provide the major intervening variables.

In his study of the Tio, for example, Vansina notes that initially 'land was without value and anyone could always leave and build his own home where it pleased him'.[52] As a consequence, 'the losers could leave the game when they wanted to . . . People would split up long before they reached the level of actually fighting with one another.'[53] But, he notes, with denser populations, 'the situation was different. There existed a limitation on favorable sites . . . and the struggle may have been more intense, with . . . strife and warfare occurring much more frequently.'[54] A major response of the Tio, he indicates, was the provision of political officials to adjudicate disputes and to mediate conflicts over scarce resources. A similar evolution is suggested by Roberts in his discussion of the Nyamwezi. 'Until the later nineteenth century', Roberts argues, 'there was little pressure for chiefs to exercise authority over large numbers of people. There was no serious competition over land-use such as might call for regulation by superior authority.'[55] With the growth of population, however, the situation apparently changed, and there was a movement toward the creation of more powerful chieftaincies.

34

I attempted to test the demographic argument. Direct tests were difficult, however, for estimates of population and area were often lacking and, when they did appear, they fluctuated widely between different sources. There was no remedy for the first problem; to cope with the second, I simply abandoned any confidence in 'point estimates' and instead recorded both highest and lowest estimates of population density. As seen in Table 7, there was sometimes a strong relationship between the estimates of population density and the measures of political centralization; and, save in one case, the higher the population density, the greater the level of political centralization.[56]

The arguments thus far suggest that favorable resource endowments attract large populations and that population density promotes the formation of political systems by generating a demand for the vesting of property rights over scarce resources. Another possibility is, of course, that population density promotes political centralization not by creating a need for property rights over resources but by promoting the growth of markets and trade. The question naturally arises: are not our previous findings, summarized in the Smithian argument, then spurious? Do we not simply have a variant of Le Roy Ladurie's 'great demographic cycle', wherein economic and political change covary as a consequence of their shared relationship to population growth? The answer to this question lies in the use of statistical controls. While the small number of observations available very severely frustrated attempts to control for the effects of population density, in a few cases, enough observations were available to introduce such controls. Although the small number of cases severely devalues the significance of the relationships, we may none the less note that, as illustrated in Table 8, economic and political factors tend to be related, even after controlling for the density of population.

RENT SEEKING

The desire for economic prosperity can be linked to the employment of coercion in a variety of other ways. One is through the factor of rents. Rents represent an economic value over and above what could be obtained in competitive markets. They can be created purposefully; monopoly rents, for example, accrue to those who restrict competition in product markets. Or they can be created by nature. Special sites confer particular advantages upon people fortunate enough to be located on them; being inherently scarce and non-mobile, these sites favor a fortunate few, and competitive forces cannot erode their locational advantage. Rents accrue to those who occupy particularly fertile soils, a favorable geographic location, or an area with mineral deposits, for example. Material advantages are conferred upon those who control such resources and they generate incentives for others to attempt to seize them. The existence of rents thus gives rise to tensions and conflict and motivates the organization and employment of force for economic purposes.

Exemplifying these dynamics is Birmingham's discussion of the salt and copper mines of Central Africa. Control over the mines, Birmingham asserts, made possible the levying of revenues; those who 'controlled the area allowed some neighbouring peoples in to work the mines on payment of a fee, but others ... were excluded from the area'.[57] Moreover, it made necessary the organization of defense. For, in response to the existence of these rents, he indicates, 'the Portuguese tried to move inland and gain control of the mines'. And in response to the Portuguese incursions, 'resistance forces of a far greater magnitude were mobilized'.[58] The existence of rents in the form of mineral deposits thus increased the demand for the organization of force and the ability to mobilize resources by which to supply it.[59]

Earlier figures show the relationship between land quality and centralization (Table 6) and between trade and centralization (Table 2). The data in Table 9 show the relationship between the possession of mines and the level of political organization. In nearly all of the sixteen tests of the argument possible with the data, the relationships run in the right direction. The presence of mineral deposits tends to associate with political centralization.

THE STATE AS MEANS OF PRODUCTION

States not only assist in the performance of markets; they are also directly productive. For this reason as well, those seeking economic gain may seek the formation of states.

For example, states produce public goods. We have already analyzed their role in producing security and property rights. They also produce infrastructure. This apparently was as true in pre-colonial Africa as it is elsewhere. For, as seen in Table 10, the data generally support the contention that political centralization correlated with the supply of public goods – roads, bridges, canals and pontoons being the ones recorded.

The states of pre-colonial Africa were productive in another sense. For it appears that in some instances they operated as economic agencies: ones that secured inputs, organized them into productive enterprises, and generated a final product for exchange with other economic actors, thereby generating profits.

In some areas, the state simply traded on its own account. Thus the Asante government maintained from time to time a state trading corporation, the Batafo, which marketed kola, gold, and slaves in both the northern territories and the coast. But the states usually lacked a relative advantage in such activities, and found that they could more efficiently generate needed revenues by leaving the conduct of trade to private entrepreneurs and by taxing them.[60]

The states did hold a relative advantage in some kinds of economic affairs, however: ones in which organized violence could be utilized as a profitable activity. One such area was in the securing of slaves. Labor was a relatively scarce factor; compared to other factors, the marginal return to labor was high. With abundant and freely obtainable land, able-bodied people could in many cases assure themselves of a prosperous subsistence livelihood; the opportunity costs of labor were therefore high and labor was costly in the marketplace. There were thus strong incentives to use coercion to secure workers at below the market price. By forcibly extracting workers from the relatively prosperous subsistence sector and by compelling them to work at reduced levels of remuneration, those with control over the means of coercion could appropriate much of the returns to this scarce factor.[61]

Sometimes slaves were used domestically in plantations, gold mines, or the public service. In other cases, they were sold abroad. In either instance, warfare was used to generate economic advantage. As Vansina writes: 'The real reason . . . that Angola needed wars [was] because they bred slaves.'[62] And as Roberts reports for the Bemba: 'In the old days, at least, they took a positive pride in "cultivating with the spear".'[63] The close connection between state power and the slaving industry is underscored by the rise of such societies as the notorious Yeke – ones whose state systems specialized in the production of slaves.

Conventional historiography sees the slave trade as leading to a major decline in the political and economic systems of Africa. More recent work questions this assessment.[64] While those societies which were conquered and enslaved clearly were weakened by the slave trade, there are few signs that those who initiated the capture of slaves 'disintegrated' either politically or economically. Instead, using the export of slaves and the import of guns as indications of participation in the slave trade, our analysis suggests that the tendency to re-evaluate the disintegrative effects of the slave trade may be correct. For, as seen in Table 11, it was never the case that societies which participated in the slave trade more frequently tended to exhibit the traits of political decentralization; and it was often the case that they more frequently were politically centralized. Moreover, as seen in Table 12, measures of participation in the slave trade correlate with measures of economic prosperity: the presence of craft specialists and trade, for example. Furthermore, as seen in Table 13, while the importation of guns associates with the tendency toward internal feuding, the exportation of slaves does not, save in a negative fashion (neither relation would be statistically significant, however). The slave trade was clearly harmful – indeed, disastrous – to some societies; but it thus appears not to have been politically or economically harmful to others. Indeed, it appears to have played a role in their economic prosperity; and rather than weakening their internal unity, it appears instead to have promoted the forces of political centralization.

It will be recalled that in earlier sections we noted evidence of conflict between economic and military interests. Measures of military centralization sometimes failed to correlate with measures of economic activity; and historical accounts revealed tension between military and trading interests in the pre-colonial societies of Africa. Our present analysis, which stresses the relation between economic activity and the forceful appropriation of slaves, would appear to contradict the earlier arguments. But the contradiction is only superficial. For in many periods slaving was profitable. And it was when it failed to remain so that the economic interests moved into opposition to those who organized the means of plunder. As Wilks notes for Asante:

> The decline in the maritime markets for slaves ... had the effect of making warfare less profitable and therefore less popular.[65]

> There can be little doubt that it was the sharp decline of the maritime markets for slaves at the beginning of the nineteenth century that was one of the principal reasons for the failure of the imperial or war party to maintain control over the Asante councils.[66]

Further evidence for the link between profit maximization and slaving is the work of LeVeen and Gemery and Hogendorn; they report significant positive relationships between changes in price and changes in the supply of slaves from West Africa, thus establishing a necessary condition for arguing that the slave trade represented profit-maximizing behavior.[67] Given that the slave trade and profit seeking were so closely combined, we can thus comprehend how economic interests could both support and oppose the military, depending upon whether the economic climate favored raiding or other economic endeavors. The relationship between economic interest and military power is thus not systematic, and the weak correlations which we obtain are therefore to be expected.

THE STATE AS MEANS OF REDISTRIBUTION

With obvious exceptions, many of the arguments thus far presented in this chapter stress the role of the state in securing economic prosperity. Inevitably, however, the chapter has entered another realm of political explanation: one in which the power to coerce is seen not as a means of establishing a framework for common prosperity but as a means for redistributing income. Redistribution, as well as efficiency, is commonly a goal of political action; and this was as true in pre-colonial Africa as it has been in other periods and places. In this section we examine arguments which stress the political basis of economic redistribution. We do so in large part by focusing on stratification in African societies.

One of the classic explanations for the formation of African states emphasizes the role of domination between divergent modes of agricultural production. While more recent scholarship calls this interpretation into question, many scholars have stressed the role of the state in enabling 'pastoralists' to rule over 'agriculturalists'.[68] Such arguments feature in the ethnography of the intra-lacustrian areas, of course, but also in studies of the Shilluk, Rosvi, and Zulu.[69] In these and other societies, it has been held, pastoralist populations, with their valuable herds and their mastery of techniques of warfare, employ the state to exact tribute and services from the sedentary agriculturalists. Alluding to the argument of Oppenheimer, scholars have thus interpreted the traditional state in Africa as a mechanism of pastoralist domination.[70]

The data only partially support this argument. They clearly indicate that domination by those who practice one form of agricultural production over those who practice another does indeed necessitate political centralization (Table 14); three of the four measures of centralization correlate with domination by one or another of these groups. Contradicting the argument, however, the data suggest that the pattern of domination can favor either group; the 'warlike pastoralists' are not always pre-eminent. Even more to the point, either pattern is very rare; cohabitation rather than domination commonly characterizes the relationship between pastoralists and agriculturalists.

Political centralization and internal stratification can relate in other ways, however. Through the power to levy tribute, to collect taxes, and to structure property rights, those in charge of the state can employ it to induce patterns of inequality. Agrarian states commonly underpin stable patterns of collective advantage in the form of estates and castes. As seen in Table 15, this appears to have been true in pre-colonial Africa as well; with but two exceptions, the greater the degree of political centralization, the more frequent the occurrence of an aristocracy or a system of castes.

In earlier sections, we have noted the relationship between the formation of states and the growth of specialization and trade. Relevant to the present argument is another side of the relationship. Not only can the state be used to promote trade; it can also be employed to restrict it. With more highly centralized polities, not only can craft specialization develop (as seen in Table 5) but also craftsmen can better employ political power to restrict entry into their trade (i.e. form guilds), to limit output, or to set prices. Our data give limited support to this argument; the possession of monarchies and centralized bureaucracies does tend to associate with the adoption of restrictive practices (Table 16), although the relationship is neither significant nor clear cut, and military indicators of centralization fail to behave in a similar manner. Materials from historical and anthropological accounts provide further evidence. They suggest not only that states help to form and maintain market places – as seen in Table 2 – but also that centralized governments are in a position to impose non-competitive prices by abetting collusion among traders. In one famous account, for example, Karl Polanyi documents (and lauds) the existence of such procedures in Dahomey;[71] a more lurid discussion is provided by the Tardits, who describe the sanctions imposed upon Dahomean marketers by the *zangbeto* society, a secret society operating with the specific authorization of the state:

> *Zangbeto* watches the merchants and if they find that a woman trespasses the law, the members of the association walk through the village for seven nights, cursing the woman who disregarded the [customary price] ... If she does not

39

comply, *zangbeto* will come out again, curse her for sixteen more nights and carry through the village a banana tree branch wrapped in a white cloth representing a corpse in a shroud . . . The tradition says that the lawbreaker dies shortly afterwards.[72]

The governance of the market places by the state thus not only facilitates trade, it also facilitates the restraint of trade and the securing of a redistribution of income.

Marketers are not the sole beneficiaries of state support for non-competitive practices, however. The rulers themselves also secure the advantages conferred by state power. Thus our data indicate that in over 80 per cent of those societies which had governmental structures, as opposed to merely structures of kinship, the chiefs possessed monopoly rights of one kind or another (Table 17). Table 18 indicates the most common forms of this practice.

Despite the arguments of many that little by way of economic advantage separated the political elites of African states from their followers, the data (Table 19) strongly suggest that the rulers lived better: they were better housed, better clothed, better fed, and had greater access to productive resources. Government and inequality go together, it would appear, in pre-colonial Africa just as they do elsewhere.

CONCLUSION

The literature on traditional states confronts us with a stark choice: we are invited to subscribe either to the 'neo-contractarians', who see the state as a mechanism for securing collective advantage, or the 'neo-Marxists', who see it as an agency of expropriation.

Exemplifying the first would be scholars such as Elman Service. As with many whose arguments have been examined here, Service stresses the benefits of political organization. He argues that these benefits alone would help to explain the adoption of centralized political systems.[73] As we have seen, in pre-colonial Africa, the states underpinned specialization and trade; they terminated feuds; they provided peace and stability and the conditions for private investment; they formed public works; and they generated wealth, if only in the form of plunder. In these ways, the states secured prosperity for their citizens. Service and others would argue that that is why they exist.

Arguing against this position would be scholars such as Fried who see the state as essentially redistributive.[74] The need to protect stratification, inequality, and privilege, it is held, provides the principal impetus to political organization. As we have seen, in pre-colonial Africa, states provided means for expropriation and redistribution. They underpinned slavery. They supported an aristocracy and a system of castes. Their rulers were relatively wealthy. And the prosperity they generated was unequally shared.

40

In the literature at large, then, we are exhorted to join the camp that sees the state as the source of collective prosperity or the camp that sees the state as the source of oppression. But the evidence forces us to realize that in pre-colonial Africa states were both.

For too long, it would appear, the literature has offered a false choice. The African materials suggest that the origins of the state lie in a blend of the forces cited by the competing theories of state formation. Those who seek power seek private advantages; they, like the rest of us, seek more of the good things of life, and they turn to the exercise of power to gain them. But, to win and retain political power, political aspirants must attract followers, and to do so they must offer advantages, such as the opportunity to prosper. To secure disproportionate benefits, they must generate benefits which can be shared. This account would appear to be closer to the truth than either the neo-contractarian or the redistributive theories.[75]

What makes the two sides of state formation so apparent in the African case is that the relative bargaining power of the masses strongly highlights the necessity for sharing by those who sought political privilege. We have noted that in central and southern Africa, at least, land was relatively uniform in quality; moreover, being abundant, it was practically free. In societies where people derived their incomes from farming, this meant that they could readily move from one society to another. As Colson notes, the result was that 'Given provocation, subjects could migrate beyond the borders as well as within the boundaries of a kingdom. Malcontents [could] join ... some [other] polity.'[76] Being mobile, the citizenry could thus bargain for favorable treatment by their rulers. Not only did they possess the means to exit, however; the evidence suggests that they also possessed institutionalized means of giving voice and thereby securing more favorable policies from their governments. Commoners often controlled particular offices, such as the 'prime ministership', the principal administrative office in the nation. Chiefs often had to rule through councils dominated by non-royals. The Oyo Mesi is an extreme example; it repeatedly deposed the Alafin and often compelled his 'suicide'.[77] In many cases, commoners kept the selection and appointment of administrative personnel out of the hands of the king; the rule of hereditary succession to headmanships or territorial chieftainships insured that lineage elders could control the selection of administrative personnel.[78] The fact that in most states the people *were* the army and that the monarchs had no independent full-time forces of his own also placed limits on central power. And the commoners sometimes exerted considerable influence upon public officials through the agency of secret societies.[79]

The extent to which commoner institutions prevailed even in centralized societies is suggested in the data. Commoner councils to debate policy existed in 36 per cent of the central monarchies and chieftaincies; and commoner councils to try cases existed in over 75 per cent of the chieftaincies and in virtually all of the central monarchies. Moreover, as

41

shown in Table 20, the existence of privileged strata, such as aristocracies or castes, failed to diminish the likelihood of the existence of such councils. Indeed, the data suggest the opposite; rather than being antagonistic tendencies, stratification and the institutionalization of commoner councils appear either to have been independent phenomena or to have systematically gone together!

The citizenry thus possessed both the option to exit and the capacity to give voice to their interests. Further enhancing their bargaining power was the level of competition for office within the political elite.

Long ago anthropologists studying African political systems discredited the notion that rules of descent placed unambiguous constraints upon the selection of rulers. Instead, as Gluckman writes, 'rarely in Africa do we find rules which indicate clearly and definitely a single heir ... Or if the rules themselves were clear, they operated uncertainly in practice. The result was that almost every succession could raise rival claimants.'[80] Contestants for office had to gather a following; and, in competing for supporters, they used their elite positions to generate benefits for the citizenry and made pledges of further benefits in the event that they should acquire power. Competition took place during succession disputes, which were contested by branches of the royal clan, by the sons and the nephews of former kings, or by prominent regional chiefs. It also took place between the members of the ruling elite – the cattle and army and administrative chiefs in Burundi, for example;[81] between regional elites, such as Chitimukulu and Mwamba, his regional rival, among the Bemba; or between segments of the royal lineage, as among the Kanuri. As Ronald Cohen writes:

> The major internal opposition to the monarch lay within the other segments of the royal lineage, that is to say, among his competitors for the royal office. These men and their followers, using whatever support they could obtain among the titled nobility, presented a constant danger of usurpation and even assassination to the ruling monarch. Excessive tyranny, continual lack of military success, local uprisings, or even weakened physical condition through ill-health or old age stimulated such opposition.[82]

The citizenry could thus exit. Through institutionalized means of access to power, they could oppose. Given the presence of vigorous competition for public office, they could bargain and exact. The evidence suggests that, while there was inequality in the states of pre-colonial Africa, those who held positions of privilege had to insure that the benefits created by the states were widely shared. For the bargaining power of the masses, relative to the elites, was strong, and to retain power the elites had to serve the interests of their followers, if only because they would otherwise lose their followers, physically or politically, or other elites would displace them.

Table 1 *Political structure and ecological variation (Percentages)*

Ecologically diversified area:

Political structure		Central bureaucracy		National army		Army commanded at	
Kinship	17	Absent	40	Absent	40	Local level	40
Chiefs	50	Present	60	Present	60	Regional level	20
Centralized						National level	40
monarch	33						
N =	6		5		5		5

Society abuts on an ecological divide:

Political structure		Central bureaucracy		National army		Army commanded at	
Kinship	12	Absent	25	Absent	38	Local level	62
Chiefs	38	Present	75	Present	62	Regional level	0
Centralized						National level	38
monarch	50						
N =	8		8		8		8

No significant ecological variation:

Political structure*		Central bureaucracy*		National army		Army commanded at	
Kinship	40	Absent	67	Absent	50	Local level	50
Chiefs	20	Present	33	Present	50	Regional level	10
Centralized						National level	40
monarch	40						
N =	20		18		20		20

*Chi squared significant at .10 level

The pre-colonial period

Table 2　Relation with measure of trade

Societies possess market centers? (Percentages)

Political structure*	Yes	No	Central bureaucracy*	Yes	No	National army	Yes	No	Army commanded at	Yes	No
Kinship	15	32	Absent	42	87	Absent	54	50	Local level	15	6
Chiefs	31	42	Present	58	13	Present	46	50	Regional level	54	50
Central									National level	31	44
monarchs	54	26									
N =	13	19		12	16		13	16		13	16

Societies possess trade caravans? (Percentages)

Political structure**	Yes	No	Central bureaucracy*	Yes	No	National army	Yes	No	Army commanded at	Yes	No
Kinship	0	43	Absent	44	79	Absent	45	56	Local level	18	0
Chiefs	45	24	Present	56	21	Present	55	44	Regional level	46	56
Central									National level	36	44
monarchs	55	33									
N =	11	21		9	19		11	20		11	18

Was trade mainly local (L) or long distance (LD)? (Percentages)

Political structure***	L	LD	Central bureaucracy*	L	LD	National army	L	LD	Army commanded at	L	LD
Kinship	53	6	Absent	60	31	Absent	47	47	Local level	6	13
Chiefs	0	50	Present	40	69	Present	53	53	Regional level	47	47
Central									National level	47	40
monarchs	47	44									
N =	15	16		15	13		15	15		15	15

*　　Chi squared significant at .10 level
**　Chi squared significant at .05 level
*** Chi squared significant at .01 level

Table 3 *Political centralization and feuds*

Are There Feuds? (Percentage 'Yes')

Political structure***		N	Central bureaucracy***		N	National army		N	Army commanded at		N
Kinship	89	9	Absent	72	9	Absent	69	16	Local level	100	2
Chiefs	78	9	Present	27	18	Present	43	14	Regional level	69	16
Centralized monarchs	23	13							National level	42	12

*** Chi squared significant at .01 level

Table 4 *Political structure and private investment*

Are there instances where large capital investments are made by private groups? (Percentage)

Political structure	Yes	No	Central bureaucracy	Yes	No	National army	Yes	No	Army commanded at	Yes	No
Kinship	0	36	Absent	50	52	Absent	50	52	Local level	50	44
Chiefs	33	32	Present	50	48	Present	50	48	Regional level	17	4
Central monarchs	67	32							National level	33	52
N =	6	28		6	28		6	25		6	25

Table 5 *Political centralization, craft specialization and the holding of inventories*

Carrying of large inventories? (Percentage)

Political structure**			Central bureaucracy**			National army			Army commanded at		
	Yes	No		Yes	No		Yes	No		Yes	No
Kinship	8	45	Absent	45	84	Absent	38	61	Local level	15	6
Chiefs	31	30	Present	55	16	Present	62	39	Regional level	39	61
Central									National level	46	33
monarchs	62	25									
N =	13	20		11	21		13	18		13	18

Craft specialists? (Percentage)

Political structure***			Central bureaucracy**			National army			Army commanded at		
	Yes	No		Yes	No		Yes	No		Yes	No
Kinship	21	45	Absent	43	100	Absent	46	75	Local level	12	0
Chiefs	25	55	Present	57	0	Present	54	25	Regional level	46	75
Central									National level	42	25
monarchs	54	0									
N =	24	11		21	10		24	8		24	8

** Chi squared significant at .05 level
*** Chi squared significant at .01 level

Table 6 *Soil fertility and political structure*

Is the quality of soils high by comparison with the soils in surrounding areas? (Percentage)

Political structure			Central bureaucracy			National army*			Army commanded at*		
	Yes	No		Yes	No		Yes	No		Yes	No
Kinship	17	50	Absent	62	83	Absent	35	83	Local level	12	0
Chiefs	33	17	Present	38	17	Present	65	17	Regional level	35	83
Central									National level	53	17
monarchs	50	33									
N =	18	6		16	6		17	6		17	6

* Chi squared significant at .10 level

Table 7 *Population density and political centralization*

Using upper estimates of population density: population density (Percentage)

Political structure	Low(1)	High(2)	Central bureaucracy*	Low	High	National army***	Low	High	Army commanded at***	Low	High
Kinship	33	25	Absent	56	71	Absent	75	29	Local level	75	29
Chiefs	22	25	Present	44	29	Present	25	71	Regional level	0	0
Central									National level	25	71
monarchs	44	50									
N =	9	8		9	7		8	7		8	7

Using lower estimates of population density: population density (Percentage)

Political structure	Low(3)	High(4)	Central bureaucracy	Low	High	National army*	Low	High	Army commanded at	Low	High
Kinship	60	17	Absent	80	20	Absent	100	0	Local level	100	0
Chiefs	20	17	Present	20	80	Present	0	100	Regional level	0	0
Central									National level	0	100
monarchs	20	66									
N =	5	6		5	5		5	5		5	5

Upper estimates of population density:
(1) Low: 40 persons or less per sq. mile
(2) High: over 40 persons per sq. mile
*   p < .10, Fisher exact test
*** p < .01, Fisher exact test

Lower estimates of population density:
(3) Low: 10 persons or less per sq. mile
(4) High: Over 10 persons per sq. mile

Table 8   *Measures of centralization and trade: controlling for population density (Percentage)*

Population density low (1)

	Caravan traffic?			Market centers?	
	Yes	No		Yes	No
Political structure			Central bureaucracy		
Kinship	0	50	Absent	25	100
Chiefs	50	17	Present	75	0
Central monarchs	50	33			
N =	2	6		4	4

Population density high (2)

	Caravan traffic?			Market centers?	
	Yes	No		Yes	No
Political structure			Central bureaucracy		
Kinship	0	40	Absent	50	100
Chiefs	0	20	Present	50	0
Central monarchs	100	40			
N =	2	5		4	2

(1) Low: 40 persons or less per square mile
(2) High: Over 40 persons per square mile

Table 9   *Mining and centralization: does this society's territories include*

Gold mines? (Percentage)

Political structure**	Yes	No	Central bureaucracy**	Yes	No	National army	Yes	No	Army commanded at	Yes	No
Kinship	0	35	Absent	25	76	Absent	25	56	Local level	25	8
Chiefs	0	31	Present	75	24	Present	75	44	Regional level	25	56
Central									National level	50	36
monarchs	100	31									
N =	4	26		4	25		4	25		4	25

Copper mines? (Percentage)

Political structure*	Yes	No	Central bureaucracy**	Yes	No	National army	Yes	No	Army commanded at	Yes	No
Kinship	0	37	Absent	0	77	Absent	50	54	Local level	0	8
Chiefs	0	30	Present	100	23	Present	50	46	Regional level	50	54
Central									National level	50	38
monarchs	100	33									
N =	2	27		2	26		2	26		2	26

Salt mines? (Percentage)

Political structure	Yes	No	Central bureaucracy*	Yes	No	National army	Yes	No	Army commanded at	Yes	No
Kinship	0	37	Absent	0	74	Absent	0	50	Local level	0	8
Chiefs	50	26	Present	100	26	Present	100	50	Regional level	100	50
Central									National level	0	42
monarchs	50	37									
N =	2	27		2	27		2	26		2	26

Iron mines? (Percentage)

Political structure*	Yes	No	Central bureaucracy*	Yes	No	National army	Yes	No	Army commanded at*	Yes	No
Kinship	25	37	Absent	50	82	Absent	42	56	Local level	25	0
Chiefs	8	37	Present	50	18	Present	58	44	Regional level	42	56
Central									National level	33	44
monarchs	67	26									
N =	12	19		12	17		12	18		12	18

*   Chi squared significant at .10 level   ** Chi squared significant at .05 level

Table 10 *State formation and public goods*

Were there roads? (Percentage 'Yes')

Political structure**		Central bureaucracy		National army		Army commanded at	
Kinship	0	Absent	14	Absent	27	Local level	27
Chiefs	20	Present	88	Present	50	Regional level	50
Centralized						National level	50
monarch	75						
N =	30		29		29		29

Were there bridges? (Percentage 'Yes')

Political structure*		Central bureaucracy		National army*		Army commanded at*	
Kinship	0	Absent	0	Absent	0	Local level	0
Chiefs	0	Present	40	Present	17	Regional level	0
Centralized						National level	20
monarch	22						
N =	27		26		26		26

Were there pontoons? (Percentage 'Yes')

Political structure*		Central bureaucracy		National army*		Army commanded at*	
Kinship	0	Absent	10	Absent	7	Local level	7
Chiefs	0	Present	50	Present	27	Regional level	0
Centralized						National level	33
monarch	50						
N =	26		25		25		25

Were there canals? (Percentage 'Yes')

Political structure*		Central bureaucracy*		National army*		Army commanded at*	
Kinship	0	Absent	5	Absent	13	Local level	13
Chiefs	11	Present	40	Present	17	Regional level	0
Centralized						National level	20
monarch	33						
N =	28		26		27		31

*   Chi squared significant at .10 level
** Chi squared significant at .05 level

Table 11   *Slave trade and political structure*

Trade in slaves? (Percentage)

Political structure**	Yes	No	Central bureaucracy***	Yes	No	National army***	Yes	No	Army commanded at	Yes	No
Kinship	0	40	Absent	25	83	Absent	11	65	Local level	11	30
Chiefs	22	32	Present	75	17	Present	89	35	Regional level	22	4
Central									National level	67	65
monarchs	78	28									
N =	9	25		8	23		9	23		9	23

Import guns? (Percentage)

Political structure	Yes	No	Central bureaucracy**	Yes	No	National army	Yes	No	Army commanded at	Yes	No
Kinship	10	38	Absent	29	79	Absent	50	50	Local level	40	41
Chiefs	40	25	Present	71	21	Present	50	50	Regional level	10	9
Central									National level	50	50
monarchs	50	38									
N =	10	24		7	24		10	22		10	22

** Chi squared significant at .05 level
*** Chi squared significant at .01 level

Table 12   *The slave economy*

	Trade in slaves? (Percentage)		Import guns? (Percentage)	
Are there:	Yes	No	Yes	No
Market centers?				
Yes	50	41	56	38
No	50	59	44	62
N =	8	22	9	21
Craft specialists?				
Yes	100	60	90	63
No	0	40	10	37
N =	9	25	10	24
		**		*
Caravans?				
Yes	88	17	56	27
No	12	83	44	73
N =	8	23	9	22
		***		
Was trade mainly local?				
Yes	25	59	30	57
No	75	41	70	43
N =	8	22	10	21
		*		
Was there carrying of inventories?				
Yes	89	21	70	26
No	11	79	30	74
N =	9	24	10	23
		***		**

*   Chi squared significant at .10 level
**   Chi squared significant at .05 level
*** Chi squared significant at .01 level

Table 13   Slave trade and feuds

	Trade in slaves? (Percentage)		Import guns? (Percentage)	
	Yes	No	Yes	No
Are there feuds?				
Yes	38	62	62	52
No	62	38	38	48
N =	8	21	8	21

Table 14   Social domination and political centralization

	Pastoralists dominate (Percentage)	Agriculturalists dominate (Percentage)	No domination (Percentage)
Political structure based on:			
Kinship	0	0	24
Chieftaincies	0	0	38
Central monarchs	100	100	38
N =	1	1	29
Central bureaucracy			
Present	100	0	35
Absent	0	100	65
N =	1	1	26
National army			
Yes	100	100	44
No	0	0	56
N =	1	1	27
Army organized at			
National level	100	100	33
Regional level	0	0	56
Local level	0	0	11
N =	1	1	27

Table 15   *Stratification and centralization*

Are there castes? (Percentage 'Yes')

Political structure		Central bureaucracy**		National army		Army commanded at	
Kinship	10	Absent	27	Absent	35	Local level	50
Chiefs	30	Present	50	Present	29	Regional level	35
Central						National level	25
monarchs	43						
N =	31		30		31		31

Is there a class of nobles or an aristocracy? (Percentage 'Yes')

Political structure***		Central bureaucracy**		National army		Army commanded at	
Kinship	0	Absent	37	Absent	46	Local level	50
Chiefs	57	Present	87	Present	69	Regional level	46
Central						National level	73
monarchs	92						
N =	28		27		26		26

**   Chi squared significant at .05 level
*** Chi squared significant at .01 level

Table 16   *Do craft specialists have the right to set prices, restrict entry or limit output? (Percentage 'Yes')*

Political structure		Central bureaucracy		National army		Army commanded at	
Kinship	33	Absent	33	Absent	67	Local level	67
Chiefs	0	Present	67	Present	33	Regional level	57
Central						National level	17
monarchs	50						
N =	16		15		18		16

Table 17   *Chiefs and economic redistribution*

Do chiefs have monopoly rights? (Percentage 'Yes')

Yes	57
No	11
Not applicable	31
N =	35

Table 18   *Most frequently mentioned objects of chiefs' monopoly*

Object	No. of mentions
Ivory	6
Kola	2
Slaves	6
Cattle	2
Skins	2
Parts of game killed	10

Table 19   *Chiefs and inequality (Percentage)*

Do kings or chiefs have:	
More luxurious homes?	
Yes	66
No	6
Not applicable	29
N =	35
More livestock?	
Yes	58
No	6
Not applicable	36
N =	33
More slaves/retainers?	
Yes	59
No	6
Not applicable	34
N =	32
Greater lands?	
Yes	62
No	9
Not applicable	29
N =	34
Better diets/more food?	
Yes	61
No	6
Not applicable	32
N =	31
More luxurious clothes?	
Yes	59
No	9
Not applicable	31
N =	32

Table 20   *Commoner institutions and stratification*

	Were there aristocrats?		Were there castes?	
	Yes	No	Yes	No
Was there a commoner council to:				
Debate policy?				
Yes	40	15	40	22
No	60	15	50	39
Not applicable	0	69	10	39
N =	15	13	10	23
Try cases?				
Yes	93	31	78	63
No	7	69	20	38
Not applicable	0	0	0	0
N =	15	13	9	24
		***		

*** Chi squared significant at .01 level

Table 21   *Societies and documentation*

Name of society	Number of pages of documentation	Name of society	Number of pages of documentation
Bambara	1,127	Chagga	1,986
Dogon	1,132	Ngondo	1,474
Mossi	942	Pygmies	1,350
Mande	605	Azande	3,264
Tallensi	964	Mongo	773
Ashanti	3,523	Rundi	1,314
Katab	352	Mbundu	847
Nupe	856	Bemba	830
Tiv	2,891	Ila	998
Yoruba	1,637	Lozi	1,635
Fang	1,117	Tonga	1,616
Nuer	1,541	Ngoni	1,123
Shilluk	1,073	Thonga	1,231
Ganda	2,261	Yao	555
Dorobo	354	Bushmen	1,259
Kikuyu	1,950	Hottentot	1,339
Luo	463	Lovedu	455
Masai	2,085	Tanala	354

Table 22   *Government and crafts*

	Is government the major consumer of crafts?	
	No.	percentage
Yes	4	11
No	15	42
Not applicable	15	42
No information	2	5
Total	36	100

Part II

The colonial period

3

Pressure groups, public policy, and agricultural development: a study of divergent outcomes

Under the impact of European colonization, two forces assumed new importance in the rural areas of Africa: the market and the nation-state. Both combined to promote the commercialization of agriculture and they thereby fundamentally altered economic, social and political relations in the African countryside. The next two essays focus on significant aspects of this transformation. The first analyzes the basis for contrasting patterns of agricultural development; the second the agrarian origins of political protest in the colonial period.

Ghana and Kenya constitute two of the most prominent cases of the agricultural development in colonial Africa. In the one case, producer interests became paramount in the colonial period; in the other, the interests of producers were sacrificed to those of other sectors. This essay examines the divergent patterns of growth of commercial agriculture in Ghana and Kenya and tries to account for the contrasting outcomes of the process of agrarian development.

MAJOR MARKETS FACING PRODUCERS

By examining the major markets faced by producers and by noting the major distortions that prevailed in each, we can establish the economic standing of the two classes of producers relative to each other and to other segments of their respective industries, thereby providing a baseline for the rest of the analysis.

Inputs into farming

Commercial farming requires access to factors of production. In this section I will examine and compare the conditions under which they were acquired.[1]

One of the major contrasts between the two cases arises in the market for labor. We know a lot about the relationship that the Kenyan commercial farmer bore to the market for labor; we know very little about that of the Ghanaian cocoa farmer. The apparent reason is instructive. The behavior of the settler farmers is well known because they struggled against the wage

61

rate set in the private market and repeatedly entered the public arena in attempts to set prices advantageous to themselves; their behavior is thus a matter of public record. By contrast, the Ghanaian cocoa farmers rarely, if ever, left the private sector to advance their wage demands.

Much of the politics of the early period of Kenya revolved around attempts to lower the supply price of labor. The commercial farmers sought to limit competition for labor from the government and the railway; this is revealed in their repeated efforts to limit the quantity of government hiring. The settler farmers sought to limit the access of African farm families to land. Thus, the land committee of 1905, which was dominated by commercial farmers, urged that the government confine the farming rights of natives to explicitly demarcated reserves and 'forecast that normal growth would result in an African population in excess of the physical carrying capacity of reserved areas. Such persons would then be available to enlarge the labour supply of the European farmers.'[2] The commercial farmers also sought to limit the variety of crops grown on native farm lands, and did so at least in part to depress the price of labor. As van Zwanenberg notes, 'the stimulation of cotton-growing [by the subsistence farmers] by the officials of the Administration was severely criticized by [the commercial farmers] which argued that "the cotton growing and the results accruing therefrom, carried to the extent which it has been in Uganda is very detrimental to the ... welfare of the native and means undoubted ruin to the European farming community ... [We] therefore urge ... [the] government both in the Colony and at Home to desist from encouraging the native to grow cotton." '[3]

Through political action, the farmers imposed taxes on the native population so as to increase the willingness of subsistence farm families to work in the commercial sector. As one leading official phrased it, 'we consider that taxation is compelling the native to leave his Reserve for the purpose of seeking work ... [Through taxation] the cost of living [can] be increased for the native, and ... it is on this that the supply of labour and the price of labour depends.'[4] And, in one of the most notorious events in the early politics of the colony, the farmers secured the support of the public administration in recruiting labor for their private enterprises; the potential for coercion was apparent to all, and was occasionally realized.[5] In all of these ways, large-scale commercial producers sought to extract a labor supply from the subsistence sector at a price below the one that was being set by the unconstrained operation of the labor market.

By contrast with the market for labor in Kenya, we know very little about the labor market in Ghana. The cocoa producers simply never organized concerted action to alter market conditions to their advantage. Instead, through 'share-cropping' types of arrangements (the *abusa* system) and the hiring of migrant labor from territories to the north, they obtained their labor through arrangements privately arrived at in the marketplace. The major reasons for the contrasting behavior of the Ghanaian and Kenyan cash-crop producers in the labor market underlie the differences in their behavior in other markets as well, and so will be discussed in a later section. But it may be instructive to note one set of factors that affect this market in particular: the different relationships between the commercial and subsistence sectors in the two agricultural economies.

In the cocoa industry the development of commercial farms and the production of food and cash-crops are not competitive productive activities; rather, they are complementary. In establishing cocoa farms, food crops, such as plantains, cocoyams, and peppers, are used to provide shading for the young cocoa trees.[6] Young cocoa trees require very little care; reports on the early years of the industry implied that the young trees were simply left to grow in a natural way in small clearings in the forest. Because they required little extra care, and because cocoa production was complementary to food production, the cocoa farmers felt little need to bid labor inputs away from subsistence activities.

Once established, the cocoa farms possessed another important property: their peak period of labor demand, which takes place at the time of the main harvest (November–February), complements, rather than rivals, the period of peak demand for labor in the production of food crops. In the case of cereals, the demand for labor reaches its maximum at the time of weeding and harvesting. These periods fall in May to July and February to March, respectively, in the grain-growing areas immediately to the north of the forest; and the further north the area, the later in the year these periods arise. In the case of root crops, which are grown in the forest itself, there is no peak period of demand for labor; root crops can simply be stored in the ground. Once established, the cocoa farms thus rarely face the maximum market price for labor. The commercially oriented cocoa industry could thus comfortably coexist with the market for labor in the subsistence sector.

The case of Kenya was different, however. In *developing* their estates, the commercial farmers did in fact successfully use subsistence production as an input into the growth of cash crops; they simply 'allowed' African farmers to utilize their rotational forms of subsistence food production on their commercial sites as a means of clearing them of bush. But, unlike the cocoa producers, the settlers themselves specialized in the production of food crops; and, once their farms were established, the production cycle of their commercial farms precisely matched that of the subsistence producers. To secure a labor supply they therefore had to bid against the peak-period price of labor. In this sense, the commercial farmers of Kenya faced a less favorable labor market than did their counterparts in Ghana, and so had stronger incentives to seek to override the operations of market forces.

Land

In analyzing the relative economic fate of producers in Ghana and Kenya, we cannot merely analyze the operation of the land market and the way in which its performance influenced the benefits to be derived from cash-crop

63

production. Instead, we must analyze the establishment of the market in the first place; and this entails studying the creation of rights in land.

The history of Kenyan land law is a complex one. Essentially, however, it developed in three stages. The first was the alienation of land from indigenous to colonial jurisdiction. This was achieved in the 1899 ruling by law officers of the Crown on behalf of the foreign office that all waste lands and lands not under actual occupation in Kenya were Crown lands, and therefore alienable under terms and conditions to be devised by the colonial state, which was the agent of the Crown in East Africa. Because of the famines of the 1880s and 1890s, and the pestilences that followed each, the indigenous population of both people and livestock in Kenya had declined precipitately just prior to the incursion of the Europeans; many lands were therefore unoccupied. In addition, the technology of local producers was such that at any given time a large percentage of the land actually being farmed would appear to be unused. Because of the recent loss of population and because of the nature of subsistence technology, the colonial government brought enormous quantities of land under its jurisdiction when it applied the definition of Crown lands devised by its legal officials. The laws of Kenya thus allowed the uncompensated expropriation of large quantities of land from the subsistence sector.

The question then arose: under what conditions would this land be alienated? A key issue underlying this question was the degree to which the state, which now held the rights to land, as opposed to the commercial operators, who wished to put it into production, would capture the rents to be derived from the growing value of this factor. This issue arose in the form of debates concerning the length of the leases the state was willing to grant private users; the rental prices it would charge for leases; the frequency with which it could revise these rents; and the degree to which the leases would be freely transferable once they were assigned to private individuals.

It is extremely difficult to determine what an equilibrium mixture of rental prices, lease lengths, and frequency of rent revisions would be. All we know for certain is that in the final legislation (the Lands Ordinance of 1915), the leases were much longer, the rents lower, and the number of permissible rent revisions less frequent than the state had initially proposed. As Sorrenson states: 'The 1915 Ordinance was an almost complete victory for the settlers and the local officials who supported them'.[7] Because of the potential for strategic behavior in this situation, as well as the potential for mistaken judgements, the initial stand of the state does not provide insight into its preferred maximum; as a consequence, neither does it give much insight into how the final legislation apportioned the benefits between the state and the private sector. More informative, perhaps, is that the Ordinance allowed the free transfer in the private market of lands leased by the state to private individuals. Were the value of the land to rise more rapidly than the revision in rents to be paid to the state, private individuals could then appropriate the difference, and this is apparently what in fact happened.[8] Lastly, we also know that a very high percentage of the land that was leased by the European farmers was in fact not put into immediate production, but held for future use or sale; figures from the early 1920s show less than five per cent of the land leased by private users had been put into cultivation.[9] It would therefore appear that the commercial farmers secured a structure of land law that left them in a position to capture a large proportion of the rents which were to be generated by the growing returns to cash-crop production.

In the process of establishing land rights in Kenya, then, land was secured in a manner that allowed the commercial producers, as opposed to the subsistence producers or the state, to capture the rents created by the growing of commercial agriculture. By contrast with Kenya, the establishment of land rights in Ghana did not involve a forceful redistribution of land from subsistence to commercial producers. Instead, the commercial producers had to compensate fully at free market prices those who controlled access to this productive resource.

Prior to the rise of the cocoa industry, much of the land of the forest was in fact vacant and not utilized. Such 'waste' lands were held as 'stool' lands: that is, they did not belong to any private individual or family, and access to them was regulated by the 'stool', i.e., by the chief. With the growth in demand for primary products, there arose a demand for rights to the forests of the interior. People from the coast were the best informed concerning the opportunities for production for the world market. And it was commercially oriented coastal people who journeyed inland and obtained concessions from the chiefs for land rights in the forests.[10]

Some of these coastal entrepreneurs were already wealthy. Businessmen like Robert Hutchinson, who worked for Swanzy, and lawyers such as Joseph Brown were prosperous members of the coastal elite; and through their purchase of the leases to inland gold deposits and cocoa farms, they increased their fortunes.[11] Others possessed more modest endowments. In particular, many of those who purchased cocoa lands were not of very great wealth, and in fact had to pool their assets and borrow to secure farm lands in the forest.[12] In any case, the growth of the opportunities for wealth in the interior in fact led to the exchange of land for cash. Among the primary agents in this exchange were the chiefs. And, briefed by the coastal lawyers, they virtually transformed the collective property of the forest – the stool lands – into private property: mining concessions, lumber concessions, and private farms.

Rather than supporting the formation of private property rights in the interior, the colonial government sought to forestall it. The government feared the depredation of the forest; it protested against the 'corruption' of collective rights; it sought to conserve timber resources; and it sought to protect the inland chiefs and tribes from being 'robbed by the concession hunters'. Moreover, the government was uncertain of the legal status of many of the concessions made outside the structure of British law. It therefore sought, through a series of land bills, to appropriate to the state the 'waste' or unused lands of the interior. These measures were vigorously resisted by both the chiefs and the coastal entrepreneurs. Thus, Hancock, discussing testimony given to a commission to investigate the land 'problem', notes that 'every chief and every African lawyer who gave evidence before the commission expressed complete satisfaction with the flourishing trade in concessions. "It is beneficial all around", declared the president of the Aborigines Protection Society' – the political movement organized to resist the land legislation.[13]

Following defeat of the land bills, the colonial government introduced further measures which would allow it either to appropriate the remaining unused lands or to control the circumstances under which they were leased or sold. In the end, all such measures failed save two: one that helped preserve forest reserves and one which allowed for the registration of exchanges of land rights, and thus secured the enforceability by territorial law of rights in private property.[14]

By contrast with the development of land law in Kenya, the establishment of land rights in Ghana entailed no confiscation of land from subsistence producers and no appropriation of land rents by commercial producers. Instead, in securing land, the commercial users found themselves operating in what was virtually a private market and they had to compensate at the going market rate those who controlled access to subsistence lands. Moreover, the market in land seemed to operate efficiently.[15] At the very least, it did not function in a way that conferred a significant subsidy upon the agricultural producers, as had been the case in Kenya.

Transportation

In the late nineteenth and early twentieth centuries, the form of transport that most significantly affected the profitability of inland farm production was the railway. The evidence suggests that in Kenya commercial farmers secured many of the advantages of this service and the costs of providing it were distributed in a way that enhanced the relative profitability of farming. By contrast, in Ghana, the cocoa farmers appear to have been compelled to pay a price for transport services that lay above the competitive market rate, with the result that the relative profitability of farming declined.

As is well known, the initial location of the railway in Kenya was not chosen with economic objectives in mind; it reflected the political imperatives of the colonial rivalries between the British, French, and Germans in East Africa – rivalries that gave strategic importance to controlling the headwaters of the Nile. More informative is the later location of spur lines. One of the first and most important was the route for the extension of the railway into Uganda. While such apologists for the commercial farmers as Elspeth Huxley debate the point,[16] the Director of Public Works in Kenya at the time persuasively argued that the route was chosen out of a regard for the benefits which it conferred on the land holdings of some of the largest commercial farmers in the territory.[17] In the 1920s, the railway, with government backing, borrowed £17 million to develop other spur lines. One account suggests that over 73 per cent of the total mileage of these extensions ran through commercial farming areas.[18] By the end of the 1920s, the construction of spur lines had brought nearly all of the commercial farmers within twenty-five miles of the railway.

While locational decisions in Kenya reveal the emphasis placed on the development of the commercial farming sector, those in Ghana suggest that priority was placed on the development of other industries, and in particular on the development of mining. In 1893, the British Government dispatched one J. I. Lang to Ghana to survey possible routes for rail lines in that territory. Lang's report offered two candidates: one that would open up the forest zone, which already was showing every evidence of developing into a prosperous farming region, and another that would promote the development of the mining centers in the west. Subsequent studies based on Lang's report in fact advocated the development of the first of these routes; but, following a visit of the governor to the mining centers in 1896, the western route was chosen.[19] Two decades later, a similar choice was made, this time with respect to the location of a deep-water port to serve as a terminus for the railway. Because of its natural geological structure, the bay at Takoradi qualified as the least costly site for such a harbor; but, being located in the west, while the major centers of cocoa production lay in the east, it was not clear that Takoradi provided the port site that would generate the greatest economic benefits. None the less, the government chose that location.[20]

It should be noted that, in its subsequent management of the harbor facility, the government revealed not only a willingness to favor the mines by comparison with the cocoa farmers, but also a willingness to favor the development of the mines at their expense. In constructing the Takoradi harbor, the government built on too grand a scale, and the unit costs of using the facility therefore proved much greater than had been expected. The government contemplated closing the central and some of the eastern ports so as to force agricultural exports through Takoradi. While it abstained from taking that decision it did in fact restrict road transport so as to force the cocoa crop onto the rail routes that employed Takoradi as their principal terminus. The result was to increase the volume of goods passing through the harbor – a measure that allowed the government to hold down port charges levied on the mines and other users but which achieved this result at the expense of the cocoa farmers.[21]

Thus far we have looked at the pattern of locational decisions and the distribution of services, and we have argued that they tended to confer benefits primarily on the commercial farmers in Kenya but on non-agricultural users of these services in Ghana. This bias extended as well to the allocation of the costs of transport.

Three major features of the rating structure of the Kenyan railways are relevant to this analysis. One was the 'country produce' provision: an item, if produced locally, was carried at a lower rate than if the same item were produced abroad. As in the early years of the century most local production took place in the agricultural sector, the primary beneficiaries of this provision were the farmers. For any given item, the magnitude of the benefits was greater the larger the volume of marketed production; so, within the farming community itself, it was the large-scale farmers – i.e., the commercial farmers – who benefited the most from this provision.

A second provision was the institution of a flat rate for the transport of maize. By contrast with the previous rate schedule, under which the rate charged for maize was sensitive to the length of the haul, under the new rate schedule, the rate charged was not; and the difference between the old and new rates was such that the farmers experienced a rise in the export price for their commodities. This effect was more pronounced for the inland producers, such as the cereals growers in Trans Nzoia and Uasin Gishu; and, again, the benefits were greater the larger the volume of produce. A third feature of the railway charges deserves note: within the class of imported goods, agricultural inputs were transported at a lower fee than were the inputs for other industries. Thus, imports of farm machinery were charged a lower rate than were imports of other kinds of machine equipment; and, among agricultural producers, it was the commercial farmers who could afford these farm machines. The structure of railway rates was thus used to protect and promote the fortunes of large-scale, European producers.[22]

It is more difficult to analyze the case of Ghana. In Kenya, the rate schedule often quoted, as we have seen, more than one rate for a particular item, and so there is no need to concern ourselves with the possibility that differences in the freight charges would merely reflect differences in the real costs of transportation. In the case of Ghana, however, the task of inference is more difficult. For any single commodity, there was but one rate charged for any given distance. In the absence of knowledge of the real costs of transporting different commodities, inferences thus have to be based on information other than those of the published rate charges.[23] Fortunately, we do have other kinds of information, and they suggest that transport was furnished to the cocoa farmers at a price that lay above the real costs of providing such services.

The principal evidence is contained in the response of the government and the railways to the growth of road transport. Lorries have been imported into Ghana since early in the century. Following the First World War, however, there was a boom in road transportation. Commercial firms and private entrepreneurs imported light vehicles from the United States – vehicles that were able to use the poor roads of the cocoa region without great damage to the roads or to themselves. For certain services, these lorries provided transport at a cost that was considerably cheaper than that charged by the railway; this differential was particularly pronounced for short hauls, with the result that much cocoa traffic shifted from the railway to the roads along those portions of the railway that lay near the coastal ports. What is interesting about the diversion of cocoa traffic to road transport was the government's response to it. The government passed regulations banning the transport by road of cocoa over routes running parallel to the railway and built barriers and posted inspectors at check-points to implement the measure. Moreover, where the government had begun to build roads that ran parallel to the railway, it stopped, with the result that Ghana was long characterized by a segmented road network.[24] The cocoa farmers were thus compelled to use the more expensive mode of transportation – the railway – and they could not acquire transport services at the competitive market price.

So, in acquiring transport services the commercial farmers of Kenya had access to a rail system which was designed to provide them with convenient services and which utilized a structure of rates which was designed to protect the profitability of their enterprises; the magnitude of many of these benefits increased with the volume of production and so were concentrated on the large-scale commercial farmers. By contrast, the Ghanaian producers had access to a rail system which was designed primarily to benefit other sectors of the economy; and they were compelled to pay a price for transport services that lay above the price that would have prevailed in a competitive market.

Capital

There is a last market for inputs that should be discussed: the market for capital. Unfortunately, even by comparison with the markets for land, labor and transport services, we have little knowledge about the way in which capital was acquired by the farming interests; and what knowledge we do have suggests a rather complex state of affairs.

The principal sources of capital for cocoa producers appear to have been either the local purchasing agents – those who bought from the farmers and sold to the merchant house who exported the crop – or other cocoa farmers.[25] In the case of the former, the farmers obtained credit by selling forward; they would receive cash in return for a promise to deliver an agreed quantity of output to the lending cocoa purchaser. In the case of the latter, one farmer would 'pledge' his farm to another. Under this system, in exchange for a cash loan, the borrower would allow the lender to operate one or more of his cocoa farms for a stated period of time. The lender would harvest and sell the output of the farm over the agreed duration of the pledge, and the revenues realized over that period would constitute repayment for the loan. It is to be noted that there was no special class of money-lenders in the farming community and that the evidence suggests that 'creditors must be nearly as numerous as debtors';[26] there thus appears to have been a competitive market.

In the case of both markets the interest rate was a random variable, and a principal determinant of its value was the price which the cocoa crop

69

commanded from the export houses. In the case of loans by local purchasers, the interest rate depended on the proceeds they realized when they sold the crop to the export houses. In the case of 'pledged' farms, the amount of the loan, the yield of the farm that was to be managed by the creditor, and the duration of the transfer of management rights were pre-negotiated; the rate of interest once again was largely determined by the revenues realized from the sale of the output of the farm. Divergent expectations about future prices naturally formed an important basis for this credit market.[27]

A full analysis of the structure and operations of the market for credit in Ghana must thus be based on an appraisal of the market for products. As we shall see in the next section, the degree of competitiveness in this market varied over time. From time to time, the major purchasing firms agreed to restrict competition for the cocoa crop; and, when they did, the result, naturally, was a reduction in the price of the commodity. There were major differences in the short- and long-term effects of this action.

In the market for credit, the *short-run* effect of collusion among the purchasers of the crop was to *reduce* the rate of interest. For, if two farmers had negotiated a transaction in which cash was exchanged for rights to the output of a given farm, the implementation of an agreement to hold down the price of cocoa reduced the value of the farm to the creditor and allowed the borrower to secure his cash more cheaply. Similarly, if a farmer received cash from a local purchaser by means of selling foward, and if the export houses then conspired to reduce the sales value of this produce, the former would have secured a reduction in the rate of interest he had to pay for this loan.[28]

Confining our attention solely to the market for inputs, we can conclude that, when collusion took place in the Ghana cocoa market, its immediate effect was to benefit borrowers and to penalize lenders. In so far as much of the borrowing and lending took place among the farmers themselves, the effect was to redistribute income *within* that community; its impact was thus neutral as between producers and other groups. And in so far as the farmers borrowed from local purchasers, the immediate impact of the collusion on the capital market was beneficial to the farmers who had sold forward.[29]

Whether or not the farmers benefited, net, from collusion is of course an entirely different matter. But in this perverse case the restriction of competition on the part of other agents in one of the major markets faced by the farmers had an immediate effect *on the price of their inputs* that was either neutral in terms of the relative standing of producers *vis-à-vis* other groups in the industry, or favorable to at least a major portion of them. As soon as the time period is broadened, however, the negative effects dominate. Not only is there a downward adjustment in produce prices; but also, in so far as prices for output were depressed by the purchasers' cartel for more than one season, or in so far as economic agents perceived that to be the case, for a given level of output, lenders would advance less cash. In the long run, not only did collusion result in a loss of revenues, but also, in physical terms, it thus resulted in an increase in the costs of capital.

During periods of competitive cocoa buying, the Ghanaian farmer paid a price for capital that was set in a competitive market, and the market price of capital was a random variable. During periods in which the farmer faced a cocoa-buying cartel, he had to give up a greater amount of his crop to secure a fixed amount of cash. Save for very short-term periods following the imposition of cartels, the Ghanaian cocoa farmers never faced a rate of interest that offered a subsidized price for borrowing.

The settler farmers of Kenya, by contrast, achieved such a subsidy. We know very little about the early capital market in Kenya, particularly that utilized by the cereals producers. We do know that persons like Delamere borrowed extensively on the private market in England, using his family estates as collateral; we have no comparable information for 'lesser' figures. But we know that in later periods, particularly in the 1920s, the cereals farmers did borrow extensively in the commercial market, with the banks accepting mortgages on their farm lands for security. With the onset of the depression, however, land values declined and the commercial banks radically increased the price they charged borrowers in order to compensate for the decline in the security of their loans. The costs of borrowing increased and, in response, the government entered the loans market. Beginning with a series of seasonal loans to cereals farmers, the government formed a land bank to make medium- and long-term loans at subsidized rates of interest. Unlike their Ghanaian counterparts, the commercial farmers of Kenya thus came to operate in a capital market in which they were charged prices that were set well below the market price. And the manipulation of prices in this market allowed them, other things being equal, to operate more profitably.

The market for output
The Kenyan producers thus appear to have enjoyed considerable subsidization in their acquisition of land, labor, capital and transport, while the Ghanaian producers at best paid the competitive market prices and at worst paid prices which contained monopsony premiums. The relative standing of the two classes of producers in the market for inputs also characterizes their standing in the market for their products. For, in this market, the large-scale cereals producers organized a mechanism for colluding in an effort to force a rise in the price of cereals; by contrast, the Ghanaian farmers faced cartels organized by purchasers and shippers of their products – cartels which sought to depress the prices received by the producers of cocoa.

From an early period, the Kenyan settlers attempted to promote the marketing of their products. The basic instrument of their efforts was the Kenya Farmers' Association – an organization first formed in the 1912–13 crop year to help dispose of the maize crop. The Association gave political support to the passage of regulations that made the provision of maize

71

rations compulsory for all employers of labor – and then signed bulk delivery agreements with the two largest employers: the government and the railways. It helped to organize, finance, and manage processing mills for the cereals produced by its members. The Association also lobbied for, and got, a mixture of policy measures which helped it in its efforts to raise the domestic price of grains: import duties behind which to shelter the domestic price and the use of public funds to assist in the disposal of surplus production at a loss in foreign markets.

A major difficulty facing the Association in its efforts to inflate domestic prices was that of establishing effective collusion among its own members. It was difficult to prevent price competition; as Huxley noted: 'Members were all too apt to sell their crops through the Association only when it pleased them.'[30] And those outside the Association could of course take advantage of the higher price established by it; they could undercut that price and so increase their sales. Particularly troublesome in this regard were the subsistence producers. Responding to higher prices, they rapidly turned to supplying the commercial market; as Huxley notes, as early as 1913 these new entrants 'had taken to growing maize with surprising enthusiasm and the local markets were glutted'.[31] Without legal backing, there was little the Association could do either to compel cooperation by its own members or to exclude new entrants.

The Association's response was to seek the support of the state. Two periods of political crisis provided the opportunity for its efforts: the depression and the Second World War. In response to the threat posed to the commercial farming sector by the depression, the Association secured legislation (the Marketing of Native Produce Act) which strengthened its ability to control the behavior of the subsistence producers. This act provided for the regulation of the purchase of products grown by 'subsistence' producers through the issuance of permits and licenses. In particular, the act was used to restrict private trading in that market, particularly by the 'Asian merchants who bought extremely cheaply, and often without mercy, in the reserves'.[32]

There remained the problem of restraining the competitive behavior of the members of the Association. Again the depression provided impetus for the securing of legislation to promote the interests of producers. One such measure was an act which gave legal underpinning to bylaws enacted by cooperative societies. This act was used to compel wheat growers to market exclusively through the Kenya Farmers' Association. In addition, through the Sale of Wheat Ordinance, the Government required every farmer to market his crop through an officially designated agency; the agency appointed was the Kenya Farmers' Association.

A second major crisis – the Second World War – provided maize producers with comparable mechanisms for curtailing competition. During the war, the government of Kenya agreed to supply British forces in the Middle East with bulk deliveries of maize. Under the terms of wartime legislation – the produce control ordinances – the government established a Maize Control Board, which served as the sole legal buyer of the maize crop. The first Maize Controller was Colonel Griffith – an executive in the Kenya Farmers' Association. As Huxley ingenuously comments: 'It was inevitable that [Colonel Griffith] should look for staff to men he knew, and who knew about maize . . . No less than 26 members of the K.F.A. staff, at all levels, left to join Maize Control.'[33] Later the Kenya Farmers' Association was made the official designated agent for the purchase of maize at 'a price . . . fixed annually by the Government on the basis of an estimated cost of production'.[34] The producers' organization thus became the monopoly buyer of the output of its members at legally binding prices.

Through state intervention, then, the domestic producers formed a cartel. Some, like William O. Jones, are skeptical about the ability of the producers to force a price rise on domestic consumers of food crops. But we must evaluate such skepticism in light of the fact that the domestic price of maize in Kenya – albeit the price in 1959, which lies considerably out of the period discussed in this chapter – was twice the world price.[35] This suggests that the mix of policies advanced by the Kenya Farmers' Association had succeeded in achieving a highly advantageous price in the domestic market – and one that, given an inelastic demand for this product, would result in a rise in producer revenues.[36]

In Ghana also a cartel was formed of the market for cash crops; but, in contrast to Kenya, the Ghanaian cartels were formed by the purchasers and shippers of the products, and not by the producers themselves. In so far as non-competitive rents were generated by the structure of the market for the products of the commercial agricultural industry, they were extracted from, rather than by, the producers.

For a variety of reasons, there emerged strong forces leading to increasing returns to scale in the export and import business in Ghana. Foremost among them were the great risks of the trade, caused by fluctuations in the prices of primary products and the concomitant fluctuations in the demand for the imports furnished by the commercial houses. Because of the distances between Europe and Africa, and the time period involved in transactions between the two areas, large amounts of capital were tied up on goods in transit; and the value of these stocks was subject as well to price fluctuations. Only firms which were large enough to operate over a large geographic area and so hedge the risks engendered by trading in one primary product (e.g., cocoa from Ghana), with variability engendered by trading in another (e.g., palm oil from Nigeria), were able in the long-run to survive in the trading business in West Africa. In addition, the commercial houses faced strong attempts to form cartels of the shipping routes between Europe and Africa. These efforts created incentives to combine, both to enhance their bargaining power in bids for better rates and services and to make credible threats of entry into the shipping business.[37] For these reasons, large firms did better in the export–import business in West Africa.

An important result was the consolidation of the merchant houses. In the 1880s, several important trading houses merged to form the African Association. In 1919, the established firms of Millers and Swanzy combined with the African Association to form the African and Eastern Trading Corporation Limited. And, with the influx of capital from Lever Brothers into the Niger Company in the 1920s, this corporation was able to engineer further mergers which eventually led to the formation of the largest trading house of them all: the United Africa Company. By the early 1930s, the import and export business in Ghana was dominated by a few major firms; in 1934, four of them handled over two-thirds of the total purchases of Ghana's cocoa crop, and one firm, the United Africa Company, handled over 40 per cent of it.

This pattern of consolidation facilitated attempts to restrict competition. Repeated efforts were made to form purchasing agreements among the firms and thereby lower the price offered cocoa farmers for their products. One investigation reveals the formation of at least seven such agreements prior to the 1930s.[38] The basic principle underlying these agreements was that each firm be allotted a share of the market, the relative shares being based on past performance. Like all such agreements, these efforts at collusion faced a basic problem: the incentives created by the attempts to form the cartel operated in a way that threatened to lead to its destruction. For, with every other party restricting their purchases, a firm could radically increase its own by offering marginally better terms; and, with a decline in prices being forced upon the farmers, new firms could enter the industry and capture the market by offering higher prices. It was thus in the interests of all parties to the agreement to cheat; it was in the interests of new purchasers to enter the market; and the results of either action would be an increase in price and a defeat of the purpose for which the cartel was formed.

The forces operating to destabilize the buying agreements were thus clear; and so too is the historical record. The frequency with which the agreements were made suggests the frequency with which they were broken. And such new entrants into the market as Raccah, who broke the ground-nut pool in Nigeria, and Levantis, who was making strong inroads into Ghanaian cocoa trade at the time of the Second World War, also underscore the vulnerability of the purchasing cartels. As Hancock pungently phrased it: 'If West African commerce is a record of imperfect competition, it is also a record of imperfect monopoly.'[39]

As had been the case in Kenya, a period of political crisis was exploited to engineer the formation of an effective cartel in Ghana; again, it was the Second World War that provided the opportunity. But, unlike the case in Kenya, it was the merchant houses, and not the producers, that seized the opportunity. With the outbreak of the war, Ghana lost much of the market for cocoa; it was cut off from Germany, which had purchased much of its crop, and the impounding of shipping for war purposes limited its access to other markets. The British feared that political turmoil would break out should the cocoa industry collapse. The government therefore pledged to purchase the Ghanaian cocoa crop in its entirety for the duration of the war. In seeking to implement this pledge, the government organized the Cocoa Control Board, later called the West African Produce Control Board. By statute, the Board was made monopoly buyer of the cocoa crop. The government chose as its official agents the merchant houses and it called upon the Association of West African Merchants to draw up the procedure for the purchase of the cocoa crop. The procedures devised by the Association were precisely those which the merchant houses had tried to implement in the period of imperfect competition. Each merchant house was allowed to purchase on behalf of the government its 'historical share' of the cocoa crop. To be noted is that these shares were calculated in such a way that they significantly curtailed the share of at least one recent entrant into the industry – Levantis, the firm whose entry into the market just prior to the war had undercut earlier attempts to form a purchasing cartel. In 1940, the Board offered producers a price which lay at 50 per cent of the London spot price for cocoa.[40]

Before concluding this section, it should be noted that the merchant houses were not the only group that attempted to form cartels and thereby extract revenues from the nascent agricultural industry. Such efforts were also made by the shipping companies. In the early days of the agricultural industry in West Africa, two major lines – the African Steamship Company and the British African Steam Navigation Company – competed for West African trade. Under the leadership of E. L. Jones, these firms merged to form the Elder Dempster line. In 1894, Elder Dempster, in cooperation with a German firm by the name of Woermann Line, formed the West African shipping conference. Through a system of deferred rebates, the conference attempted to control the regional market for shipping services. A rebate of ten per cent would be given on the cost of any shipment made with a conference member if and only if the party in question confined all his patronage to the member companies for a full year following the date of shipment. For a firm doing a lot of business, significant amounts of capital would thus be lost were it to fail to ship exclusively through the conference. In this way, the conference shippers sought control over the transport of producers between West Africa and its major external markets.[41]

Sources such as McPhee tend to accord the shippers great market power. McPhee notes the small number of natural harbors on the West Coast of Africa, which make it difficult for tramp steamers to operate. He notes the treacherous conditions in what harbors there were, and the fact that Jones put the vast majority of the local pilots under contract with his firm. He notes as well Jones' attempts to monopolize the lightage and warehouse facilities and his founding and management of the major bank of West Africa – the bank that provided credit for most of the merchant houses in the area.[42] And yet there simply is too much evidence of the ease of entry into the shipping industry to sustain McPhee's inference of significant market power by the shipping interests. Thus, we know that Jones' early monopoly was broken by Woermann, and that the latter's entry is what provoked the formation of the conference in the first place. We know that before the Second World War Lever gained access to non-conference vessels.[43] And we also know that the conference lines' unwillingness to provide adequate service to the United Africa Company led in 1929 to the formation by that company of its own shipping capacity, with the result that the conference lost 40 per cent of its business.

The Ghanaian producers thus eventually faced a cartel in the form of government-backed collusion among the merchant houses. The shipping industry attempted also to form a cartel, but it failed. At no time, however, did the producers themselves succeed in forming an institution capable of altering prices for their products to their advantage.

DISCUSSION AND ANALYSIS

We have examined the major markets faced by the cocoa producers of Ghana and the large-scale commercial farmers of Kenya, and we have compared the relative standing of the two classes of producers in these markets. We find that *at best* the cocoa producers faced competitive market prices in these markets; often they faced prices which were set against them. By contrast, the large-scale cereals growers *at worst* faced competitive market prices in the major markets of relevance to them; most often they were able to set prices in these markets to their advantage.

In this section I seek to explain the divergent patterns in these two industries. In particular, I examine a series of factors which influenced the perceived costs and benefits of organization and I examine the way in which these factors helped to account for the relative ability of different groups to form in defense of their economic interests. These factors include considerations arising from the structure and operation of colonial institutions, from the size distribution of different segments of the two industries, and from the nature of the commodities produced in them.

Of these factors, those arising from the structure and operation of colonial political institutions were obviously of fundamental importance. No government run by British public officials and paid for by British taxpayers was going to intervene in the cocoa industry to promote the interests of indigenous producers against those of British merchants and manufacturers. Nor, save under exceptional circumstances, was a British government in East Africa going to try to undermine the interests of its own citizens in the agricultural industry of that nation. The fact that the agricultural industries operated within a colonial political system thus had a fundamental bearing on the ultimate distribution of the gains.

Despite the primacy of political considerations, I shall discuss them at the end rather than the beginning of this section. For there were other factors at work, and, in the face of the glaring significance of the political fact of colonialism, their importance is often ignored. Moreover, these non-political factors tended to influence the desire and ability of organized interests to form. And it was these interests which, once formed, set the colonial system in action.

Properties of the commodities

One of the major non-political factors influencing the relative standing of the two classes of producers were differences in the incentives to organize. A variety of factors influenced the incentives, but among the most important were differences in the commodities which they produced. The Kenyan farmers specialized in the production of cereals which were largely destined for the domestic market; the Ghanaian farmers produced a confectionary item which was destined for the world market. From differences in the commodities which they produced there arose differences in the incentives for collusive behavior; and this is particularly true with respect to their incentives to collude in the markets for products.

Because cereals have a low value-to-weight ratio, they are expensive to transport. Consumers will tend to find domestically produced cereals relatively cheap by comparison with those produced abroad. This was particularly true for a place like Kenya in the early years of this century, for the major rival grain-producing economies were located at a considerable distance from the Kenyan market. Were the settler farmers to collude, then, and were they able successfully to constrain the behavior of the African producers, they could easily capture the local market. It was therefore reasonable for them to believe that they could force a price rise upon the domestic consumer.

Rather than producing for a relatively small home market, by contrast, the Ghanaian producers marketed their output on the world market; and within that market there were alternative sources of supply. Granted that by 1911 Ghana was the largest producer for that market; and also that she accounted for over 15 per cent of the world's output in that year. None the less, the very speed of her rise to ascendancy among the world producers underscored the rapidity with which new entrants could undercut any attempts by Ghana to raise the price of her cocoa. And because the market faced by Ghanaian producers was world-wide, and not national, the behavior of these other producers lay outside Ghana's jurisdiction. In effect, the Ghanaian producers faced what appeared to be a highly elastic demand for their product; the incentives to form a producers' cartel were therefore weakened.

Other differences in the commodities which the two sets of farmers produced help to account for the differences in the strength of the incentive to collude. One is that cereals are widely regarded as a necessity whereas cocoa is not; the effect once again is to create a relatively lower price elasticity for the products of the Kenyan farmers and thereby enhance the prospects of returns from collusive behavior. Another attribute is import-

77

ant. Cereals can be preserved with relative ease; the farmers can store them and withhold them from the market. Moreover, they can divert them to other uses – their own consumption or consumption by livestock, for example. By contrast, cocoa tends to ferment and to spoil, and this is particularly true in the tropical conditions under which it is grown. A farmer contemplating holding his crop off the market thus finds that the rate of loss due to deterioration seriously offsets the prospective gains to be derived from an increase in price.[44] In addition, cocoa has little use outside the confectionary market; it cannot be profitably diverted to other activities nor can it be consumed on the farm. Differences in the technical properties of the two crops thus create differences in the perceived gains and losses from collusive behavior.

An interesting test case for this analysis is offered by the behavior of the producers of export crops in Kenya, coffee and tea in particular. Clearly, these producers received greater assistance from the state, particularly in the form of research and extension services, than did their Ghanaian counterparts. But it is also clear that they failed to form a producers' lobby approaching in power that of the lobby formed by their cereals-growing fellow nationals; nor were they able to compel the government to intervene on their behalf to the degree attained by the latter group. Evidence of this contention is that, within the European farming community, it was only the producers of export crops who were subject to direct taxes by the government. Moreover, when the interests of the producers of food crops directly conflicted with interests of export producers, as they did over the issue of the price of food to be supplied to the employees of the producers of export crops, the interests of the cereal growers prevailed.

A variety of factors is obviously at play in determining the relative political power of these groups. But the pattern that obtains is in conformity with what would be expected if the nature of the commodity itself, in addition to the role of citizenship and race, were an important factor in influencing the ability of groups to form in support of their economic interests.

Properties of the producers as a group
Another difference helps to account for variations in the readiness and ability of the two sets of producers to collude in defense of their interests. And this is the difference in the size distribution of the farms. We lack good data on this point. But what data we do have indicate that the settler farms in Kenya were relatively small in number and large in size, while cocoa production in Ghana was engaged in by a fairly large number of small-scale farmers.

Brett's figures disclose that there were 1,183 settler farmers in Kenya in 1920; in 1929, the number was 2,035; and in 1934, 2,027.[45] Given the total area occupied in those years, the average farm size was about 2,500 acres. We also know that there was considerable inequality in the farm sizes.

Delamere alone, for example, is reported to have owned 100,000 acres;[46] and in 1915, 13 occupiers – or roughly one per cent of the commercial farmers – are reported to have owned 20 per cent of the land.[47]

If the data on Kenya are poor, those on Ghana are worse; but they none the less suggest a distinctly different pattern. For it is the overwhelming consensus of all reports on the cocoa industry that cocoa is produced by a very large number of relatively small producers. Illustrative of this fact are the figures published by the Nowell Commission. According to the commission report, the Department of Agriculture estimated that there were approximately 300,000 cocoa producers in Ghana in the later 1930s; this figure is not based on an actual survey, however. The report also cites an estimated average farm size of 2.5 acres in Ashanti; this estimate is based on survey data.[48] Beckett's work in Akokoaso in the 1930s also reports an average farm size of 2.5 acres;[49] other surveys report an average farm size of 4.2–5.2 acres; the largest estimate reported for this era was 16.7 acres for the area about Suhum-Kibi.[50] More recent work, and especially that of Polly Hill, has demonstrated that there is significant variance in the size distribution of the cocoa farms, and that some of the producers are very large and very wealthy indeed. While Hill's data do compel us to recognize that there is more inequality among the cocoa producers than hitherto had been thought, they in no way lead us to infer a size distribution of farms similar to that which prevailed in Kenya.

The difference in the size distribution of farms in the two agricultural industries could have influenced the relative strength of the incentives to engage in non-competitive behavior. A given farmer in Kenya, being one of a relatively few large farmers, could have believed that his behavior would have an impact on the market prices which he confronted. By contrast, a Ghanaian farmer, being one of 300,000 small-scale producers, could not have reasonably believed that his individual conduct would have such an impact.

The difference in the size distribution of the two industries may have influenced not only the perceived benefits but also the relative costs of collusion. The fewer the number of farmers and the larger their average output, the easier it would be to detect the evasion of common agreements. We know, for example, that in Uasin Gishu, the members of the Kenya Farmers' Association knew full well that the other farmers were not cooperating in selling their produce; for it did not take sales by very many of these farmers significantly to depress prices in the local market.[51] By contrast, it must have been extremely difficult for the organizers of the cocoa boycotts, which I discuss below, to detect individual violations of withholding agreements; hundreds could have sold their produce before a sufficient volume entered the market to have a significant impact on the price.

The number of producers would influence the costs of organizing in another way. Irrespective of the effect on the incentives to cooperate, the larger the number of farmers, the greater the costs of reaching potential

79

members of a collective enterprise, of communicating with them, and of coordinating their behavior. A good example of the effects of these costs is offered in the attempt of the cocoa farmers to boycott the 1931 market in an effort to drive up prices. Organized by people from the coast, the boycott movement sought to reach and incorporate the multitude of small-scale inland producers. The leaders of the boycott succeeded in reaching the farmers in Akim Abuakwa, the heartland of the cocoa industry at the time; but they failed to reach the numerous producers in the interior, and in particular those in Ashanti. Once it was realized that the Ashanti farmers had not been brought into the movement, and that they were therefore capitalizing on the rise in prices being created by the cooperative efforts of the producers on the coast, then the farmers on the coast re-entered the market with their produce and the boycott collapsed. The costs of making contact with so large a number of small-scale producers appears to have been too high; and failing to organize all of the producers, the movement could retain the allegiance of none of them.[52]

The factor of size appears as well to have had a significant bearing on the development of leadership among the farmers of the two territories. In both cases, leaders were drawn from the large farmers. In Kenya, Delamere and Grogan provided much of the leadership for the commercial farming community. While I have been able to find out little about the economic activities of the latter, through the work of Elspeth Huxley we know a good deal about the former.[53] What with 100,000 acres of farmland, over 1,200 acres under wheat, 40,000 sheep, a herd of exotic cattle, and interests in a creamery, milling operations, and timber, it is clear that for any given cost of organizing to provide favorable conditions for the farming industry, Delamere would stand to secure considerable private benefits from such measures. There were thus strong private incentives for him to secure collective benefits.

A similar pattern arises in the Ghanaian material. Thus Rhodie, in his study of the 1931 boycott, isolates the large farmer as the active agent in the attempts by the cocoa producers to drive up the market price.[54] And one of the leading spokesmen of the cocoa farmers in this period was Nana Ofori Atta. We know that, at the time of the 1931 boycott, he had some 20 tons of cocoa in storage.[55] We also know that because of his political position, he had access to the profits of a large number of very prosperous cocoa farms. As Omanahene of Eastern Akim (later Akim Abuakwa), Nana Ofori Atta manipulated traditional political obligations – payments for land rights, rental fees for the use of stool lands, and tax obligations on the part of immigrant farm communities – to divert the profits from the cocoa industry to the treasury of his native authority.[56] Because his domains included the richest cocoa lands of that time, he stood to gain a great deal privately from the increased collective well-being of the local producers. He therefore had strong private incentives to champion their interests.

The size distribution of farms thus appears to have had a significant bearing on the development of leadership among the farmers. In both cases, leadership was drawn from the large farmers. Contrasts in the size distribution of the two industries suggest that the incentives to take the initiative in organizing were stronger in Kenya. And the relative strength of the incentives to invest resources in organizing thus helps to explain the comparative vigor of collective action in support of producer interests in Kenya.

Before turning to a discussion of a third set of factors – those having to do with the structure and operation of political institutions in Kenya and Ghana – it is important to note that the factors we have discussed thus far help to explain the capacity of other groups to organize collectively in attempts to manipulate the market to their advantage and to the disadvantage of farmers. A case in point is the Ghanaian merchant houses.

Conditions in the industry made it credible for the merchants to believe that, in the short run at least, they faced a relatively inelastic supply of cocoa. The tendency for cocoa to spoil when stored on the farm was one reason for this. Equally important was the perception that there existed relatively large rents for the Ghanaian cocoa producers. In part these rents derived from the superior natural conditions under which cocoa was grown. Factors such as: the rich, as yet unexploited, and therefore highly fertile soils of the forest; the shelter from the winds offered by the forest; the retention of moisture and the dampening of temperature variations by the forest – and other factors, many of which are poorly understood – created growing conditions that were apparently unrivaled elsewhere. And, because the crop had only recently been introduced in Ghana, diseases had not yet extensively developed. The result was that Ghanaian producers appeared to enjoy an enormous natural advantage in the production of cocoa. Other crops whose production would be favored by these same factors compared unfavorably with cocoa on other grounds. In the years under discussion, the price per ton offered for cocoa was from two to five times greater than the price offered for palm oil.[57] Moreover, the costs of production were much lower. Cocoa production thus offered much greater profits. As Dickson states: 'By 1910, farmers in some areas ... were not merely ignoring the oil-palm trees but felling them to make room for cocoa.'[58] That the production of cocoa bore such an enormous economic advantage by comparison with the production of alternative commodities supported a conviction on the part of purchasers that cocoa supplies would be forthcoming over a wide range of prices.[59] This conviction furnished an incentive to collude.

The size distribution of the merchant houses has already been noted; information from the Nowell Commission suggests that the top four firms marketed two-thirds of the cocoa crop.[60] Moreover, the position of one dominant firm – the United Africa Company – provided an incentive for that firm to furnish leadership. That the United Africa Company in itself handled over 40 per cent of the crop helped to insure that a favorable adjustment of the price of cocoa would yield it a substantial private return, despite the costs

81

that it may incur in organizing the price reduction. The set of factors which helped to explain the relative disorganization of the Ghanaian producers thus helps as well to account for the ability of the merchant houses to organize in pursuit of their interests in the major markets of the Ghanaian agricultural industry.

The structure and operation of political institutions

We have argued throughout this paper that the political context of the agricultural industries had a decisive bearing on the capacity of producers to manipulate their market environment. In this section, we therefore conclude by examining the structure and operation of political institutions and the way in which groups within the industry manipulated the colonial state to enhance their fortunes in the market place.

The role of coercion

When scholars analyze the political-economy of colonialism, they rightfully analyze the use of colonial political institutions by groups to extract resources from others and to appropriate them for themselves. The importance of this phenomenon is obvious. And only access to the coercive powers of the state enable groups to effect this redistribution.

Far less obvious, but equally important, is the use of state power by members of a group *to coerce others of their own kind*. Indeed, in order for the first kind of coercion to exist – coercion between antagonistic groups – the second kind of coercion – coercion between members of the same group – had to take place. Members of a single social category have first to use the power of the state to compel themselves to act cooperatively in pursuit of common interests; only then can they advance their common interests. Access to the state, in short, provides means for organizing.

Access to coercion is essential to the organization of interest groups, and for several reasons. The most basic is the need to resolve the problem of inappropriate incentives – something which is aptly referred to as the 'free-rider problem'. The problem arises in the case of public goods – goods which are available to any actor irrespective of whether the actor has contributed to the costs of their provision. As we have seen, public goods can exist in private markets. All actors in the marketplace confront the same prices; and an artificially manipulated price is available to all irrespective of whether they contributed to the costs of establishing it. The price is thus a public good; and as each actor believes he can 'free ride' on the efforts of others and enjoy the beneficial price for free, no actor is willing to make the sacrifices required to obtain favorable prices. The free-rider problem also arises in the public sector where publicly mandated freight rates, rates of taxation, or regulations that affect the price of land and labor create benefits for all members of an economic sector, irrespective of whether they have paid the costs of securing them.

In the presence of the free-rider problem, it is thus extremely difficult to secure voluntary efforts to attain collective objectives. Given the failure of incentives to provide voluntary collaboration, the public good will not be supplied; and everyone may therefore be better off if they were coerced to contribute to its formation. Access to means of compelling compliance therefore becomes critical. Groups, such as the settler farmers in Kenya or the merchant houses in Ghana, which can use the state to coerce their members to sell at the same price or to refrain from bidding up the price of the goods they buy, will then operate at a higher level of profits than if they had not employed the coercive power of the state in their attempts to manipulate markets.

In explaining the divergent fortunes of large-scale producers in Kenya and Ghana we must pay attention to their relative access to public institutions. We will therefore scrutinize the structure and operation of public institutions in the two territories, examining the differences in the constitutional structures which they held in common and noting as well the features which distinguished them.

Constitutional provisions for the representation of interests

The interests of the agricultural producers were but one of a diverse collection of local interests; a necessary determinant of the responsiveness of the colonial state to the interests of the farmers, then, was its level of responsiveness to local interests in general. Over the period under discussion, political institutions in Kenya gave far greater weight to local interests than did those in Ghana. And it was precisely here that the racial and national considerations that underpinned the colonial system were decisive; the government of Kenya was more willing to devolve power locally because, when it did so, it was conferring power largely upon British citizens who had sought to make their fortunes abroad.

As in the vast majority of British colonial possessions, the governments of Kenya and Ghana consisted of a governor, an executive council, and a legislative council. In both cases, the governor was appointed by the metropole. So, a key factor determining the responsiveness of the colonial institutions to 'local' interests was the extent to which local interests were represented in the two councils. Over the period covered in this chapter, 'local' interests in Kenya achieved much greater access to these institutions than did those in Ghana. In both territories, the representatives of local interests – unofficials, in the constitutional terminology of the period – sat in the legislative councils; and until the end of the First World War, they held an equal proportion of the seats – one-third of the total. Thereafter, the situation in the two territories rapidly diverged. Following the First World War, unofficials in the Kenya legislative council achieved parity of numbers with the representatives of the colonial administration; not until after the Second World War did the proportion of unofficials equal the proportion of officials in the legislative council of Ghana. After the First World War, unofficial representation was added to the executive council in Kenya; a similar status was not achieved in Ghana until the Second World War.[61]

A second factor influencing the responsiveness of the colonial state to local interests was the way in which local representatives were chosen. Those who owed their selection to election by local constituents would more likely seek to make the public-administration response to local interests than would those who were selected through nomination by the governor – the head of the colonial bureaucracy. The electoral mechanism was adopted in Kenya in 1919; 17 of the 20 representatives of local interests in the legislative council were then chosen by election. Not until 1925 were elections used to choose members of the Ghanaian legislative council; and then, only 3 of the 14 unofficials were directly elected, 6 others being 'elected' by the chiefs who were themselves officials in the colonial bureaucracy.

Also important in determining the responsiveness of the colonial administration to local interests were the practices which were adopted in conducting public business. A review of these practices strongly suggests that the conventions which governed the conduct of public business in Kenya amplified the numerical weight accorded to its local representatives. In 1923, the government of Kenya adopted the practice of establishing a Finance Committee 'to scrutinize the budget in private before its final submission to the [Legislative] Council';[62] the committee consisted of all the elected representatives of the local interests and only three representatives of the public administration. As Dilley comments: 'This Committee is one development which has made it possible for unofficials to exercise the influence beyond their constitutional position.'[63] While there was a Finance Committee in Ghana as well, it did not have an unofficial majority, and its powers appear to have extended only to the deliberation of supplementary estimates.[64] For much of this period, the government of Kenya allowed what amounted to a caucus of the unofficial representatives the right to request the attendance of heads of departments so that the unofficials could probe the way in which they were conducting their agency's affairs; no such practice was followed in Ghana. From the period 1912–21, public business in Kenya was conducted under an understanding that has been described in the following terms:

> [The] Government and settlers bound themselves to cooperate to the fullest possible extent ... The Government would not introduce a controversial measure by springing it on the country without warning, steam-rollering it through Legislative Council with the official majority ... An important measure was, by agreement, outlined to the elected members before being introduced into Council so that they could express opinions and, if necessary, suggest modifications.[65]

No such practice characterized the conduct of public affairs in Ghana. Instead, the official majority was occasionally used to pass legislation despite the unanimous opposition of African members; in Wight's words, the government 'took the view that the African community had not yet reached the stage where its representatives might be given the power of obstruction in Council'.[66] And indicative of the unwillingness to engage in prior consultation with the representatives of local interests is the reaction of the local representatives to legislation introduced to terminate the cocoa boycott of 1937–8: 'There was much dissatisfaction that a bill dealing with so crucial an issue should be presented in this way ... Mr Kojo Thompson argued that a bill of such import and magnitude, dealing with the existing crisis in the country, needed serious and close discussion; moreover, that there was no need for rushing it through the Chamber.'[67]

The distribution of offices in public institutions and the way in which persons were selected to fill these offices thus gave greater weight to the representation of local interests in Kenya than in Ghana. And the practices which were adopted in making public policy amplified this distinction. Local interests in Kenya therefore had greater access to the state and a greater ability to use its power of coercion to their advantage.

The distinction between Ghana and Kenya in fact goes even deeper. It is clear that not just local interests, but the interests of farm producers in particular, received greater weight in the political institutions in Kenya than they did in those of Ghana; and, conversely, sectors whose interests were opposed in critical respects to those of the producers received disproportionate weight in the public institutions of the West Coast territory.

Under the constitution of 1906, of the three representatives of local interests in Kenya, two were farmers; and under the constitution of 1919, of the eleven local unofficials representing the interests of Europeans in the territory, a full eight represented the rural farming constituencies. As Bennett states, in designing the constitution 'electoral areas were to be delineated to represent interests rather than numbers ... it was generally realized that constituencies based on numbers would have meant control by Nairobi and Mombasa ... Instead the South African principle of weightage in favour of the rural areas was taken to a more extreme conclusion.'[68] In Ghana, by contrast, *there was no explicit representation of farming interests*. The chiefs did serve as representatives of rural interests in the high councils of government, and it may be granted that their interests were in many respects consonant with those of the farmers. But in matters of taxation and the levels of rent to be charged stool lands, their interests were often in conflict; and in any case, even with enthusiastic backing of the chiefs, the interests of the farmers could easily be out-voted by the representatives of the merchant houses and mining companies. Until 1916, of the four representatives of local interests, two were European – one representing the mining interests and the other the interests of the merchant houses – and two were African – one representing the urban educated classes and the other the chiefs. The expansion of local representation in 1916 did little to help. Again making the unwarranted assumption of an identity of interests between the chiefs and the cocoa producers, farming interests could be construed as holding only three of the nine local votes. Under the constitution of 1925, the chiefs held six positions. But, once again, they were a minority in a legislative body that allocated three positions for the coastal municipalities, one for the United Africa Company, one for the merchant houses not owned by the United Africa Company, one for the Chamber of Mines, one for the shipping interests, and one for the Bank of West Africa!

Wight's tabulation of the questions posed in the Gold Coast legislative council over 1933–41 reveals that the cocoa industry provoked more inquiries than any other subject. From all we have said, it is clear that in so far as this assembly made policy in the area, it would not do so with as high a regard for producer interests as was given by the legislative council in Kenya. One is hard pressed to believe, for example, that any governor of Kenya could have commented to the Kenyan legislative council as contemptuously as did the governor of Ghana: 'You will never find a farmer who is really satisfied. It is the same in England as it is here. If the weather is dry they want it wet, and if it is wet they want it dry.'[69] In Kenya, pandemonium would have followed; in Ghana, the governor was talking about interests who held no seats in the audience which he was addressing.

Thus far we have looked at variations between Kenya and Ghana in the structure of the constitutional forms which they, and other British territories, shared in common. We have seen how within the same constitutional framework the Kenyan political system gave greater weight to local interests in general and to farming interests in particular. It is clear that the structure and operations of the political institutions in Kenya were such as to introduce a stronger bias in favor of producer interests in the making of public policy. In addition, the two political systems possessed distinctive characteristics, and these too influenced the way in which different groups could utilize the states' control of coercion to advance their interests in the developing agricultural industry.

Centralization of power
In Ghana, more than in Kenya, organized economic interests in Britain influenced the colonial government. They employed their political power within the metropole to maximize the economic returns which they could secure from their commercial operations in the colonial territory.

These interests were the commercial houses. Their headquarters were in London, Manchester, and Liverpool. In Britain, their interests were represented through the chambers of commerce in those towns – chambers which took an active role in influencing public policy, including British policy overseas, on behalf of their members. Each chamber had a section on West African trade; and the leadership of these sections repeatedly combined to form delegations to lobby the foreign and colonial offices on behalf of their trading interests in Africa.

The major merchant houses were active in the chambers of commerce; the name of Swanzy, for example, appears in the minutes of numerous delegations dispatched by the chambers of commerce.[70] Using the combined influence of their head office in England and their local representatives in Ghana, the merchant houses were able to manipulate colonial institutions to mobilize the coercive powers of the state in support of their interests in the emerging agricultural economy.

It should be noted that the combination of access to policy-making institutions in both London and Accra was not fortuitous. We find, for example, the Board of Directors of the Manchester Chamber of Commerce supporting 'the merchants' proposal' to Lord Kimberley at the Colonial Office 'that the merchant element in the various legislative councils [of West Africa] should be considerably strengthened'.[71] On the other hand, we find scholars such as Martin Wight commenting that the merchants' representatives in the legislative council of Ghana 'hold a watching brief, remaining silent until their immediate interests are touched, and they never speak except to their book. They are businessmen, not politicians.'[72] The merchant houses thus had access to both the metropolitan and local centers of public policy making, and they did so on purpose. The advantages of this arrangement were perhaps best revealed in the attempts of the merchant houses to appropriate a larger share of the revenues generated by the agricultural industry in Ghana by forming cartels in the cocoa market in 1937.

The market-sharing agreements that formed the basis for the cartel were not negotiated by the firms in Ghana; rather, they were negotiated by the head offices in England. At the initiative of the United Africa Company, purchasing agreements were negotiated in the late summer and early fall of 1937. In September of that year, in the words of the United Kingdom report: 'Mr Frank Samuel, a Director of the United Africa Company, Ltd., and Mr John Cadbury of Messrs Cadbury Brothers, Ltd., called at the Colonial Office on the 24th of September, 1937 . . . to offer an explanation of [the agreement] and to request that the information might be conveyed to the West African Governments concerned.'[73]

The firms then notified their local representatives in the Gold Coast of the terms of the agreement and cabled detailed purchasing instructions to secure its successful implementation. The colonial office, for its part, sent dispatches to the Governor of the Gold Coast detailing the agreement and expressing 'the view that the Agreements were justifiable on economic grounds'.[74]

The local officials appear in fact to have had deep reservations concerning the purchasing agreements, these reservations being based on their assessment of its unfavorable impact on local politics. Despite these reservations, they none the less supported their implementation. The most credible characterization of their behavior is that they felt it necessary to implement an unwise policy foisted on them by their superiors in London. Indeed, given the dispatches received from their superiors, they had little choice but to accept the agreements as forming a legitimate basis for public policy. The local administration therefore biased the application of its coercive powers in favor of the incipient cartel. It never opposed the implementation of the collusive agreements on the part of the merchant houses; but it did rule that the use of state power to enforce the withholding of cocoa from the market in response to the formation of the buyers' cartel constituted an illegal restraint of trade.[75]

In some areas critical to the development of commercial agriculture in the territory, public institutions in Ghana were thus characterized by a high degree of centralization of policy formation in the metropole. By contrast, Kenya was characterized by a high degree of decentralization within the policy-making process. And, whereas the structure of decision making in Ghana appears to have biased the process of interest representation in favor of the buyers of agricultural products, the decentralized structure of interest representation in Kenya appears to have given greater access to coercive power to the producers of agricultural commodities.

In the case of almost every market of interest to the agricultural producers, there existed in Kenya a government board or policy-making committee; and, through these institutions, the representatives of farmers' interests gained access to public policy. We have already observed this in the case of the market for products; the Maize Control Board in fact operated as a state-sponsored cartel managed by the leaders of the producers' interests. A similar situation existed in the market for land. The government formed a lands committee to review its proposed land laws. The committee contained representatives of the farmers' interests and was chaired by Delamere, their leading spokesman. Its report urged modifications that favored the interests of the commercial farmers.[76] The government later formed a consultative body called the Land Board to aid in the development of the fundamental ordinances governing land development in the territory; farmers' interests were represented on the board and they used their access to secure a 'considerable influence on policy formation' in the area.[77]

A similar pattern obtained in the supply of transport services. In financing the expansion of these services in the 1920s, the railway sought government backing to secure its loans; this gave the public sector considerable control over the operations of the railway. The location of railway branch lines, for example, was in part made by a select committee of the legislative council. The representatives of local interests had a majority on the committee.[78] In the formation of rates, the railway management again had to consult with a public body, the Railway Advisory Council; again, the farmers' representatives dominated this institution. As one report noted: 'There is more than suspicion that unofficial members are nominated [to the Advisory Council] to forward certain popular policies, and not on account of the help they can give to the railway management.'[79] The government representative on the Advisory Council was the Director of Agriculture; as one expert noted, following his investigation of the operation of the railway: 'I think the Directors of Agriculture are too much interested in the success of their various agricultural schemes and are too inclined to seek assistance for these schemes through railway rates to be . . . advisers on railway policy.'[80]

The decentralized structure of policy formation thus promoted control by the farmers' interests of the conditions under which major inputs – those of land and transport services – were supplied to cash-cropping operations. Their control extended to more than just the regulation of major markets, however; it extended as well to the making of commercial policy. The most famous example of this is the so-called Bowring Committee. In the early 1920s, the colonial secretary, named Bowring, formed a committee to promote the development of exports. Chaired by Bowring himself, the committee was composed in large part of the representatives of farmer interests. Its behavior was instructive. Rather than supporting the development of those crops, such as coffee, in which Kenya had a relative advantage in the world market – the policy it should have followed had the committee sought to fulfill its public mandate in a socially optimal way – the committee instead adopted a series of policy measures that promoted those crops which were grown by the majority of the commercial farmers, such as maize and wheat – crops in the production of which Kenya in fact held a relative disadvantage in the world market.

The committee reduced the railway rates for maize to help subsidize exports of the crop. As Huxley notes: 'In September, 1922, railway rates were lowered to Shs. 11/20 a ton, and a shipment of 18,708 tons, the first since before the war, followed.'[81] And it imposed duties on dairy products, meats, wheat, and wheat flour. As Wrigley states: 'the cultivation of wheat and the raising of cattle had become technically feasible, but the costs of production were such that neither wheat nor dairy products could compete even on the East African market . . . To overcome this difficulty, it was now decided to secure the local market for local producers.'[82] Exploiting its mandate to develop commercial policies, the committee thus manipulated the instruments under its control to help dump inefficiently produced cereals on the world market and to shelter the domestic market against foreign competition in the production of agricultural commodities. Through this committee and others the agricultural producers thus exploited the decentralized procedures for public policy-making in Kenya to develop policy measures that secured them a position of advantage in the emerging commercial agricultural industry of East Africa.

Indirect rule

The policy-making process in Kenya was thus distinguished by its degree of decentralization. In Ghana there was greater involvement of the metropolitan center. The system of special-interest boards and committees did not exist in Ghana to the same degree as in Kenya; and it was therefore unavailable as a means of securing the power of the state to secure objectives in the market place. But, as we have noted throughout, the farmers did have access to public power through the leaders of rural interests: the chiefs.

We have already noted that the chiefs had close economic ties with the cocoa industry. They controlled the sales of stool lands, and often personally

89

pocketed the proceeds of these sales; and a primary determinant of the demand for this land was the profitability of cocoa production. Much of their income came from taxes and fees collected from the cocoa farmers. In addition, the chiefs themselves often owned farms, served as creditors, or otherwise had a deep personal stake in the industry. For all these reasons, they shared with the producers an interest in securing higher cocoa prices. Unlike the purely private producers, however, the chiefs also exercised control over legal sanctions. Thus, in the boycotts of both 1931 and 1937–8, the chiefs played an important role. They issued public edicts giving official support for the boycotts; they promulgated local statutes making it a punishable offense to market cocoa during the boycott; and, in some instances, they invoked their traditional sacred powers, making it an act of sacrilege to market cocoa.

Despite their powers, however, the chiefs were a highly imperfect instrument for securing the interests of the producers. The problem was that, while they possessed local power, they lacked national power; within the domain of the markets characteristic of the colonial era and the scope of the incipient nation-state, they were politically ineffective. Each chief had legal power over the behavior of only a small portion of the cocoa producers. Effectively to control the cocoa market, *national* political control was needed; for unless all the farmers acted in concert it was in the interests of none to cooperate. As we have seen, however, the chiefs were in no position to command majority support in the national political arena. Indeed, the national government reversed the policies which they selected, and condemned their attempts to give official backing to farmers' movements as an illegal restraint of trade. Without the backing of the state, the efforts of the chief were doomed to failure. The state's apportionment of power among the competing interests was a decisive factor in determining which interests prevailed.

CONCLUSION

The penetration of colonial powers into the interior of Africa brought in its train the forces of the market and the state. The spread of the market promoted the commercialization of agriculture; the operations of the state biased the resultant distribution of economic gains. Political forces shaped the operation of economic forces in such a way as to determine the pattern of economic rewards which came to distinguish the various societies of Africa.

Colonialism is a political system which is designed to bring economic benefits to foreign nationals. Political systems allocate access to force and they provide mechanisms for altering the operation of markets. Clearly, politics provides a means whereby groups can use coercion to levy resources from others: colonialism led to the redistribution of resources from indigenous to foreign interests. But, less obviously, access to state power also provides a means whereby the members of a group *can coerce themselves*; and it is by coercing themselves that they attain the capacity for collusive behavior. *In so far as state institutions apportion access to coercive power, they then allocate the means to organize.* The importance of the political order is that it provides differential access to the means of organizing economic interests – groups can then act to bias the operation of markets to their advantage.

The political dimension of the problem is thus fundamental. The cases revealed the importance of other factors, however. One was the nature of the commodities and their markets. Another was the size distribution of groups in the industry. Both helped to determine the relative power of producer intersts.

The colonial state thus put in place economic forces and political frameworks within which the commercialization of agriculture took place in Africa. While oppressing local interests, the impact of colonialism was none the less by no means uniform. Instead, the state system set a framework within which the pursuit of wealth in the market place, augmented by political means, led to the emergence of strongly contrasting agrarian societies in Africa.

4

The commercialization of agriculture and the rise of rural political protest

This chapter explores the relationship between the commercialization of agriculture and the rise of rural political protest in the colonial period in Africa.[1] It does so by examining several of the major issues which arose in the countryside during the colonial period in Africa. These issues include protests over governmental regulation of agricultural production, protests concerning the structure of markets, conflicts over land tenure, and disputes over taxes. Taken together, confrontations over these issues made up much of the rural political agenda in Africa during the colonial period.

Some of these issues were more significant in some places than in others. Disputes over the structure of markets most frequently arose in the forest areas of West Africa and in the cotton-producing regions about Lake Victoria, whereas conflicts over land-use regulations most frequently arose in the savannah farmlands of East Africa. The relative significance of the issues varied over time as well. Disputes over land tenure were most important at the onset of the large-scale commercialization of agriculture, that is, in the late nineteenth and early twentieth centuries; while the conservation issue rose to prominence after the intensification of agricultural production had begun to make a major impact on the environment and ecology of the farming areas – in the 1930s and 1940s.

The importance of these issues thus varied over space and time. But, over the continent as a whole and over the colonial period in its entirety, these issues accounted for a large portion of the political grievances of the African countryside. And the successful exploitation of these issues by nationalist politicians enabled them to mobilize rural political support for the movements which made Africa ungovernable by foreign powers and thereby led to political independence in sub-Saharan Africa.

THE STRUCTURE OF MARKETS

One of the primary issues which promoted agrarian protest in colonial Africa was the structure of the markets faced by the producers of cash crops. The commercialization of agriculture promised significant economic gains;

but, as we have seen, in some cases, the producers faced cartels which sought to appropriate these gains by engaging in price-setting behavior. Collusion on the part of the purchasers of the cash crops furnished an incentive for the producers to combine and so achieve market power in an effort to increase their profits.

One example of this kind of behavior is provided by the cocoa producers in the Gold Coast. As we have seen, in 1937, the merchant houses had organized a price-setting arrangement for the producers of Gold Coast cocoa. In retaliation, the cocoa farmers, led by the large-scale producers, the chiefs, and agents who had loaned money in anticipation of the sale of cocoa to the merchant houses, attempted to form a producers' cartel and so rival the price-setting power achieved by the merchant houses. The resultant boycott led to the large-scale politicization of the rural interior of the Gold Coast, and furnished one of the historical legends that shaped the nationalist consciousness of the colony's rural population.[2]

A similar situation arose in East Africa, where the producers of cotton also faced a non-competitive market – one that was used by the purchasers and processors of the commodity to lower the price they paid for the farmers' output. Again, the structure of the market furnished an incentive for the producers to combine. In the case of East Africa, the farmers' combinations took the form of cooperative societies – agencies which the farmers tried to use to break the power of the purchasers and thus to realize higher profits from cash-crop production.

In the production and processing of cotton in East Africa, economies of scale tended to concentrate in the ginning, as opposed to the growing, of cotton. The ginners had relatively high fixed costs: the buildings and machinery of the ginneries represented significant capital investments. Moreover, the machines, at least, could be used for no other purpose than ginning and so stood idle for much of the year. An important consideration for a prospective investor in ginning, therefore, was the certainty of a high volume of cotton for processing at the time of harvest.

To promote cotton production in East Africa, the governments of the area sought to promote investments in ginning capacity; and, to secure such investments, they sought ways of guaranteeing to prospective investors a high rate of utilization for each gin. In the case of both Uganda and Tanganyika, the major cotton-growing areas, the governments therefore passed ordinances requiring ginning licenses, and they restricted the number of licenses that could be issued. Moreover, they formed marketing zones. In a specified area surrounding each gin, only buyers who sold to that gin were permitted to operate and no shipping across the zones was allowed. The curtailment of competition on the part of the ginners naturally led to a decline in the price offered to the farmers for their produce.[3]

One result was protest on the part of the producers. In 1934 'all the *saza* chiefs in Busoga signed a letter to the provincial commissioner expressing ... their dislike of zoning, which "gives an opportunity to the cotton buyers to reduce the prices of cotton, knowing that people cannot remove their cotton and sell it in other neighboring districts".[4] Another result was the formation of the cooperative movement. The farmers sought to form cooperatives which would buy and gin cotton; by entering the market, the farmers sought to insure for themselves better prices than those offered by the ginners belonging to the cartel and to reap more of the gains from cash-crop production. One movement of this kind was the famous Victoria Federation of Cooperative Unions in Tanganyika – a society that helped to form the nucleus of the nationalist movement in the northeastern regions of that territory.[5] Another was the Uganda African Farmers Union. The Farmers Union made the grievances of the cotton producers a central issue in the 1949 disturbances in Uganda – disturbances that laid the foundation for the post-war period of national protest in that territory.[6]

PRODUCTION EXTERNALITIES, GOVERNMENT INTERVENTION, AND POLITICAL PROTEST

Producers of cash crops in Africa thus sometimes faced a market structure which threatened to divert much of the gains to be had from commercial agriculture to other parties in the industry. Collusion on the part of others served as an incentive for the producers themselves to combine. And attempts to achieve the power to influence prices in the marketplace thus motivated collective action in the countryside of Africa.

A second group of issues arose around externalities generated in the production of cash crops. Externalities occur when the activities of one producer directly influence the production possibilities of another. If the activity of one producer adversely affects the profits of another, in the absence of market mechanisms for creating incentives to adjust his behavior, the first producer will engage in more of that activity than is desirable; greater total profits could be secured by producers as a whole were he to reduce the degree to which he engaged in that activity. If the activity creates beneficial effects for the second party, in the absence of market mechanisms for creating incentives for the first producer to provide the beneficial externality, he will engage in less of the activity than is desirable. Under such circumstances, there are gains to be made if the government were to intervene in the market and provide the incentives for the first producer to increase the level at which he employs the activity which generates external effects.

In the case of cash-crop production in Africa, negative externalities appear to have been more common than positive ones; and the colonial government had frequently to contain activities which were privately profitable but socially undesirable. A major result was protest on the part of cash-crop producers who benefited from the use of externality-producing production techniques and a willingness to turn against the colonial government.

One common source of production externalities was erosion. During the Second World War, the colonial government promoted the production of cash crops and at a maximum rate, irrespective of the effects on the ecology or the environment. In East Africa, for example, they vigorously championed the production of maize, largely as a way of securing food for troops in the Middle East and North Africa. One result was extreme monocropping, with the attendant depletion of the soils; another was the extension of cash-crop production into increasingly marginal lands. The result of both trends was increased soil erosion.

An example of this problem arose in the Uluguru mountains of northeastern Tanzania. The mountains formed an important watershed and were the sources of several streams and rivers. In response to the increased demand for food, producers had moved up the mountains and cleared them of trees, shrubs, and groundcover in order to put them into production. With less groundcover, the soils of the hills retained the rain waters for shorter periods than before. One result was downstream flooding and the loss of crops by those who planted alluvial gardens. Moreover, with the more precipitate release of the waters deposited by the rains, the dry-season level of the rivers declined. Salt water from the ocean therefore moved further upstream; the result was increased salinization and a loss in the fertility of the soils near the rivers. The effect of increased production on the hills, therefore, was decreased production downstream. As is true everywhere in Africa, in northeastern Tanzania the major concentrations of population were located along the rivers, and the loss of crops due to the increased run-off from the hills more than offset the increase in the production of foodstuffs by the mountain producers.

The colonial government was unable to devise mechanisms whereby the downstream producers could make it to the advantage of the hillside producers to clear less land, or whereby the mountain producers could compensate the downstream farmers for the damage which they inflicted by bringing the hillside into production. Instead, the government had to attempt to use political power to alter the productive practices of the hillside farmers. Using its legal powers, the government sought to compel the hillside farmers to make bench terraces to curtail run-off from the hills. The farmers resisted the government's efforts. At first, they attempted to bribe the government's agents; when that failed, they turned to violence. In 1956, riots broke out, troops were called in, and people were killed in the confrontation which followed. A new group of rural dwellers joined the anti-government coalition formed by the nationalist movement.[7]

Erosion is one source of externalities, and measures taken to control it led to political protest throughout East Africa.[8] Another source of externalities is crop diseases. The attempts of the colonial governments to control the spread of diseases through the West African cocoa industry furnished an important source of rural protest in that region.

In 1936, officials of the department of agriculture of the Gold Coast first noted the death of cocoa trees in the older producing areas: New Juaben and Akim Abuakwa. They were sufficiently concerned to investigate further and, upon doing so, they discovered that significant infestation had taken place over an area of 200 square miles. Because of the physical marking which it left on the trees, the disease was called 'swollen shoot'. At first it was misdiagnosed, and only after the completion of a new research station – the first agricultural research station to be built in the Gold Coast – was the government able to diagnose the disease as a virus whose vector was the mealie bug. What made the virus so difficult to control was that ants served as hosts for the mealie bugs and provided protective shelters for them – shelters which made the insects inaccessible to sprays. The only viable control was the destruction of diseased trees; included in these efforts were adjacent, apparently healthy trees, but ones which may well have provided shelter for the infected insects. Following the Second World War, the government launched its control program.[9]

A major problem faced by the government was the resistance of the farmers themselves. And a principal reason for the clash between the farmers and the government was that each farmer evaluated the control measure from the point of view of his own private gains and losses, whereas the government took into account the effects of his behavior on other cocoa producers. A farmer who kept diseased trees in production – and trees often would continue to produce for several harvests after infection – would continue to earn profits, but he would be imposing costs on other farmers in terms of increasing the probability of the infestation of their farms.

Had there been a way that other farmers could charge a farmer with diseased trees for the injury he inflicted on their healthy ones, then control measures could perhaps have been voluntarily implemented. Moreover, had the governments understood the externalities problem, they might have been more ready at the outset to reward the afflicted producers for lessening the probability of infesting the farms of others. But the West African governments did not understand this aspect of the problem, and they refused to give compensation; as one Nigerian official put it, why pay compensation when 'the farmers are receiving the cutting out services for free'?[10] Instead, using their legal powers, the governments simply coerced the farmers. Government agents would move from one farm to the next. Locating diseased trees, they would mark the farm. Then the work gangs would arrive and, in the words of one farmer: 'The farms became a plain field within an hour.'[11] In the Gold Coast, the cutting out program began in January 1947; by 1948 over 600,000 trees had been removed from over 2,500 acres.[12] And in that year, the farmers rose against the government's program. Protesting against cutting out, they joined in the 1948 disturbances that led to basic constitutional reforms. Mobilized in large part through the issue of disease control, they joined the political coalition that brought an end to British rule in that colony.[13]

In agriculture, externalities can arise in other forms. They arise, for

96

example, under conditions of common property. Under conditions of collective grazing, for example, if one producer restricts his herd size to a level that is optimal, given the carrying capacity of the land, he confers a positive externality upon the other producers who share in the rights to graze livestock on that land. Without means of rewarding such behavior, the other grazers cannot evoke such socially optimum behavior, and private incentives therefore fail to produce the correct choice of herd size; in the absence of external intervention, the lands are overgrazed. Attempts to reduce herd sizes lead, however, to clashes between the government's vision of the public good and the producers' perception of their own best interest. Captured by the power of the incentives created by such externalities, de-stocking often became an issue that led to the mobilization of the arid-land farmers against their colonial governments.[14]

Collective rights to fisheries also led to the politicization of rural populations. Thus, in Zambia, conflicts between the fishermen and the government which imposed regulations in an attempt to prevent the depletion of the Lake Mweru fishery – controls over net sizes, fishing during spawning season, etc. – furnished a basis for incorporating the Luapula fisheries into the nationalist movement.[15]

Externalities also arose in the establishment of quality standards. The purchasers of many of the export crops of Africa were willing to offer only one price – one that reflected their appraisal of the average quality of the crop. In so far as it was cheaper to produce a low-quality product, each farmer was better off marketing a low quality of output while being paid the price for an average quality product. But, when all farmers behaved in this way, the average quality of output declined. The rational behavior of each farmer thus imposed costs on all farmers in the form of a lowering of the market price. In the absence of a willingness on the part of the purchasers to offer a spectrum of prices for a variety of quality standards, the governments in cash-crop-growing areas felt compelled to intervene and to maintain by administrative methods a high standard of marketed output. The result, once again, was conflict between cash-crop producers and the government.[16]

The colonial governments' attempts to promote soil conservation, control grazing, fishing and crop diseases, and increase the quality of production thus led to increased state intervention in the agricultural industries of Africa. In the absence of mechanisms that would secure voluntary compliance with rules that would maximize the profits of the producers as a whole, the colonial governments felt compelled to constrain administratively the behavior of the African farmers. Under the impact of government regulation, producers who generated negative externalities experienced a decline in their private profits. They resented being coerced into accepting a lower level of economic reward. And they therefore were willing to turn against the colonial governments and to back the efforts of nationalist politicians to overthrow the colonial regimes.[17]

THE STRUCTURE OF LAND RIGHTS

With the prospects of profits from agriculture came an increase in the value of land. The allocation of this benefit among competing claimants was largely determined by the allocation of land rights, and the ultimate adjudicator of that allocation was the state. Control over the state and its legal system was therefore sought by those seeking to gain economic benefits from commercial farming. Disputes over land rights thus led to political action in rural Africa.

Struggles between indigenous peoples and highly capitalized foreign immigrants constituted one set of such disputes. As we have seen, one such case arose in Kenya. Both the indigenous human and livestock populations had declined precipitately as a result of famines and pestilence in the 1890s; and, as indigenous agricultural technology depended in any case on long and extensive land rotations, much of the land in Kenya *appeared* to be waste or unoccupied. Employing a legal ruling which vested rights to such lands in the Crown, the colonial government appropriated vast acreages from the indigenous farm families and rapidly transferred ownership to immigrant commercial farmers. Protests over the loss of land rights subsequently formed the basis for much of the nationalist movement in Kenya.[18]

In Ghana, too, although the outcome was different, attempts by the state to seize rights to 'waste' lands also gave rise to popular movements of political protest against the colonial order. The indigenous population, led by the rural chiefs and the legal and commercial elites of the coastal towns, vigorously defended the rights of the native population to their lands, and argued that, though lands may presently be unexploited, rights over them were well defined under the traditional legal system. A major reason for their resistance to the transfer of land rights to the Crown was that an active market in land, and in concessions for its use, had begun in the Gold Coast – a market that allowed chiefs and the coastal elites to share in the economic benefits deriving from control over this valuable input into commercial cash-crop production.[19] To promote their resistance to the alienation of lands to foreign control, the chiefs and the coastal elites formed the Aborigines Rights Protection Association – the first nationalist political party in West Africa.

Disputes over the control of land also arose in the Congo, where the Belgian government gave large-scale concessions to foreign capitalists.[20] They also arose in Tanzania, Zambia, Rhodesia, and South Africa, where foreign settlers, backed by the colonial state, appropriated large acreages. In almost every area in Africa, these disputes formed a prominent basis for rural resistance to colonial rule.

It should also be noted that disputes over land rights led to splits within the indigenous community, and the way in which these political cleavages formed in any African territory gave a special character to the nationalist movement of that area. One of the major characteristics of the nationalist movement in several territories, for example, was that it sought as much to depose the indigenous political elites, the chiefs, as it sought to displace the foreign administration; and, where such movements arose, they often did so in areas where the chiefs and the peasants were at odds over land rights.

In the Gold Coast, for example, where there were waste and unoccupied lands, they remained stool lands. That is, they remained the lands of the community and rights to these lands could be alienated only by the administrative head of that community, the chief, who was said to occupy the stool or throne. With the rise of the demand for cash crops from Africa, there arose a demand for rights to land; and the chiefs, in conformity with their traditional role, sold rights to the stool lands. The problem was that, rather than channelling the profits from their sale to the communal treasury, the chiefs diverted many of the profits to their private pockets. Increasing indignation over their corruption led to splits between the chiefs and the masses, and these conflicts lent a radical character to much of the nationalist politics of that territory. It also led to major cleavages within the nationalist forces. The chiefs and the commoners, having split over this and other issues, tended to back different factions of the nationalist movement, the chiefs tending to be drawn to the United Gold Coast Convention while the commoners tended to support the more radical Convention People's Party.[21]

A similar polarization emerged in Uganda. In negotiating the final terms of their settlement with the encroaching colonial power, the Kabaka and his subordinate chiefs evoked a recasting of land rights in terms of freehold tenure. Each major chief secured freehold rights over large estates in exchange for acknowledging British sovereignty. The actual occupants of these lands then became tenants of the chiefs. With the growth in the commercial values of these lands – a growth which principally resulted from the spread of cotton production in Uganda – the chiefs were able to use their control over land rights to divert revenues from the producers themselves. They did so by raising the rental fees on the land and by increasing the burden of services required of the tenants. The result was the emergence of a major cleavage between the traditional elites and the peasant farmers – a split that was only partially healed by the passage of rent control laws.[22]

Other kinds of political cleavage arose in disputes over land rights. Some occurred between adjacent localities, as major indigenous communities filed competing claims over lands.[23] Others took the form of conflicts between different levels of government; these often *appeared* to be communal in nature. Groups which in the past had conquered others responded to the growing profits to be gained from agriculture by attempting to increase the extent and value of tribute obligations; as these obligations were paid from what amounted to property taxes at the local level, such disputes often took the form of conflicts over the jurisdiction over land.[24] So-called 'age-old' disputes between different indigenous communities thus often fundamentally revolved around the allocation of legal rights to this productive resource.

One last kind of dispute over land rights is of interest – conflicts over collective as opposed to individual forms of tenure. Collective rights assure access to land, or to the profits to be realized from its use in commercial agriculture, to all members of a community. In insuring everyone access to these benefits, however, such rights also reduce the ability of entrepreneurs to secure maximum returns from commercial agriculture. Those who sought to maximize their private advantage in the emerging agricultural industries of Africa therefore sought private rights in land; those who were more concerned with securing guaranteed access to a subsistence level of production favored establishment of collective rights.

This conflict appears to have been most frequently joined in East Africa. In Uganda, for example, it took the form of the militant reassertion of traditional clan rights over the lands that had been alienated to the chiefs under freehold tenure. The dedication to clan rights formed much of the basis of the Bataka Association – a movement of the farmers and the clan heads who opposed the power of chiefs in general and their private rights over the *mailo* lands in particular.[25] Analogous disputes broke out among the Kikuyu. Prosperous farmers sought to advance their claims to individual tenure, while others sought to emphasize collective rights to *mbari* lands out of fear of losing their rights to land in the Kikuyu reserves.[26] The assertion of private rights over collective property by the chiefs of the Gold Coast underlay much of the rural politics in that area. And, in the contemporary period, the attempts by the state in Tanzania to promote collective rights to land in the cash-cropping regions of that territory has apparently found favor among the rural poor, who fear the loss of land rights in the countryside, while meeting with resistance on the part of the prosperous farmers, who naturally see such measures as threatening the gains which they seek to secure through cash-crop production.[27]

TAXATION

There is a last set of issues which arose in conjunction with the commercialization of agriculture: those which revolved around taxation. As is well known, taxation was repeatedly used by public policy makers to induce subsistence farmers to exchange produce or labor for cash; as such, its introduction met with resistance by African rural dwellers. More relevant to this chapter, however, was the behavior of the farmers once they had begun to produce for the market. For a variety of reasons, they continued to engage in political protest against the levying of taxes.

Leaving aside consideration of the properties of public goods, we can view the payment of taxes as an exchange. The private citizen relinquishes the power to purchase a basket of commodities provided in the private marketplace in exchange for a collection of public goods and services provided by the state. In making this exchange, the rural dwellers in Africa have repeatedly protested that the rate of exchange was unfavorable, and that the goods and services received from the state failed to equal in value the private commodities forsaken due to the payment of taxes.

One example of this reaction arose in early tax rebellions of the 1850s. In the Gold Coast, for example, the colonial administration had convened a series of local assemblies to announce that in order to provide a variety of services – roads, schools, and hospitals, for example – the government would be imposing a capitation tax. For a brief period, the tax was successfully collected; but then resistance broke out. Opposition grew to the point of large-scale rebellion and no serious attempt was made to collect the tax after 1852. Upon investigating the resistance to taxes, the colonial administration determined that 'only about one-fifth of the amount collected ... had been spent on the objects for which it was given'.[28] A major grievance was that 'the stipends and expenses of collection swallowed up nearly the whole revenue, and the people became restless at the failure to provide the promised benefits'.[29] The people protested against taxes because they felt that the taxes made them worse off; the loss in income which they suffered from taxation had not been compensated for by public services of comparable value. So strong were their feelings on the matter, and so successfully did they act upon them, that the Gold Coast government was unable to impose direct taxes until 1943.

A second major source of grievance over the collection of taxes often fed into and exacerbated the split between the chiefs and the masses that arose with respect to land rights. In the absence of an ability to provide satisfactory services, the colonial government's exercise of its power of taxation in the countryside led, in the minds of many taxpayers, simply to a redistribution of income between the taxpayers and the holders of public office. Protests over taxation thus frequently became protests against rural office holders, the most prominent of whom were the chiefs. Kilson's analysis of the rural basis of the nationalist movement in Sierra Leone emphasizes these dynamics.[30] So do many of the studies of rural protest in Ghana. Thus Tordoff notes that, with the commercialization of agriculture in the inland areas of the Gold Coast, the chiefs used their powers of taxation to build up the public treasury; the funds of the Native Authorities were supposed to be used to provide public goods, but the rural public authorities largely failed to supply these amenities. The result was that 'the number of destoolments increased rapidly and underlined the basic insecurity of the chief's tenure of office. Malcontents were quick to seize the opportunity of accusing their ruler of misappropriating stool money, and the failure of most chiefs to keep proper accounts made this charge difficult to rebut.'[31] In his analysis of the changing role of the chief in the Gold Coast, Busia makes a similar point and provides data on local government finances which help to substantiate the argument. Busia's data show that during the early to mid 1940s over 80 per cent of the expenditure of the Native Authorities was for 'administrative expenses',

101

i.e., for salaries, by and large, and less than 20 per cent for education, medical services, capital works, and other improvements.[32] Because of the failure to provide services, the payment of taxes thus appeared to involve not a creation of public benefits but a redistribution of income between cash-crop producers and those who drew their incomes from the state; and, naturally, the rural producers resented this transfer.[33]

Two other features of the taxation of cash-crop producers generated political protest in colonial Africa: first, the inherent nature of public goods. In the case of public goods and services, such as roads or law and order, it is reasonable for citizens to misrepresent the value they place on them and to protest that they are being charged too much for them. Being public goods, the goods provided by the state will be available for consumption by the taxpayer irrespective of the amount he actually pays for them. The taxpayer would in fact do best by letting others pay for the public goods, which he could then consume for free. The African cash-crop producers, like taxpayers everywhere, were thus simply behaving in a way that maximized their own private welfare when they denigrated the value of the services which they received from the government as being of too low a quantity or quality, and when they condemned as excessive the level of taxation which they were asked to pay for these services.

Second, the power of taxation is the power to coerce, and this power can be used to redistribute income. Redistribution makes some people better off by making other people worse off; and the latter group will not voluntarily consent to redistributive measures. When taxes are used in this way they will lead to political protest, be it in rural Africa or anywhere else.

This pattern is clearly revealed in the political conflicts between small-scale subsistence and large-scale commercial farmers in Kenya and in the emergence of anti-colonial politics in that country. The commodities boom of the early twenties increased the commercial farmers' demand for labor. The government's recruitment of laborers for railway construction and the effects of the loss of population in the First World War and in the post-war outbreaks of influenza had reduced the supply of labor. The commercial producers were unwilling to increase the level of wages which they paid and they therefore experienced a shortage of labor. In response to this shortage, they championed an increase in the level of taxes on subsistence-farm families as a means of redistributing labor power from the subsistence to the commercial-farm sector. In 1920, the government raised the tax rate; because of a change in the budget year, the new tax was collected twice in a single calendar year. Largely in response to this tax, Harry Thuku organized the first African political party in Kenya: the Young Kikuyu Association.[34]

It was not only labor that was forcefully redeployed between the two farming sectors. The costs of providing services were concentrated in one sector; the benefits from using them were reaped by the other. The use of tax laws thus to redistribute income is revealed in the politics of the 1920s in Kenya. In 1920, the colonial government introduced an income tax and the commercial farmers resisted it. Forming a Taxpayers Protection League, they opposed the measure in the legislative council and organized the withholding of tax payments. Finally, in May 1922, they secured the repeal of the income tax and secured as well the passage of a substitute financial measure: a schedule of customs rates which was designed to generate revenue by imposing duties on items consumed in large part by the native population and to provide protection for the commodities produced by the commercial farmers.[35]

The power of taxation was thus used in Kenya to facilitate the redistribution of resources between different sectors of the farming community; and much of the politics of that area centered around efforts to alter the structure of taxes and the allocation of the services which they financed. Similar patterns obtained in West Africa. One of the main reasons for the taxpayers' revolt in mid-nineteenth-century Ghana, for example, was that the rural communities perceived that the fisc was being used to redeploy resources among different sections of the population. Explaining their resistance to taxes to which they had formerly assented, Kimble notes: 'The original Assemblies had thought that they were taxing themselves for purely local purposes, and the Accras, for example, "never could have conceived that their money was to be applied in making roads and supplying medical aid for Fantees".'[36] The Accras therefore joined the tax rebellion.

The redistributive nature of taxation emerged in another form, and this also promoted political unrest. Through public financial institutions, groups can achieve particular benefits while transferring the costs of supplying them to the political community as a whole. As each group can potentially secure all the benefits of a particular measure while paying only part of the costs, each group will therefore demand that the political community provide those services in which it has a particular interest, even though the benefits of the measure are outweighed by the total costs. This dynamic appeared to underlie a series of financial crises which beset rural political institutions in Africa. I refer to the fiscal crises that bedeviled the native authorities of twentieth-century Ghana.

As we have discussed, the rise of cocoa production in the Gold Coast increased the tax base of the rural chieftaincies. The rise of cocoa farming also increased the demand for public services, and, in particular, the demand for secure rights in land. The cocoa farmers obtained their farm lands by purchasing land rights from the chiefs; and, where the jurisdiction of the chiefs was uncertain, it was in the interest of the farmers to demonstrate through a court of law the jurisdictional primacy of the chief that had sold them their lands. The disputes between cocoa farmers thus became disputes between different local chieftaincies.

With the increased density of farms in the cocoa-producing forest lands, the number of conflicting land claims multiplied; the cocoa farmers therefore had more frequent occasion to seek clarification of their chiefs' jurisdictions. The costs of these disputes were borne by all of the taxpayers who fell under the jurisdiction of the chief; the benefits were reaped by a particular group of farmers. The result of these factors was apparently to

103

increase further the volume of litigation, both by raising the likelihood of disputes being pushed that had a low probability of winning and by increasing the number of appeals against adverse rulings. It was therefore not surprising that the costs of litigation rose to an alarming degree in the cocoa-farming areas, and in fact imposed a major fiscal burden upon native authorities throughout the area.[37] Much of the political unrest in the cash-cropping areas of the Gold Coast reflected dissatisfaction with the mounting stool debts and the apparent mismanagement of public finances by local governments.

The rising stool debts, and the attempts to remove them through general levies, represented a transfer of resources to the farmers – who would benefit from the establishment of their rights to the full capital value of their lands – from present and future taxpayers – who would have to pay the costs of litigation involved in establishing their chiefs' jurisdiction over these lands. Farmers, however, were not always the primary beneficiaries of the redistribution of resources through fiscal measures; indeed, they have increasingly become the victims of such measures. And this has become increasingly true as ambitious political elites have sought to secure for public purposes the private resources being amassed by those making profits from commercial agriculture. This trend emerges more clearly in the post-independence period, and I therefore leave the discussion of it to the last essay in this volume.

CONCLUSION

With the onslaught of colonial rule, rural Africa was subject, to a greater degree than before, to the impact of market forces. And, as has been true elsewhere, the commercialization of agriculture was intimately linked with the rise of political protest in the rural areas. Farmers, concerned with the value of their incomes, not only engaged in the production and marketing of agricultural products but also engaged in politics. In this essay, I have explored the relationship between the market and the political arena and analyzed why rural producers were impelled into political action in defense of their economic interests.

The politicization of the African peasantry made the farm families of Africa 'available', as it were, to the movements which would ultimately dislodge the European colonial powers from that continent. In the post-independence period, the governments of Africa set terms for the incorporation of the peasantry into the nation state and the national economy. These terms reflect a turning away from the peasantry and a reluctance to confer economic rewards commensurate with the magnitude of their contribution to the movements of national liberation. The subjects to which we now turn are the nature of the policies of African governments toward their rural sectors and the way in which these policies reflect an abandonment of the peasantry in the post-independence era.

Part III

Agrarian society in post-independence Africa

5

The nature and origins of agricultural policies in Africa

In this last essay I examine the location of rural dwellers in the political economies of the post-independence states of Africa. I do so by exploring the agricultural policies of these states and the position to which they assign the economic interests of farmers.

Agricultural policy is made up of those decisions by governments which alter the prices farmers confront in the markets which determine their incomes. To explain agricultural policy – and thus the assignment of farmers to official positions in the political economies of the African states – one must explain patterns of market intervention engaged in by governments. It requires as well an explanation for the biases which governments introduce in the performance of these markets and hence in the allocation of economic resources.

As will be seen, the post-independence states of Africa – like their counterparts elsewhere in the third world – adopt agricultural policies which possess certain distinctive features. They both tax the output of farmers and subsidize agricultural inputs. The policies are project-based rather than price-based. They seek to promote increased agricultural production without strengthening economic incentives by offering higher farm prices. They introduce economic inefficiencies in the form of price distortions, non-competitive rents, and poorly designed development projects. And, above all, they violate the economic interests of most farmers.

To explain the content of agricultural policies and the patterns of bias which they engender, I explore several basic models of policy formation. Each makes certain assumptions concerning the state. Each accounts for some features of agricultural policy. Each also exhibits major shortcomings. Taken together, however, these models help to account for many of the characteristic features of these policies and thus for the standing of rural interests in the political economies of contemporary Africa.

In a prescient essay, Frantz Fanon set much of the agenda for the analysis of the role of the peasantry in post-independence Africa. 'The men at the head of things distrust the people of the countryside', Fanon wrote, and their 'distrust takes on serious proportions'.[1] The peasantry is politically isolated, he wrote, it is 'looked down upon' and 'kept at a distance'.[2] None the less, its revolutionary potential remains strong. Few common interests tie it to the elite and the urban masses, and the countryside constitutes a refuge for those who are disaffected by the prevailing social order. 'It is [therefore] understandable', Fanon concluded, 'that the meeting between the ... militants with the police on their track and these ... masses of people, who are rebels by instinct, can produce an explosive mixture of unusual potentiality.'[3]

In this last essay, I will demonstrate that indeed the peasants are politically isolated and economically oppressed. But I will disagree with Fanon in one critical respect. Fanon equates structural position with revolutionary potential: to be isolated and oppressed is to possess the tendency to rebel. But I will argue that the very policies which oppress the peasantry may well undermine their capacity to organize in resistance to them. Properties of the oppressive policies themselves help to account for the inability of the peasantry to alter their structural location in the political economies of Africa.

POST-INDEPENDENCE AGRICULTURAL POLICY

Farmers derive their revenues from the sales they make in the markets for agricultural products. Their profits are a function of these revenues but also of the costs incurred in a second major market: the market for factors of production. And the real value of these profits, and thus the real value of their incomes, is determined by the prices which they must pay in a last major market: the market for consumer items and, in particular, the market for goods manufactured in the city. So, the analysis of agricultural policy involves an examination of the nature and form of government intervention in the markets for agricultural commodities, for inputs into farming, and for the goods which farmers buy from the urban-industrial sector.

A review of agricultural policies in tropical Africa suggests that governments intervene in markets in order to depress the prices of agricultural products. They intervene to increase the prices which must be paid for manufactured items. And, while they subsidize the costs of farm inputs, these subsidies tend to go to a small number of large-scale farmers. Agricultural policies tend to be adverse to the economic interests of most farmers.

Markets for products

With some violence to the facts, the marketed products of African farmers can be classified into two kinds: cash crops largely destined for export and food crops destined for domestic consumption. In the case of both products, governments adopt policies which attempt to depress prices.

Cash crops

Cash crops include the beverage crops: coffee, tea and cocoa. They include crops which yield vegetable oils: palm oil, palm kernel oil, cotton seeds and groundnuts. They also include such fibers as sisal and cotton.

Most governments in Africa maintain publicly sanctioned monopsonies for the purchase and marketing of these crops. While the existence of international boundaries and the frequent absence of border controls allow some farmers to evade the exactions of their own national agency, the best most farmers can often do is to sell their crops to the monopsony run by an adjacent government. By one estimate, at the time of independence, government marketing agencies handled 90 per cent of the exports of palm kernels, 80 per cent of the exports of coffee, 65 per cent of the exports of tea, and 60 per cent of the exports of raw cotton.[4]

Most African governments inherited these monopsonistic marketing structures from their colonial predecessors. The historical origins of these agencies differ in important respects. Some were created by the producers themselves; this was most frequently the case in East, Central and Southern Africa. Others were erected by the colonial governments in league with private trading firms; this pattern tended to prevail in Western Africa.[5] Whatever their origin, however, the agencies have increasingly been employed by the governments of Africa to levy revenues and foreign exchange from the producers of cash crops.

The governments use the monopsonistic power of the marketing agencies to set a domestic price. They then sell the crop on the world market at the prevailing international price. The difference between the two prices allows the accumulation of a trading surplus. This surplus represents a tax on the agricultural producers.

I have attempted to collect data on the level of the financial burden placed on the producers of export crops by the dual-price policy of the public marketing agencies. In most cases the data represented the prices offered in the domestic market expressed as a percentage of the price f.o.b. at the nearest major port. In some cases, they represented the percentage of the income generated by the sale of the crop in the international market which is actually secured by the producers. In either case, they documented that the producers almost invariably received a price which lay below the world market price. In most instances, they obtained less than two-thirds the potential sales realization. And, in many cases, they received less than one-half.[6]

Initially, it was held that the farmers themselves were to benefit from the accumulation of trading surpluses. Monies levied at times of high international prices, it was held, would be returned at times of low prices, thereby stabilizing farmer incomes. Rarely, however, have marketing board surpluses been used in this fashion. Indeed, as seen most vividly with the fall of cocoa prices in 1960–1, when the world price fell, the governments of West

Africa cut the local price proportionately. What was stabilized was the off-take of the marketing boards rather than the incomes of farmers.[7]

The beneficiaries of the dual-price policy are best revealed by noting who gains access to the trading surpluses. A prime recipient is the state; the marketing boards have become important instruments of taxation. Soon after self-government, for example, the governments of Ghana and Western Nigeria committed themselves to major development plans. In order no longer to be constrained to employ the funds raised by the marketing boards for the benefit of the farmers, the governments altered the laws governing the allocation of the trading surpluses.[8] In the first years of self-government, the marketing agencies tended to loan funds to the public treasury; in later years they simply turned the funds over to their governments in the form of grants.[9] In these ways, the marketing agencies have become the source of over a third of the revenues of some of the states of Africa.

Another major beneficiary has been the urban-industrial sector. In part, this sector has benefited as a consequence of the ways in which the governments have allocated public resources. Governments have employed the revenues generated by the marketing agencies to construct projects of primary benefit to the urban industrial sector: hydroelectric schemes whose power is used by urban industry but not for rural electrification, the building of industrial parks, or the construction of intra-urban transport systems.[10] And while there has been little systematic research into patterns of governmental expenditure, what little there is suggests that it concentrates disproportionately in urban and industrial centers.[11]

Industry has benefited in other ways. The monopsonistic marketing structures which generate state revenues have also been employed to depress the price of agricultural products in efforts to attract investments in processing industries. Low prices for raw materials are employed to lure and retain industrial investments. This trend has been noted for sisal and coffee in Tanzania;[12] sugar, cocoa, and vegetable oils in Ghana;[13] cocoa in Nigeria;[14] pineapple production in Kenya and Zambia;[15] and vegetable oil production in the Sudan.[16] Moreover, the resources levied from the rural sector have been employed to create capital which is then loaned to new industrial projects. The best-documented instances of such transfers originate from Nigeria, where the well-known Coker Commission recorded the transfer of capital from the marketing boards to the projects of private investors. The loans were made at subsidized rates of interest; in many cases, they were simply not repaid; and in most instances little was requested by way of security.[17]

The marketing boards are not the sole means by which resources are redistributed from export agriculture to the urban industrial sector. Also aiding in the transfer is the overvaluation of the rate of exchange between local and foreign currencies. By overvaluing their currencies, governments in Africa seek to make it easier for industries to import capital equipment; they thereby attempt to promote domestic industrialization. But in so doing they also lessen the purchasing power of those who earn their incomes in foreign markets. For, with the overvaluation of their currency, earnings of foreign exchange convert into lesser amounts of local 'dollars'. The maintenance of an overvalued currency thus represents a tax on exports; export agriculture is hurt in an effort to assist the growth of the industrial sector.

Government and industry are not the sole beneficiaries of the levies from export agriculture; another beneficiary is the bureaucracy which manages the public monopsonies which tax agricultural exports. The bureaucracy consumes an increasing portion of the resources secured from export agriculture; evidence is the inflation of the costs of marketing.[18] Among the most rapidly increasing components of these costs are salaries. In part, this is because the number of persons employed has increased; as noted by a commission of inquiry into cocoa marketing in Ghana:

> The evidence before us suggests that the [agency] used the profits obtained from its monopoly cocoa operations to . . . provide funds for the dance band, footballers, actors and actresses, and a whole host of satellite units and individuals . . . [T]he State Cocoa Marketing Board itself is not free from . . . this type of practice. The CMB's area of operation . . . embraces activities and involves a staff which would have appeared absurd only ten years ago.[19]

In part, too, the increase in salary represents simply the growth of the pay and perquisites given to those in charge of the marketing agencies; as reported in *West Africa*, for example:

> Cmdr Addo, former chief executive of the Cocoa Marketing Board, told the committee investigating its affairs that the CMB spent nearly ₡1 m. on drinks alone between August 1977 and July 1, 1978. Giving evidence, Cmdr Addo said during his tenure of office he instituted certain measures to boost the morale of the directors. As part of these measures, he said, all the eight or ten directors were given a bottle each of whisky, brandy, and gin at the end of every month in addition to receiving a . . . table allowance.[20]

In addition, Commander Addo stands accused of the fraudulent appropriation of hundreds of thousands of *cedis* of the Board's trading profits.[21] The bureaucrats who staff the marketing agencies thus capture a major portion of the non-competitive rents generated by the marketing structure.

Food crops
Governments in Africa not only intervene to depress the price of cash crops; they also intervene in attempts to secure low-priced food.

In part, they intervene by attempting directly to manipulate the price of food products. Their commercial policies, for example, help to secure low-priced food. Overvaluation of the domestic currency cheapens the price of foreign foodstuffs; and governments tend not to offer tariff protection to domestic producers in order to offset the effects of overvaluation. As a result, the lower world price tends to prevail on the urban markets; Africa

111

has become a major importer of food. Moreover, when the world price lies above the domestic price, governments often ban the export of food items. Exports of meat from the Sudan and Kenya, of tea and dairy products from Kenya, and of maize from Zambia have, for example, been terminated from time to time to prevent domestic shortages. The effect, of course, is to prevent the domestic price from rising to the world price, thus preserving the lower local price for the domestic consumer.

Governments also attempt directly to administer prices in food markets. Many attempt to establish price controls; the floggings of persons failing to abide by government prices under Rawlings' regime in Ghana is but a vivid, if pathological, illustration of a common policy commitment. Some governments attempt to secure low-cost food through the establishment of monopsonistic marketing channels. In Kenya, Tanzania, and Zambia, and throughout the Sahelian countries, public agencies are empowered to operate as the sole legal purchasers of staple food crops. Through elaborate controls over the movement, storage and marketing of the crops, they seek to depress the prices paid to farmers and thereby secure low-cost food.[22] Governments also seek low food prices through the conferral of subsidies; government subventions to millers, for example, help to keep down the price of bread in Nigeria, Zambia, and Tanzania.

None of these policies has proved satisfactory, however. In the face of competing demands for foreign exchange and shortfalls in its supply, African governments find it increasingly costly to spend this scarce resource on food imports. Repeatedly they have mounted programs to secure self-sufficiency in food. Subsidies are resisted by governments faced with shortages of public revenues. Lastly, by comparison with the marketing of export crops, the marketing of food crops is difficult to control. There are several reasons for the relatively greater difficulty of regulating food marketing. In the case of most export crops, the number of consumers is limited; they must have access to foreign markets or to expensive processing equipment. Food crops, by contrast, place no particular restrictions on consumers; they can be bought and processed by almost anyone. Export crops must be moved through well-defined spatial locations: ports and harbors, for example. Food crops can be transported along almost any road or path. Lastly, cash crops are often grown in ecologically specialized zones; food crops, by contrast, are grown by all subsistence farmers. It is therefore simply much harder to implement controls over the marketing of food crops than is the case with export crops. By some estimates, in countries with food-crop monopsonies, as much as 90 per cent of the crop moves outside officially regulated government channels.[23]

As a consequence of the weakness of these policy measures, governments try other means of lowering food prices. Most commonly, rather than directly manipulating food prices, they manipulate food supplies. Rather than employing price-based policies, governments employ production-based policies. In many of the nations of Africa, governments in effect set themselves up as competitors with the peasantry and try, by increasing food supplies, to lower the price of food.[24]

In the market both for export crops and for food crops African governments have adopted policies which seek to depress the price of farm products. While it is the generally draconian nature of these pricing policies which I wish to emphasize, it is useful and important to point out as well variations within the general trend. The major sources of variation appear to be twofold: historical and structural.

One source appears to derive from the political origins of the governments which came to power with the end of colonial rule. In particular, the location of farming interests, with respect to the coalition seizing power from the colonial government, appears to have made a major difference in the pricing policies of the post-independence regimes. In Ghana and Zambia, for example, the parties which seized power had a strong urban base; in Ghana, the Convention People's Party tapped the political militancy of the coastal cities, and in Zambia, the United National Independence Party drew the vast preponderance of its organized base from the urban centers of the copperbelt. Moreover, in both cases, the political movement which seized power had earlier broken away from and subsequently out-maneuvered more conservative political factions which had been based upon commercial agriculture – the cocoa farmers of Ashanti in the one case and the maize producers of the southern plateau in the other. By contrast, in the Ivory Coast and Kenya, the political movements which seized power at the time of independence remained strongly centered on a political base made up of commercial farmers. At the core of the Parti Démocratique de la Côte d'Ivoire in the Ivory Coast stood the indigenous planters; and, in Kenya, the Central Province farmers, and particularly the farming elite in Kiambu, occupied a controlling position within the ruling party. Since independence, Ghana and Zambia have adopted pricing policies which have been remarkably adverse to the interests of farmers;[25] the governments of Kenya and the Ivory Coast have adopted policies which, by comparison, are highly favorable to farmers.

A second and related historical factor is the origin of the marketing systems which have been called upon to implement post-independence pricing policies. As we have seen, in East Africa agencies were formed by producers themselves in an effort to defend and advance their economic interests. In West Africa, by contrast, the agencies were formed by governments and trading interests who sought to employ their monopsony power to capture a portion of the profits to be gained from commercial agriculture. The origins of the agencies appear to have created an enduring institutional bias. The governments of East Africa tend, in general, to have imposed less-adverse domestic prices for export crops. And, by contrast with the performance of the grain marketing boards in Tanzania and

Zambia, the Maize and Produce Board of Kenya – which, as we have seen, began as a producer cartel – has set domestic producer prices at levels which are far more favorable to producer interests.[26]

Historical forces are thus important in explaining variations in pricing policies. So too are structural factors and, in particular, those having to do with the pattern of rivalry for the resources generated by commercial agriculture.

The producers themselves are a major claimant for the proceeds of agriculture. And, where the industry is characterized by large-scale production, governments tend to confer more favorable prices upon the producers. In Kenya, for example, estates receive no less than 90 per cent of the world market price for coffee, whereas small-holders receive no more than 66 per cent.[27] In Ghana, rice production takes place on large-scale mechanized farms; producers receive a price in excess of the international price. Cocoa production, by contrast, takes place on small-scale peasant holdings; it is severely taxed.[28] The structure of production thus appears to influence the pattern of pricing decisions.

Another claimant is the government. Faced by the imperative of securing revenues, governments impose taxes; and the greater their access to non-agricultural sources of revenue, all else remaining equal, the lower the taxes on farmers and the less adverse to producers the pattern of their pricing decisions. In nations with major extractive industries which can produce revenues and foreign exchange, we should thus expect to see lower levels of taxation. Exemplifying this is the case of Nigeria; when the oil industry in Nigeria came 'on line' in the mid-1970s, the level of domestic prices for agricultural crops rose by comparison with those in the international market.[29]

Local processing industries which employ agricultural crops as raw materials form the last major claimant. The larger the portion of output consumed by local processors, it would appear, the less willing are governments to allow domestic price levels to move to the level of international prices. For example, while the government of Nigeria altered its pricing policy, it none the less failed to confer increases in the level of cotton prices and virtually banned the export of groundnuts, thus keeping domestic prices well below world market prices. A major reason for these actions, it would appear, was that in both the cotton and groundnut industries, domestic processing industries consumed a large portion of the crop. To protect the interests of the local textile and oil-extracting industries, the government attempted to insure that they retained access to low-priced materials – a consideration which did not arise, for example, in the cocoa-producing sector, where domestic processors consumed an insignificant portion of the crop.[30]

A last structural factor which helps to explain the form of price intervention is the presence of units to which the costs of the policies could be transferred. This is particularly relevant in the area of food prices, where governments seek means of subsidizing the price of food. Some governments have access to the resources of major extractive industries; where this is the case, they often employ these revenues to subsidize the price of food. This was the case in Zambia, where copper revenues were used to subsidize millers who in turn were required to market flour at low official prices; the fall of copper prices in the 1970s led to a cutback in the subsidies and to a rise in urban food prices. In other cases it is export agriculture that assumes the fiscal burden; the takeover of the Sierra Leone Rice Corporation, with its heavy commitments to the importation and subsidization of the domestic price of rice, by the Sierra Leone Marketing Board, which raises its revenue from the export of cash crops, represents a direct effort to employ resources levied from the producers of export crops to subsidize the urban consumers of food crops. In other cases, foreign donors pick up the bill; in the later 1970s, this pattern prevailed throughout the Sahel. Elsewhere, governments lack sources of revenues by which to finance low-cost urban food and they are far less able to employ subsidies as a policy instrument.

Within Africa governments seek to depress the prices of agricultural commodities. It is that general trend which I wish to emphasize. But we have also seen that important variations take place within that overall pattern – variations which result from differences in historical background and from differences in the structure of the economic and political environments within which agricultural production takes place and governments make decisions.

Market for inputs

We have noted that, particularly in the case of food crops, African governments themselves engage in farm production. In some countries special units of the Ministry of Agriculture manage farms. In many, irrigation authorities grow and market food. In others, units of the governing political party or its youth brigades staff government farms. In still others, efforts are lodged in special public agencies: those in charge of mechanization, water management, river-basin development, or the promotion of designated crops. In at least one case, the department of prisons is used to grow food. African governments have thus become major food producers.

In addition to growing food themselves, governments attempt to promote private production. They do so not by offering higher prices for products but by attempting to lower the costs of production. While taxing farmers in the market for products, they subsidize them in the market for farm inputs.

Attempts to lower input prices take various forms. Governments provide subsidies for seeds and fertilizers, the level of the last running from 30 to 80 per cent (30 per cent in Kenya and 80 per cent in Nigeria). They provide tractor hire services at subsidized rates, up to 50 per cent of the real costs in Ghana in the mid-1970s.[31] They provide loans at subsidized rates of interest for the purchase and rental of inputs. And they provide highly favorable tax treatment for major investors in commercial farming ventures.[32] Moreover, through their power over property rights, African governments have released increased amounts of land and water to commercial farmers at costs that lie below the value they would generate in alternative uses. The diversion of land to large-scale farmers and of water to private tenants on government irrigation schemes, without the payment of compensation to those who employed these resources in subsistence farming, pastoral production, fishing, or other ventures, represents the conferring of a subsidy upon the commercial farmer – and one that is paid at the expense of the small-scale, traditional producer. This process has been documented in Northern Ghana,[33] Nigeria,[34] Kenya,[35] Ethiopia[36] and Senegal.[37] It was common in settler Africa as well.

So, in the case of land and water, a major effect of government intervention in the market for inputs is to augment the fortunes of large-scale farmers at the expense of small-scale farmers. To some degree, this is true of programs in support of chemical and mechanized inputs as well.[38] Even where there is no direct redistribution, however, it is clear that government programs which seek to increase food production by reducing the costs of farming reach but a small segment of the farming population: the large farmers. In part, this is by plan: the programs are aimed at the 'progressive farmers' who will 'make best use of them'. In part, it is because the large farmers share a common social background with those who staff the public services; the public servants therefore aim their programs and services at those with whom they feel they can work most congenially and productively.[39] And, in part, it is because the favoring of the large farmer is politically productive. I will elaborate this argument below.

Markets for manufactured items

While subsidizing the cost of farm inputs, most African governments pursue policies designed to lower the price of agricultural products. By contrast, they follow policies toward industry and manufacturing whose effect is to raise the price of goods.

In promoting industrial development, governments adopt commercial policies which shelter local industries from foreign competition. To some degree, they impose tariff barriers between the local and international markets. To an even greater extent, they employ quantitative restrictions. Quotas, import licenses, and permits to acquire and use foreign exchange: are all employed to conserve foreign exchange on the one hand, while on the other hand protecting the domestic market for local industries. In connection with the maintenance of overvalued currencies, the trade barriers create incentives for investors to import capital equipment from abroad and to manufacture goods domestically which formerly had been imported from abroad.[40]

Not only do government policies shelter industries from low-cost foreign competition; they shelter them from domestic competition as well. In part, protection from domestic competition is a by-product of protection from foreign competition. The policy of allocating licenses to import in conformity with historic market shares provides an example of such a measure. The limitation of competition results from other policies as well. In exchange for commitments to invest, governments guarantee periods of freedom from competition. Moreover, governments tend to favor large projects; seeking infusions of scarce capital, they tend to back those proposals which promise the largest capital investments. Given the small markets typical of most African nations, the result is that investors create plants whose output represents a very large fraction of the domestic market; a small number of firms thus come to dominate the industry. Lastly, particularly where state enterprises are concerned, governments sometimes confer virtual monopoly rights upon particular enterprises. The consequence of all these measures is to shelter industries from domestic competition.

One result is that inefficient firms survive. Estimates of the use of industrial capacity range as low as one-fifth of the single shift capacity of installed plant.[41] Another consequence is that prices rise. Protected from foreign competition and operating in oligopolistic or monopolistic settings, firms are able to charge prices which enable them to survive despite operating at very high levels of cost.

For many leaders in Africa, the costs of these policies are justified; they are the price that must be paid to generate an industrial base for their societies. As Nkrumah is quoted as saying:

> It may be true in some instances that our local products cost more, though by no means all of them, and then only in the initial period . . . It is precisely because we were, under colonialism, made the dumping-ground of other countries' manufacturers and the providers merely of primary products, that we remained backward; and if we were to refrain from building, say, a soap factory simply because we might have to raise the price of soap to the community, we should be doing a disservice to the country.[42]

But for others the costs do not represent a price paid for a social benefit; they constitute elements of private economic redistribution. Such a view is expressed in the following letter, penned by one of Nkrumah's countrymen.

> In Ghana if a company is able to produce an inferior type of product which has been lying in a warehouse unpatronized for years, it then runs to the government claiming that . . . the government should stop the importation of such items. This is usually quickly agreed upon . . . then all of a sudden, the papers tell us that [the importation of] such and such a product is being banned forthwith since we are self-sufficient in that field . . .
> Because of Union Carbide, the importation of batteries was restricted and a torchlight battery sells at between ₵ 2.50 [and] ₵ 3.00; because of GTP and Akosombo Textiles, no importation of cover cloths, and a piece of Dumas sells at between ₵ 150–₵ 200; because of Lever Brothers (Ghana) Ltd, you can't import any type of soap, all you can get (toilet soap) ranges from ₵ 2.–₵ 2.50 . . . Yet all these factory managers claim they can meet the demands of the entire population in their vows.[43]

The effect of price increases resulting from the policies used to promote local industrialization has been a decrease in purchasing power, particularly by those groups who consume locally manufactured goods and who cannot afford to consume the more expensive commodities imported from abroad. Thus Jamal, examining the early stages of industrialization in Uganda, found that while import prices increased by 14 per cent, the overall cost of living increased by 46 per cent. Moreover, the price of the goods which formed a high proportion of the purchases of poorer people – clothing and household goods – increased 74 per cent and 94 per cent respectively. These were the kinds of goods particularly favored by protective policies.[44]

MODELS OF POLICY FORMATION

Agricultural policies in Africa are thus characterized by government attempts to lower the prices of goods produced by farmers; by measures which increase the price of goods which farmers buy from the city; and by government efforts to increase food supplies by financing a multitude of agricultural projects and subsidizing the costs of farm inputs. These last efforts produce benefits for only a small number of rural producers. Agricultural policies in Africa thus tend to be adverse to the interests of most producers.[45]

In the sections which remain I will advance several explanations for these choices. Each explanation, I argue, accounts for some of the features of agricultural policies. Each also has major shortcomings. Taken together, however, they help to account for many of the characteristic features of these policies and give insight into the political basis of policy choices toward agriculture.

Governments as maximizers of the social welfare
The first approach is most often employed by development economists. It rests on the proposition that governments are agencies whose task is to secure the best interests of their societies. According to this position, policy choices are derived from a consideration of the aggregate welfare. The choices of third world governments, in particular, reflect a determination to secure higher levels of welfare by securing development; and, in the context of how this is understood, development implies supplanting agriculture with industry.

While on the face of it hopelessly naive, this approach is surprisingly consistent with certain facts. In particular, it generates expectations which are consistent with the ways in which governments formulate policies toward export crops. For virtually all the governments of Africa seek industrial development. Most seek to create the social and economic infrastructure necessary for industrial growth and many are committed to the completion of major industrial and manufacturing projects. To fulfill their plans, governments need revenues; they also need foreign exchange. In most of the

African nations, agriculture represents the single largest sector in the domestic economy; and, in many, export crops represent the principal source of foreign exchange. It is therefore natural that in seeking to fulfill their objectives for their societies, the governments of Africa should intervene in markets in an effort to set prices in a way that transfers resources from agriculture, particularly export agriculture, to the 'industrializing' sectors of the economy: the state itself and the urban industrial and manufacturing firms.

An explanation based on the development objectives of African regimes is thus consistent with the choices made in the markets for export goods. It is also consistent with other well-known facts. The policy choices which have been made are, for example, in keeping with the prescriptions propounded in leading development theories. According to these theories, to secure higher levels of *per capita* income, nations should move from the production of primary products to the production of manufactured goods. Savings take place out of the profits of industry and not out of the earnings of farmers. Resources should therefore be levied from agriculture and channeled into industrial development. And agriculture in the developing areas, it is held, can surrender revenues without significant declines in production. These were, and remain today, critical assertions in development doctrine. Many policy makers in Africa were trained under development specialists; and important advocates of these arguments have served as consultants to the development ministries of the new African states. On these grounds, therefore, it is credible to account for the policy choices made by African governments – ones which systematically bias the structure of prices against agriculture and in favor of industry – as choices made in accordance with prescriptions of how best to secure the welfare of people in poor societies.

Such an approach ultimately proves unsatisfactory, however, and for several reasons. First of all, it is incomplete. For, to secure social objectives, governments can choose among a variety of policy instruments. And the underlying social objectives of a program often do not resolve which technique is chosen to secure the realization of these objectives. Moreover, often the approach is wrong.

An important objective of African governments is to increase food supplies. To secure greater supplies, they could offer higher prices for food or invest the same amount of resources in food-production projects. There is every reason to believe that the former is a more efficient way of securing the objective. But governments in Africa systematically prefer project-based policies to price-based policies.

To strengthen the incentives for food production, African governments can increase the price of farm products or subsidize the costs of farm implements. Either would result in higher profits for producers. But governments prefer the latter policy.

To increase output, African governments finance production programs. But, given the level of resources devoted to these programs, they often create too many projects; the programs then fail because resources have been spread too thin. Such behavior is nonsensical, given the social objectives of the program.

To take a last example: In the face of shortages, governments can either allow prices to rise or maintain lower prices while imposing quotas. In a variety of markets of significance to agricultural producers, African governments choose to ration. They exhibit a systematic preference for the use of this technique – a preference that can not be accounted for in terms of their development objectives.

A major problem with an approach which tries to explain agricultural policies in terms of the social objectives of governments is that the objectives rarely determine the particular form which the policies assume. There is a second major difficulty: given the objectives underlying agricultural policies, the policy choices are often self-defeating. It is therefore difficult to explain the choices made in terms of their objectives, for the objectives are, in fact, often undermined by the very policies which are selected to attain them.

This problem is most patently revealed in the area of pricing policy and particularly by the adoption of 'negative' pricing policies for farm products. The governments want cheaper food; they therefore lower the prices offered to food producers. But such a measure only creates shortfalls in supplies and the shortages result in higher prices. The policy chosen thus produces an effect precisely opposite to the stated objective of the program. Policy objectives thus fail to provide an adequate explanation for the policy choices. Other things are obviously at work in shaping government decisions; and other explanations – ones which put less stress on the social objectives of governments – must be employed to account for them.

There is a last and more basic problem. What fundamentally undermines the utility of this approach is its inability to deal with one of the most pervasive features of agricultural policies: the degree of economic inefficiency which they engender.

The approach rests on the assumption that the state is an agency for maximizing the social welfare and that policy choices represent attempts to secure what is socially best. Economic efficiency is a pre-condition of social welfare maximization; it is a necessary condition for it. But one of the most characteristic features of agricultural policies is that they are inefficient. As we have seen, they introduce distortions in market prices. They generate and employ non-competitive rents. And they create as well a spate of inefficient production projects. Those who employ the assumption of welfare maximization in analyzing government policy are therefore confounded by many of the most compelling features of the phenomenon they wish to explain.

One response has been to regard governments and politicians as benighted. Development economists can often be heard describing the pathologies of governments with amused incredulity. A closely related response is to regard people in markets as rational and people in political arenas as irrational. But such a schizophrenic view of human nature is a basically flawed ground from which to engage in social science. A third response is to regard inefficiencies as aberrations – ones which provoke slaps on the wrists of governments and professional advice concerning the necessity of 'getting prices right'. To engage in such a response is, however, to acknowledge that the approach is normative, rather than positive, in content. A last response – and this is the one adopted here – is to say that the approach itself is fundamentally unsound. Other models should be explored: models which do not regard inefficiencies as aberrations or signs of irrational behavior, but as central features of the policy process; and models for which the existence of such inefficiencies serves not as a source of embarrassment but as a cornerstone for the analysis.

Governments as respondents to political demands
An alternative approach would view the state as an agency for aggregating private demands and would interpret public policies as choices made in response to political pressures exerted by organized interests. Particularly in the case of food crops, this approach has much to recommend it. For, as we shall argue, it helps to account for several major features of government policy toward food production: the attempts to impose 'negative' pricing policies, to increase food supplies through input subsidies and production projects rather than through higher prices, and the adoption of measures which impose a structure of relative prices which favors industrial rather than agricultural interests.

Motivating this approach is the realization that urban dwellers are highly sensitive to their economic interests. They desire to protect the real value of their money incomes. They are willing and able quickly to organize in defense of these interests. Moreover, they are willing to form coalitions across industries and sectors in order to protest about government policies which threaten these interests.

The power of urban interests has been repeatedly demonstrated in Africa. The colonial powers were driven from West Africa by nationalist movements whose urban branches were largely drawn from organizations initially formed in protests over post-war inflation. Since the colonial period, governments have remained vulnerable to organized opposition in the cities; and this opposition tends to focus on the level of consumer prices. By way of illustration: to the surprise of most informed observers, Arap Moi peacefully succeeded Jomo Kenyatta to the presidency of Kenya; it was when urban food prices rose in 1980 that the succession was contested, with the competence of Moi's government then being contrasted unfavorably to that of his predecessor. In Zambia, the major challenges to Kaunda's government have tended to center on the urban costs of living and on the way in which the government's foreign policy has led to consumer shortages and higher prices. The Busia regime in Ghana was overthrown following changes in policy which led to sharp price increases for urban consumers. And, in Liberia, President Tolbert was assassinated and his government toppled following a protracted political struggle precipitated in large part by riots protesting about a rise in the price of rice.

Food is an essential consumer item, and a large portion of the urban consumer's budget is spent on it.[46] In protesting over the level of urban prices, consumers tend to focus on the price of food. And, in responding to urban political pressures, governments often advocate measures to secure low-priced food. To appease urban consumers, governments advocate a characteristic set of policies. They endorse low or 'negative' pricing policies. And, in efforts to create incentives for increased private production, they offer prospects for higher profits *not* by offering higher prices for farm products but by subsidizing the costs of farm inputs. The proposal of such measures is often to be found in the reports of commissions of inquiry into urban unrest.[47] Agricultural policy can thus be viewed as a by-product of governmental efforts to maintain peaceful political relations with urban political forces.

This argument can be generalized. And, in so doing, a paradoxical feature of urban protest can be explained: why it is that urban consumers, in attempting to defend the real value of their incomes, seek policy measures which promise lower prices for food but higher prices for manufactured products.

The argument is based on several key assumptions:

I   People specialize in production but 'generalize' in consumption. That is, while people derive the vast bulk of their incomes from the production of a particular good, they spend their incomes widely on a variety of commodities, devoting only a portion to the consumption of each. For purposes of exposition, call the percentage of income which the representative consumer spends on good 'i' α_i. Each good can then be characterized by its α-weight.

II   Specialization has proceeded much further in the industrial and manufacturing sectors than it has in agriculture. In the industrial sector, firms produce such items as flashlight batteries, bicycle tires, or enamel-ware. In agriculture, by contrast, firms tend to produce a wide range of commodities. Farmers tend to grow the full range of food crops necessary for their own subsistence and to market what they do not consume; they thus produce a fairly undifferentiated product which we will call 'food'.

III   People are poor. As a consequence, they tend to spend a high proportion of their incomes on food – in the range of 60 per cent in Africa, according to most surveys. Food, in other words, has a very high α-weight.

IVa   Governments have policy instruments at their command – tariffs, price controls, licensing powers, etc. – by which to influence prices. And (IVb) in employing these instruments governments respond to numbers, in the sense that the broader the coalition that demands government intervention, the larger the price increase which the government will confer.

Making these (and other) assumptions, it can be shown that, if people seek to maximize the value of their real incomes, an equilibrium coalition will form. The coalition which uses the state to secure higher relative prices will contain some but not all members of the society. In particular, it will contain those industries which produce goods with small α-weights. The greater the α-weight of a commodity, the less the likelihood that the maker of the commodity will be a member of the coalition. Agriculture, in short, is likely to fall outside the coalition and to have prices set against it in a way that redistributes income to the coalition members.[48]

The process that derives this result can be easily portrayed. By I, people specialize in production and generalize in consumption. A major consequence is that they will always favor higher prices for the goods they produce. For they derive all of their incomes from the production of that good and spend but a fraction of their income upon it; the benefits of an increase in its price will therefore more than offset the losses sustained from having to pay higher prices for the commodity. And if by IVa and IVb governments respond to petitions and respond more favorably to demands from groups than to demands from single industries, then there are benefits to be derived from forming coalitions in the search for price increases. The question then arises: How will these coalitions form?

Consideration of the effects of differences in α-weights suggests that those who make goods with small α-weights will join together in seeking the benefits to be secured from coalition formation. For, if persons combine with others who make goods with small αs, they will do better than if they combined with persons who make goods with high αs. By combining to secure price increases with persons who make goods with small α-weights, they will then have to spend a smaller portion of their incomes on the goods which receive price increases than would be the case were they to combine with the producers of goods which have high α-weights; the benefits to their incomes from higher prices are secured at the cost of lesser losses.

In closing the argument, we can now invoke assumptions II and III. These assumptions suggest that in the search for partners with whom to form coalitions in petitions for price rises, farmers will be relatively unattractive partners. Being poor, consumers spend a high proportion of their incomes on food; an increase in food prices has a larger effect on real incomes than would a similar increase in the price of commodities which possess smaller α-weights. And farmers in poor countries tend not to specialize but to grow 'food'. In the search for partners with whom to join in price-setting coalitions, persons do better combining with persons other than farmers. Food producers therefore find themselves outside of the policy-making, price-setting coalition.[49]

It should be noted that the approach accounts not only for the disadvantaged position of agriculture in the developing countries of Africa but also for the changing position of agriculture at higher levels of development. One index of development is higher *per capita* income; by Engel's law, with higher incomes, the percentage of incomes spent on food declines. Moreover, with development, specialization increases; farmers no longer produce food for subsistence purposes, but specialize in the production of particular crops. The results, of these alterations in consumption and production is to lower the α-weight of farm products. At higher levels of development, farmers, acting as producers of particular commodities, now gain control over many government pricing decisions. It is ironic that as the percentage of the population in agriculture declines, the bias in public policy shifts in favor of agriculture. A virtue of the model advanced here is that it suggests why this should be so.[50]

There is another set of factors at work. These pertain to the structure of the agricultural industry as contrasted with the urban-industrial sector; and they, too, help to explain how private interests could influence public policy in order to achieve the structure of relative prices that characterize agricultural policy in Africa.

A price in a market is a public good. If one producer secures a government policy which sets a favorable price, all other producers can enjoy the benefits of that policy for free. It is therefore difficult to organize collective action in support of price-setting measures. The magnitude of the difficulty varies, however, with the structure of the industry. And structural factors tend to conspire against the political efficacy of agriculture.

Where there is but one producer, there is no incentive to free ride. And where there are only a few producers, and where each producer markets a fairly high proportion of the industry's output, the private returns to each producer from an increase in price may more than offset the costs of lobbying. Again, the incentives to free ride are weakened. But where there are numerous producers, each generating only a small proportion of the total output, the incentives for collective action are weak. The benefits of a change in price to each producer are small; and, lacking any easy means to apportion the costs of a lobbying effort, the benefits may be exceeded by the costs of providing the change in pricing policy. As each producer would do best reaping the benefits of the change for free, the incentives not to contribute to the costs of lobbying are strong.

In addition, industries with a large number of small firms are simply very costly to organize. This is especially true where the firms are widely scattered. The costs of communicating and coordinating rise with the number of producers and their dispersion. Moreover, as the number of firms increases and the size of their output relative to total production of the industry declines, then the costs of policing price agreements rise. An individual farmer, for example, could increase his profits by undercutting the market price and his behavior would have little impact on prevailing market prices. Collective agreements in support of higher prices thus are more costly to organize and to sustain in relatively atomistic industries.

The implications of this argument are clear. In most nations and for most crops, production is undertaken by a multitude of small-scale, village farmers. The farmers are widely dispersed. By contrast, as we have seen, government policy favors high levels of concentration in manufacturing and industry; and firms tend to be concentrated in urban locations. For members of the agricultural industry, the characteristics of their industry are such that the incentives to organize to secure advantageous market prices are far weaker than for members of the manufacturing sector.

In this section, we have treated government not as an agency which seeks to maximize the social welfare but as an agency which aggregates private interests. And we have analyzed public policies not as choices made to secure what is socially best but rather as decisions made in response to organized private interests. Particularly in the analysis of food policy, such an approach has much to recommend it. It helps to account for the reason why governments prefer to strengthen the incentives for private production by lowering the costs of production rather than by increasing the prices of farm products. It also helps to explain why governments attempt to increase food supplies without increasing food prices and their strong preference for policies which emphasize the use of production schemes rather than the conferral of positive incentives through higher prices. Most important, the approach accounts for the fundamental distortion in the structure of relative prices – one which is biased against agricultural products and in favor of the products of industry. The distortion has puzzled advocates of the first approach and has been roundly denounced by them as a pathological feature and/or anomaly of the development process. This second approach, by contrast, makes the distortion an expected result of a political process in which private interests, behaving rationally, seek economic rewards through their influence over public policy.

A private demand-based model thus helps to account for many of the basic features of the agricultural policies adopted by African governments. Where this approach falls short, however, is in explaining how the governments get away with these policies. The policies tend to violate the interests of most farmers. Yet the majority of Africa's population derives its income from farming. How can the governments impose policies which violate the interests of the majority of their constituents? A third approach is needed: one that looks at agricultural programs as part of a repertoire of devices employed by African governments to secure political control over their populations and thus to remain in power.

Market intervention and political control
Governments in Africa, like governments everywhere, seek to retain political power. They shape and structure their policy programs to satisfy political claimants and nullify the political opposition. These tendencies

have already been observed in the choices made with respect to agricultural prices: attempts to lower food prices are efforts to appease organized urban interests. They can also be observed in other features of agricultural policy: the tendency to confer divisible as opposed to general benefits and to render the inefficiencies associated with disequilibrium prices a basis for political organization.

Divisible benefits and political organization
We have already seen that adopting policies in support of higher prices for agricultural commodities would be politically costly to African govern-ments. What is important is that such a stance would generate few political benefits as well. For, as we have noted, a price in a market is a public good. From a political point of view, conferring higher prices therefore holds few attractions for politicians, for the benefits of the measure can be enjoyed by opponents and supporters alike. The benefits cannot be restricted exclu-sively to the faithful and withheld from the politically disloyal. Pricing policies therefore cannot be employed by politicians to organize political followings.

Project-based policies, however, suffer less from this liability. Officials can exercise discretion in locating projects; they can also exercise discretion in staffing them. Such discretion allows them selectively to bestow benefits upon those whose political support they desire. For these reasons, govern-ments in Africa tend to prefer project-based policies to pricing-based policies in order to secure greater supplies of food.

The political utility of projects explains several otherwise puzzling features of agricultural programs. One is the tendency to construct too many projects, given the budgetary resources available. A reason for this proliferation is that governments often wish to insure that officials in each administrative district or electoral constituency have access to resources with which to secure a political backing.[51] Another tendency is to hire too great a staff or a staff that is technically untrained, thus undercutting the viability of the projects. A reason for this is that jobs on projects – and jobs in many of the bureaucracies involved with agricultural programs, for that matter – represent political plums, ones given by those in charge of the programs to their political followers. State farms in Ghana were staffed by the youth brigade of the ruling Convention Peoples' Party and the cooperative societies in Zambia were formed and operated by the local and constituency-level units of the governing party, to offer but two examples of the link between staffing and political organization. A last tendency is to have projects that are privately profitable but socially wasteful. Again and again, from an economic point of view, agricultural projects fail; they often fail to generate earnings that cover their costs or, when they do so, they often fail to generate a rate of return comparable to that obtainable through alternative uses of government funds. None the less, despite the projects' failures, public agencies revive and re-implement such projects. A major reason is that public officials are frequently less concerned with using public resources in a way that is economically efficient than they are with using them in a way that is politically expedient. If a project fails to generate an adequate return on the public investment, but is privately rewarding for those who build it, provision it, staff it, or hold tenancies in it, then political officials may none the less support it. For it will serve as a source of rewards for their followers and as an instrument for building a rural political constituency.

An approach that focuses on the role of public policy in facilitating political organization not only draws attention to those features of policy which enable governments to organize political support, however. It also highlights those features which enable governments to *dis*organize political opposition.

Divisibility and political disorganization

We have seen that government policies are often aimed at establishing low prices for agricultural products. Particularly, in the market for cash crops, governments maintain monopsonistic agencies and use their market power to lower product prices. They therefore impose deprivations on all producers. What is interesting, however, is that they return a portion of the resources which they thus exact to selected members of the farm community. Some of the earnings taxed from farmers are returned in the form of subsidies for farm inputs and these are given to a privileged few. While imposing *collective* deprivations, governments thus confer *selective* benefits. The benefits serve as 'side payments': they compensate selected members of the rural sector for the losses they sustain as a consequence of the governments' programs. They thereby make it in the private interests of particular members of the rural sector to abide by policies which are harmful to rural dwellers as a whole. By so doing, they secure the defection of favored farmers from a potential rural opposition and their adherence to the governing coalition which implements agricultural programs which are harmful to the majority of producers.

Seen from this viewpoint, we can understand the intense politicization of farm input programs in Africa. In Northern Ghana in the late 1970s, for example, subsidized credit was given to large-scale, mechanized producers who were close allies of the ruling military government. In Senegal, the rural base of the governing party is dominated by the Mourides, a religious sect that earns much of its income from the production of groundnuts; its adherence to the government in power, and to the government's pricing policies, is in large part secured by the conferral upon its leaders of massive amounts of subsidized credit, land, machinery, and other farm inputs.[52] In Zambia, access to subsidized inputs could best be obtained by most rural dwellers by membership in agricultural cooperative societies. The societies were formed by local units of the governing party and are now dominated by them; access to inputs is therefore contingent upon political loyalty. The

127

rural loans program, moreover, was run and staffed at the local level by former party 'militants' who helped to insure that the 'fruits of independence' were given to those who contributed to the cause of the party in power. In Ghana, to cite one last example, the collective resistance of cocoa producers to low cocoa prices in the 1950s was broken in part by the 'secret weapon' of the Convention Peoples' Party, the notorious United Ghana Farmers' Council. By distributing gammalin, cutlasses and other farm inputs to those who would support the government and its policies, and by restricting access to credit to the political faithful, the Farmers' Council helped to break the resistance of the farming population to the government and its agricultural programs.[53]

It should be noted, incidentally, that the bestowal of privileged access to farm inputs was a technique employed as well by the colonial governments. And the exchange of political loyalty for access to these inputs was widely recognized to be a part of the bargain. In Northern and Southern Rhodesia, for example, the colonial governments used revenues secured by their monopsonistic maize marketing agency to subsidize the costs of inputs which they then lavished upon a relatively small number of so-called 'improved' or 'progressive' farmers. The nationalist movements presciently labeled these farmers 'stooges' of the colonial regimes. They saw that the apportionment of the inputs had been employed to separate the interests of these privileged farmers from the interests of the mass of rural producers and to detach their political loyalties from those of their fellow Africans.

Conferring selective benefits in the markets for farm inputs on the one hand, while imposing collective deprivations in the markets for products on the other, governments thereby secure the deference of a privileged few to programs which are harmful to the interests of most farmers. By politicizing their farm programs and making access to their benefits contingent upon political loyalty, the governments secure acquiescence to those in power and compliance with their policies. The political efficacy of these measures is underscored by the fact that they are targeted on the larger producers: those who have the most to gain from a change in pricing policy and who might otherwise provide the 'natural leadership' for efforts on the part of farmers to alter the agricultural policies of their governments.

The political use of economic inefficiency
We have come a long way from the conventional approach, which views agricultural policies as programs designed to secure the best interests of developing societies. We are now ready to take a last step. For not only have we documented the pervasive inefficiency of many of these programs; we have noted as well their political importance. What we now wish to argue is that, in many cases, the inefficiencies persist *because* they are politically useful; economic inefficiencies afford governments means of retaining political power.

This argument can be illustrated by analyzing the price distortions which characterize agricultural programs in Africa. As part of their development efforts, African governments intervene in markets in efforts to alter prices. At least in the short run, market intervention establishes disequilibrium prices. These, in turn, generate rents. The existence of such rents has been analyzed by Krueger, Posner and others.[54] The prevailing tendency has been to regard these rents as pure social costs – inefficiencies induced by the political distortion of market forces. What has not been stressed is that the rents also represent political resources – resources which can be used to organize political support and to perpetuate governments in power.

Such rents arise in the markets for agricultural products. Public monopsonies depress the price of commodities below the world market price and below the price that would prevail were competition permitted. To those in charge of the bureaucracy that administers the market accrue the noncompetitive rents. On the one hand, they can consume the rent themselves; corruption is a widely recognized feature of the operation of these agencies. On the other, they can ration access to these rents; they can thereby grant favors and build a political following.

In this way market intervention becomes a basis for building political organizations. Those in charge of the market can bestow the right of entry upon potential political loyalists; such persons will then come to owe their special fortunes to the favor of those in charge. Members of the Cocoa Marketing Board of Ghana, for example, frequently allowed private trading on the part of persons whose political backing they wished to secure. Such persons came from the very highest levels of the Ghanaian government. And in Kenya those in charge of policing the coffee market conspired with the politically influential to evade the government mandated price for that commodity. In the Kenyan maize market, moreover, the issue of movement permits by the director of the Maize and Produce Marketing Board was used to create an indebted and loyal political following.[55] Granting access to a market where the price of commodities has been artificially lowered as a matter of government policy thus becomes a valuable instrument in the accumulation of political influence.

Disequilibrium product prices also facilitate political control by yielding the capacity to *dis*organize those most hurt by the measure: the farmers themselves. For a portion of the gains, the bureaucrat in charge of the market can turn a blind eye while farmers make sales at market-clearing prices. The structure of regulation vests legal powers in the bureaucrats; the farmers have no right to make such sales. Only by securing an individual exception to the general rule can the farmer gain access to the market-clearing price. Within the framework established by marketing policy, the farmers thus do best by securing individual exceptions. The capacity for discretion therefore allows the bureaucrat to separate the individual interests of particular producers from the interests of their class, and collective organization on the part of rural producers becomes more difficult to organize. In addition, the structure of regulations creates for the government essential elements of political power. By allowing exceptions to the rules, the bureaucracy grants favors; by threatening to enforce the rules, it threatens sanctions. Market regulations thus become a source of political control, and this, in a sense, is most true when they are in the process of being breached.

Governments establish disequilibrium prices in the markets for inputs as well; the result, once again, is the enhancement of their capacity for political control. When they lower the price of inputs, private sources furnish lesser quantities, users demand greater quantities, and the result is excess demand. One consequence is that the inputs acquire new value; the administratively created shortage creates an economic premium for those who acquire them. Another is that, at the mandated price, the market can not allocate the inputs; they are in short supply. Rather than being allocated through a pricing system, they must be rationed. Those in charge of the regulated market thereby acquire the capacity to exercise discretion and to confer the resources upon those whose favor they desire.

It is these dynamics which render farm input programs so potent a source of political patronage. On occasion, governments place political 'heavy-weights' in charge of these programs. The result often is that members of the elite then consume the rental premium; they sell the inputs at the price they can command in the market. By allowing the corruption of farm programs, the governments thus secure the fealty of potent political figures. In other cases, governments forbid such corruption and instead allocate the inputs at their officially mandated prices. The result then is the securing of political loyalty from lower-level political figures – the intended clients and beneficiaries of the subsidy program. For it is they who then secure the rental premium.[56]

Public programs which distribute farm credit, tractor-hire services, seeds, and fertilizers, and which bestow access to government managed irrigation schemes and public lands, thus become instruments of political organization in the countryside of Africa. Moreover, both 'reactionary' and 'progressive' regimes employ these measures to secure power. The basis of distinguishing between such regimes is *not* whether they do or do not intervene in markets, as classical theories would have it. Rather, the distinction turns on whether the regime confines access to the rental premium to the upper levels of society – the rulers and elites – or allows it to be reaped at the lower levels – by the farm families and the clients of the programs. The first is characteristic of conservative regimes, such as in Zaire; the other of socialist governments.

Regulated markets thus serve as political instruments. I recall an interview I held in 1978 with one rich cocoa farmer in Ghana. I asked him why he did not try to organize political support among his colleagues for a rise in product prices. He went to his strongbox and produced a packet of documents: licenses for his vehicle, import permits for spare parts, titles to his real property and improvements, and the articles of incorporation that exempted him from a major portion of his income taxes. 'If I tried to organize resistance to the government's policies on farm prices,' he said while exhibiting these documents, 'I would be called an enemy of the state and I would lose all these.' He was a rich cocoa farmer and we were discussing cocoa prices. The price of Ghanaian cocoa is indeed one of the most politically sensitive topics in African agrarian politics. But, in systems where producers operate in markets which are increasingly maintained and controlled by public agencies, his point was generally valid.

CONCLUSION

I have examined three basic approaches to understanding the content of post-independence agricultural policies in Africa. One emphasized the role of the state as an agency for fulfilling social purposes and interpreted agricultural policies as choices made in efforts to secure public objectives. This approach helps to explain some aspects of agricultural policy, most notably the burdens imposed upon cash-crop producers. But it fails to explain others, the selection of negative pricing policies in food production, for example. Moreover, it fails to account for the pervasive patterns of economic inefficiency which characterize agricultural programs. A second approach stressed the role of the state in aggregating private demands and interpreted agricultural policies as choices made in response to organized interests. Particularly in the area of food policy, this approach goes far to explain characteristic features of agricultural programs. But it fails to explain how governments which advocate such programs could retain political power in nations which are overwhelmingly agricultural in composition. The third approach focused on those features of agricultural policies which enabled them to be employed to build organized political support for governments in power and which enabled those governments to disorganize political opposition. Market intervention may create inefficiency, this approach emphasizes, but economic inefficiency may also generate the resources by which to govern.

There is an important addendum to this argument. I have emphasized the role of competition among interest groups. I have emphasized as well the importance of the competition for divisible benefits, rationed favors, privileged access, and individual exceptions to general rules. The end result has been the neutralization of the majority of the African citizenry. This form of politics, it should be noticed, could only be expected in the absence of meaningful party competition. This pattern of politics would make little sense in the face of political forces which seek the support of national majorities.

The banning of meaningful patterns of party competition is thus critical to the fate of the peasantry in Africa. In this connection, it is illuminating to refer to the evidence I collected in my study of Zambia in the 1960s.[57] In that study I found that the necessity of contesting elections led to public recommitments by the government to rural development in Zambia and to a modification of budgetary priorities in favor of capital expenditures upon rural, as opposed to urban, projects. It is also notable, however, that the emphasis, once again, was on rural development *projects*. Pricing policy never became the major issue in rural electoral contests; instead, the emphasis remained on the allocation of jobs, public works, and other divisible benefits. In the face of political parties seeking majority, and therefore rural, support, issues critical to the fate of the peasantry do arise; but even so, they selectively enter the political agenda, pricing issues being less favored than those that offer special benefits.

In describing the location of the rural peasantry in the political economies of post-independence Africa, Frantz Fanon was correct.[58] Rural producers are politically isolated; their interests are indeed separated, as we have seen, from those of workers and industrialists, politicians and bureaucrats. Moreover, the agricultural policies of the African states are such that we must concur with Fanon in viewing the peasants as oppressed. Where I must disagree with Fanon is in equating the structural position of the African peasantry with a revolutionary potential. To be isolated and oppressed is not to possess the potential for collective political action.

One reason is that the very policies which oppress the peasantry help to undermine their capacity for political action. The policies, as we have seen, promote the political disorganization of the peasantry. They divide the interests of their 'natural leaders' from those of the mass of small-scale producers and they put a premium on seeking individual accommodation with the prevailing political order. Moreover, agricultural policies create resources for organizing and thus help to promote the formation of collective support, even in the rural areas, for the governments in power.

In seeking further reasons, we may contrast the political situation of the post-independence peasantry with that of the peasantry in the period of nationalist ferment. As we have seen, in the post-independence period, farming interests are opposed in the policy-making arena by urban workers, who want low-priced food; urban industrialists, who want low wages and low prices for raw materials; bureaucrats and white-collar workers, who want higher salaries and lower food prices; and politicians, who run governments which need taxes and which are major employers and industrialists in their own right. So, farm interests stand in conflict with the interests of most other major groupings. In the pre-independence period, by contrast, many of these same groups were allied with the peasantry; the interests which now separate them were subsumed by a common interest in dislodging the colonial power. For the worker, the colonialists were employers who offered oppressive terms of service in the urban labor market. For the native capitalist, colonialism offered artificially advantaged terms to investors and industrialists from abroad. For the white-collar worker, the colonial regime underpinned a civil service which bestowed special perquisites for persons of other races and nationalities. And, for the politician, colonialism offered opportunities to consolidate these grievances and gather the worker, the capitalist, and the bureaucrat into an alliance with the rural masses in order to overthrow the prevailing political order. Under such circumstances, the peasantry could be politically active; save for the colonial government, there was no one to oppose its initiatives and, indeed, persons from other classes offered their leadership in mobilizing the rural masses.

With the triumph of the nationalist coalition, however, the conflict of interest between the peasants and others was no longer subsumed by their common objectives. Moreover, it was then that the 'development coalition' formed: a coalition of the workers, the industrialists, and the state, in league with their rural allies, the large farmers and the tenants on government development projects. In the name of development, this coalition combined against the mass of the rural interests, and, as Fanon correctly observes, the peasantry became politically isolated and oppressed. By the same token, it also became politically demobilized. For it lost both the allies and the political leadership which it had secured from other sectors during the period of nationalist political action.

For the peasants in Africa, the political route to economic ends, which formerly was attractive, is now devalued. Rather than turning to public action, they now do better forsaking the political arena. Avoiding publicly monitored markets, working private plots, and seeking refuge in the most private of all institutions – the family – the peasants pursue private solutions to the problem of economic welfare.

Conclusion

In this volume I have analyzed several of the major themes which have dominated the study of agrarian Africa. I have re-examined one of the oldest of these themes: the sources of order in stateless societies. I have addressed as well a subject long studied by anthropologists and historians: the origins of states in pre-colonial African societies. I have examined the impact of colonial rule upon African rural societies and the response of rural dwellers to the forces unleashed by the colonial order. And I have explored as well a subject of compelling contemporary interest: the nature and origins of post-independence agricultural policy.

The subjects arise naturally in the study of African rural society. In looking at such well-established topics, I have attempted not only to raise new points and to contribute new insights, but also to advance a mode of analysis. By way of concluding, I would like to make explicit the analytic framework which I have employed.

Clearly, the approach I have taken derives from the works of scholars who may loosely be grouped into the collective-choice school of political economy.[1] Three fundamental characteristics of this approach require emphasis and clarification: the premise of rational choice, the method of equilibrium analysis, and the role of institutions.

The collective-choice approach to political economy is characterized by its commitment to the individual as a unit of analysis and to the assumption of rational behavior. Rationality demands that individual decision makers choose their most preferred alternatives. Alternatives will be ranked in terms of their value in enabling the individual to secure his or her preferences; rationality merely requires that the individual choose his or her 'top' or most preferred alternative.

Note that rationality says nothing about the content of preferences. Some models of rational choice, for example, posit preferences which imply an aversion to risk while others do not; 'minimax' models, for example, require that alternatives be ranked in terms of their least favorable possible outcomes. This clearly implies an extreme form of risk aversion and, for many purposes, a bizarre form of preference. Nor does rationality require perfect information. Quite the contrary; most models of rational behavior allow for imperfect estimates of outcomes and, granting that information is costly, many allow for the acquiring of 'optimal' levels of information. The implication is clear: behaving rationally, people may well choose to remain ignorant.[2]

The concept of individual rationality is thus a narrow one. It does not impose conditions on the content of preferences. Nor does it require perfect information. It requires only that choice makers order alternative courses of action in terms of their estimates of the consequences for the values they seek to attain and that they choose that alternative which they expect to yield the most favorable outcome.[3] Were the individual systematically to choose an alternative at the 'bottom' of his or her ranking – i.e. one that would secure the least preferred result – then that person would be behaving irrationally. The systematic choice of such self-defeating alternatives lies outside the realm of behavior amenable to analysis by this approach.

The assumption of rationally maximizing individual agents represents one cornerstone of the collective-choice approach. The method of equilibrium analysis provides another. It is through equilibrium analysis that insight is achieved as to how the choices of individuals result in social outcomes.

To clarify, equilibrium analysis *does not* assume the existence of an equilibrium, much less the uniqueness of an equilibrium. Very commonly indeed, efforts to analyze the outcome of social processes – i.e. to solve for their equilibrium – will yield a proof of the non-existence of an equilibrium; alternatively, even when existence is proven, it may be impossible to prove uniqueness. In other words, the use of equilibrium analysis does not imply a conviction that the world is 'determinate'.

Nor does the use of equilibrium analysis imply a conviction that the world is orderly. By an equilibrium is simply meant a situation in which no party has an incentive unilaterally to alter its behavior. In situations of chaos, or in the making of revolutions, there may be strong incentives to behave violently; as in the case of Chapter 1, the use of violence can represent an equilibrium strategy. To *apply* equilibrium analysis is thus not to *imply* that there is social order, much less a lack of change.

To move from individual, maximizing agents to the analysis of social equilibria requires assumptions about the social and political context of choice making. Indeed, the institutional environment stands as a third basic element of the theoretical apparatus of the collective-choice approach. For, without knowledge of this environment, one simply cannot infer social outcomes from a knowledge of preferences and the use of equilibrium analysis.

Many critics contend that approaches based on the premise of rational choice are tautological: outcomes can always be explained, they contend, by invoking a proper set of preferences. What these critics fail to appreciate is that, in most institutional environments, preferences fail systematically to aggregate into outcomes. Under majority rule, for example, given a fixed set

135

of preferences, any outcome may be possible. And under other conventional voting rules, outcomes can be *defeated* which are *unanimously preferred* to the outcome chosen.[4] Clearly, the outcome cannot then be accounted for in terms of people's desires. Clearly, too, institutions help to determine the nature of social outcomes.

The collective-choice approach advanced in this volume represents a form of political economy. When applied to the study of politics, its parentage lies in micro-economics. It is important to note, however, the degree to which it represents a critique, both empirical and normative, of this tradition.

The foundation for this critique is the conviction that the conventional economic paradigm is too narrow. Rather than restricting its focus to the study of economic choices, the collective-choice approach studies social choices more generally. It recognizes that problems of choice and allocation occur in settings other than markets. And it seeks to bring the tools of rational-choice analysis to the study of these problems.

The empirical foundations for the critique of conventional economics are clear. What represents an equilibrium in a market, after all, cannot be expected to represent an equilibrium in a non-market setting. By broadening its conception of relevant choice environments, the collective-choice approach makes predictions concerning outcomes that diverge from those made by economists. The normative foundations for the critique are even more powerful. For, in considering the market as but one of a wide variety of potential institutions for fulfilling human wants, and in precisely characterizing its distinctive properties, collective-choice theorists have shown the degree to which any conviction concerning its welfare properties rests on restrictive grounds.

From at least the time of Adam Smith, the market has been analyzed as a mechanism for aggregating individual wants into social outcomes and has been extolled for its ability to do so in a highly desirable manner. The benevolent operation of the 'hidden hand' is a well-known construct. Naturally, however, allocations generated by the market are ethical in a strong sense only in so far as the initial distributions of the resources which agents bring to the market place are themselves defensible on moral grounds. Even more to the point, contemporary investigations suggest that market allocations are ethically justified, even in a weak sense – i.e. in terms of the notion of Pareto efficiency – only under an extraordinarily restrictive set of assumptions.[5] *Rational actors, operating in market settings*, it has been shown, *would make choices which produce socially rational, i.e. efficient, outcomes only under the most exceptional circumstances.* Efforts to characterize precisely the distinctive properties of markets as allocational institutions have thus led to a major reappraisal of their desirability as social institutions.

In pressing forward with its agenda – the examination of ways in which preferences of individuals aggregate into choices for society in different institutional environments – the collective-choice approach has also examined the properties of political institutions. In so doing, it has once again attacked the premises of conventional economics.

Economists subscribe to several key assumptions which are political at their very core. One is that the concept of society's 'welfare' or 'best interests' exists; a second is that the values of a society will be those values articulated by its government. Such assumptions supply the foundations for applied welfare analysis and are employed in formulating public policy. An illustration is offered by a development economist with whom, otherwise, I am in great sympathy, Michael Todaro. 'Economics', he writes, 'cannot be "value free" ... Once ... subjective values have been agreed upon by a nation or, more specifically, by those charged with the responsibility for national decision making, then specific ... public policies can be pursued.'[6] The assumptions, in short, are that something called the values of society can be distilled from the values of its members and that the values of the government reflect this composite called the social welfare.

Common sense suggests that such assumptions are not valid. For those working in the developing areas, the experiences of Vietnam, Iran, Zaire or Chile – to name but a few examples – suggest the magnitude of the separation between popular aspiration and government policy. The equation of the government's values with those of society thus makes little sense; in the light of recent history, it violates good taste.

More relevant to the discussion, however, is that early investigations of political institutions from the collective-choice framework, particularly the work of Kenneth Arrow, have disputed these assumptions on theoretical grounds. Arrow's work suggests that one may be able to derive an economically meaningful social welfare function for a society; that is, one may in fact be able to distill from the preferences of individuals an ordering of alternatives for society such that one alternative can unambiguously be revealed as socially best. But, he proves, *if this is true, then there is for certain a dictator* – a member of society who can secure his wishes as the social choice even when his preferences are unanimously opposed by all other members of society.[7] Inferring what is socially best from the preferences of governments is a dangerous business; it is 'safe' only when the governments are dictatorships.

The collective-choice approach thus offers a critique of conventional economics. In addition it has challenged conventional economics by generating significant insights in areas where conventional assumptions do not apply. Efforts have been devoted to the positive analysis of behavior in 'imperfect' markets: the study of the performance of markets in the presence of production externalities, public goods, imperfect information or imperfect competition, are standard fare for practitioners in the field.[8] Other efforts have focused on the correction of imperfect markets; the design of forms of public market intervention now represents a central concern.[9] Still other efforts have centered on the behavior of non-market institutions, and in particular those of a political nature.

137

Conclusion

Following Downs, for example, some have studied elections and attempted to characterize the equilibrium outcome of the process of electoral competition. Others have studied legislatures and attempted to assess the impact of variations in such parliamentary institutions as rules for amendment or requirements for the size of majorities. Still others have focused on legislative committee systems and characterized their impact on the nature of government programs, the capacity of parliamentary bodies to achieve 'stable' or 'coherent' outcomes, and on the quality and nature of the political representation offered to constituents. The impact of political intervention on the behavior of markets has also been investigated extensively.[10]

So far, however, few attempts have been made to employ the assumptions and methods of this approach to the study of politics outside the Western democracies. One purpose of these essays has been to attempt to broaden this range of applications by analyzing the politics of developing societies.

ALTERNATIVE APPROACHES IN ANTHROPOLOGY

In thus extending the collective-choice paradigm into the study of development, note must be taken of the alternative forms of political economy. One major approach analyzes the behavior of small-scale communities. Examples would include Godelier, Terray and Meillassoux.[11] While divided in their purposes and methods, these scholars share in common a commitment to the development of a form of Marxist political economy appropriate to the study of pre-industrial societies. What is the relationship between their enterprise and our own?

What makes the Marxist approach so appealing is the potential it offers for terminating the ceaseless frettings brought on by the wars between the formalists and the substantivists in economic anthropology. The former viewed the 'laws of economics' (by which they tended to mean price theory) as independent of particular social settings and championed the use of economic analysis in all forms of societies. The latter saw exchange behavior as imbedded in particular social structures and advocated a form of relativism, contending that economic analysis was appropriate only in capitalist societies.[12] Marxist anthropology promised to transcend this divide – a divide which for decades had paralyzed economic anthropology – by capturing key points in the positions of both parties. With the substantivists, Marxist anthropology asserted that the form of economic behavior observed in capitalist society was indeed specific to that historical form; 'bourgeois economics' could not be uncritically extended to the analysis of pre-capitalist societies. With the formalists, however, it insisted upon the universality of economic processes. Economic forces did not disappear in the pre-capitalist period; they did not become reducible to the study of kinship, culture, or ideology, as some substantivists would have it. Rather, they acted through such social relations, and did so in law-governed ways. Emphasis therefore focused on the manner in which economic forces

138

determined social, political and cultural relations in the particular historical forms characteristic of pre-capitalist societies.

The extension of a collective-choice form of political economy into pre-industrial societies shares the promise of Marxist anthropology. It too seeks to build an economic analysis of pre-capitalist societies. And it is well positioned to do so, for it takes as its agenda the application of economic reasoning to *non-market* institutions.

Some, like Godelier, have appraised this form of theorizing and found it wanting. Godelier's reasons appear faulty, however. He does not want economics to be only 'a formal theory of purposive action', as the collective-choice approach would have it, for then it is 'no longer possible to distinguish between economic activity and activity directed toward obtaining pleasure, power or salvation'.[13] Such an objection is understandable if one's goal is to specify the impact of the 'economic' upon the 'non-economic' aspects of social life. But, if one's goal is, as Godelier claims his to be, to understand the 'deeper logic of a social system – the underlying order by which the apparent order must be explained' – then the construction of predictive models through the application of rational-choice analysis is not in the least inconsistent with Godelier's program.[14]

Godelier also rejects the use of economic reasoning because of the absence of formal markets in pre-capitalist societies. But in so doing, he slips back into the fallacy of the substantivists – one of the very pitfalls he hoped to avoid. Scarcity is not confined to market economies; as a consequence, neither are problems of choice and allocation. 'Economic reasoning', in the sense of analyzing how rational persons will confront these problems in the context of a particular social environment, therefore need not be confined to societies which possess specific institutions such as markets. It can be applied to other non-market institutions as well.

The value of extending social-choice analysis into non-market settings is suggested by noting the very arguments marshalled by Dalton and others – arguments specifically cited by Godelier and noted by him with approval – against such endeavors. As Dalton and his colleagues have long pointed out, in many societies, certain goods and services cannot be traded; markets for these goods therefore do not exist. Alternatively, commodities may be exchanged but at prices that are set outside the market, i.e. by political fiat or by custom. When prices do exist, they may not be uniform; they may vary according to the social status of the parties to the exchange.

These facts are well known by anthropologists. And they have obviously discouraged Godelier and others from applying the form of economic analysis pursued in these essays. But what is less well known is that the behavior characterized by these patterns is amenable to economic analysis. In regulated industries in advanced industrial economies certain factors may not be exchanged. Prices are set and maintained at fixed levels for long periods of time and are liable to change through political, rather than market, mechanisms. Frequently, different prices are set for different categories of consumers; home owners and industries are charged different rates for the use of telephone or electrical services, for example. Nothing inherent in these facts puts the behavior of these industries beyond the reach of rational-choice analysis; and the studies of these industries should be explored by those seeking to analyze the implications of 'Polanyi-type' restrictions upon pre-capitalist economies.[15]

The collective-choice approach to political economy shares with Marxist anthropology a conviction that conventional economics is seriously flawed; when applied to the study of pre-industrial societies, it also shares a sense of the futility of the formalist and substantivist divide. It refuses, however, to confine the use of economic reasoning to the study of markets. Instead, by seeking to extend it into non-market settings, it seeks to fulfill an agenda which it shares with Marxist anthropologists: to terminate the substantivist–formalist debates by analyzing economic behavior in non-market institutions and by analyzing 'the deeper logic' that accounts for the patterns of behavior which are observed in pre-capitalist societies.

In fulfilling this mandate, it should be noted, the collective-choice perspective separates once again from conventional economic analysis. All too often, particularly in development economics, economists have assumed that income is an overriding objective; 'homo-economicus' has too often been pressed into service in situations where he simply does not belong. In moving away from an exclusive preoccupation with markets, the collective-choice approach recognizes the importance of a far broader range of human motivations; it is therefore sensitive to a wider range of human values and to the variability of cultures. Moreover, because it has grappled with the complexity of analyzing institutions other than markets, the collective-choice approach has learned that the precise specifics of institutional environments count, in the sense that they play a key role in determining the way in which individual preferences aggregate into social outcomes. Institutional environments offer choosers values in addition to economic values: membership, office, prestige, etc. They provide access to resources other than income or productive technologies: to power, followers, networks, or systems of rights and obligations. And they provide frameworks within which bargaining takes place and strategies are developed; they define, in short, the 'rules of the game' which determine the values of outcomes which can be sought by alternative courses of action. Because the collective-choice approach is sensitive to the determining power of cultural and institutional settings, it is highly resistant to any effort artificially to 'homogenize' human behavior. The gross oversimplifications, too often characteristic of conventional economic analysis, find little support among its practitioners. Rather, the approach *requires* the use of a precise and detailed knowledge of cultures, structures, and institutional environments. It requires a far more complex vision of man.

Conclusion

In anthropology, the collective-choice approach must encounter an alternative form of political economy which is being applied at present to the developing areas. In political science, it finds further competitors. No single label fully captures the character of these alternative approaches. But it is clear that they too draw a common inspiration from Marxism.

In exploring the relationships between the collective-choice approach and these alternatives, it is useful to go back to the Marxist critique of marginalist analysis. One such critique was written by Bukharin; as its brilliance warrants, it is even today pressed into service in decrying conventional economics. Bukharin's critique represents an attack on the 'Austrian school' for its 'extreme individualism in methodology, [its] unhistorical point of view, and . . . its taking consumption as its point of departure'.[16]

In two of these charges, the collective-choice approach takes essentially the same position as Bukharin. There are, however, few grounds for assenting to the Marxist emphasis on production. Marx's theory of value is too closely tied to his conception of labor for his followers to weaken the emphasis they place on the central role of production. For collective-choice theorists, the theory of value derives from preference and scarcity and the resultant operation of supply and demand. The gap yawns so widely that reconciliation can be attempted successfully only in very special cases.[17] In addition, it is from Marx's theory of value, rooted as it is in production, that radical political economists derive their fundamentally conflictual view of capitalism in particular and politics in general. Collective-choice theorists, for their part, instead tend to draw their orientation toward politics not from the analysis of production but from the analysis of exchange. They therefore emphasize the cooperative as well as conflictual properties of human interaction; and they stress the creative role of politics in transcending the limitations of pure conflict by orchestrating cooperative solutions to human problems. The magnitude of this divide may ultimately frustrate any attempt to formulate a more general political economy.

Given the importance of the subjects which divide the two schools, it is therefore particularly striking that Bukharin's other attacks on classical economics should resonate so strongly with the critique mounted by collective-choice theorists. Bukharin attacks the assumption of 'individualism' for leading to a failure to perceive the significance of social settings. He also attacks the 'a-historicism' of economic analysis; the institutional and structural frameworks within which market forces operate exist at precise historical moments, he contends. And as a consequence of being 'individualistic' and 'a-historical', Bukharin argues, economic analysis is subject to error when applied to specific cases. In particular, it fails to generate insight into the extreme irrationality – the major contradictions – of contemporary capitalist society. As Bukharin states:

> Modern society, with its anarchic structure (the theory of political economy makes precisely *this* society the object of its study); with its market forces and their elemental action (competition, fluctuation of prices, stock exchange, etc.), offers numerous illustrations in favor of the assumption that . . . the result of the motives of the individual (yet not isolated) economic men, not only does not correspond to these motives, but at times even enters into direct opposition to them.[18]

The point of reviewing Bukharin's critique is to illustrate a surprising and non-obvious contention: that, in their orientation toward social analysis, much unites the collective-choice and the Marxist approaches, despite the fact that the former's roots lie in marginalist economics. Both realize that the assumption of atomistic behavior does not hold; instead, one must recognize the existence of interdependence and analyze behavior in terms of models of strategic and interdependent choice making.[19] They share a belief in the necessity of specifying precisely the institutional setting in which choices are to be made. And, above all, they share a profound skepticism of the ability of the choices of rational individuals to aggregate into socially rational outcomes.

Distinctive to the Marxist alternative, however, is its stress on the role of collective aggregates. Classically, of course, social classes provide the motive force to Marxist analysis. In the literature on development, social classes are joined by 'modes of production' as the active agents in social change.[20] In the African setting, for example, such recent works as that of Palmer and Parsons interpret the contemporary economic history of Africa in terms of the ways in which the capitalist mode of production confronts, disrupts, and ultimately impoverishes indigenous, pre-capitalist societies.[21]

A key problem in Marxist analysis – and one that has long featured on its agenda – is the origin of these collective aggregates. Once again, there is a strong convergence in the answers given by collective-choice theorists and contemporary Marxists. What both point to is the central role of *political* power in the *organization* of *economic* interests.

The reason why the emergence of concerted behaviors is problematic is that, under most circumstances, those who stand on the same side of a market possess a dominant strategy: to compete. To illustrate from the supply side of the market, all those positioned on that side of the market do possess a common interest in higher prices; none the less, each actor also possesses a particular interest in maximizing his or her revenues by marginally undercutting the prices offered by others. Moreover, each possesses this particular interest *irrespective* of the behavior of the other parties. Should the other parties collude and raise their prices, the party that does best is the one that marginally lowers its price; and, should the others compete by lowering their prices, each party has no choice but to undercut the price offered by the other. Collusion is thus very difficult to organize in economic environments.

This argument is not of purely theoretical importance; the power of such disruptive incentives is clearly revealed in the historical record. Palmer and Parsons, for example, attribute the impoverishment of indigenous African economies to the overwhelming power of the capitalist 'core' or 'export enclave' which grew up in southern Africa. The presumed coherence of this economic system is belied, however, by the case materials which they present. Was there a natural harmony of interest between the commercial farmers and the railways? Certainly not in Nyasaland, where Vail documents the conflicts between the farmers and the railways over rating charges.[22] Elsewhere in southern Africa, the farmers 'captured' the railways and set favorable rates for the transport of their goods. Who then paid the bills? In large part, the mining companies. In the Transvaal, for example, Legassick states that: 'Through *direct* taxation, railway rating policy, and state monopolies to tax the importation of mining equipment and supplies, the Transvaal state took its share of the mining surplus for the benefit of the farmers.'[23] In Zaire, so afraid of the economic power of the commercial farmers were the mining companies that they systematically frustrated the development of large-scale farming.[24] And elsewhere so vigorously did the mines, the railways, governments, and new manufacturing firms compete for the labor services of the indigenous peoples that the price of labor rose precipitously and the indigenous populations prospered even while the capitalist sector experienced labor shortages.

It is therefore mistaken to regard the natural state of an aggregate such as the 'capitalist sector' of a developing economy as being non-competitive. On the basis of the evidence presented by Palmer and Parsons, there were clearly deep conflicts of interests and major economic rivalries within it. Competition existed and the indigenous economies were able to exploit it to their advantage.

But, clearly, despite the strength of the incentives to compete, collusion very often does occur in practice. And, despite the fact that the historical record documents the potential for internal divisiveness within the capitalist sector, this sector did come to cohere and to evoke a massive and involuntary transfer of resources from the indigenous economies of southern Africa. The formation of coherent political interests out of maximizing economic individuals may be problematic; but it does occur. Collective-choice theory points to a key element in this process; so, too, does contemporary Marxist analysis. The element is power: the capacity to coerce.

Among contemporary Marxist analysts, it is Poulantzas who lays particular stress upon the role of political power in inducing coherence among economic interests. Classes, he stresses, only become historical forces when they are organized. But they tend to be filled with discordant factions – factions which seek their particular and immediate interests, even at the expense of the common, long-run interests which they share with similarly situated economic agents. Class interests are realized only when internal compromises are secured from the constituent factions; and the agency that

143

secures concessions in the cause of common class interests is the ultimate holder of coercive power: the state. As Poulantzas contends: the role of the state is 'precisely in *making* the dominated classes *accept* a whole series of compromises which appear to be to *their* ... interest'.[25]

Collective-choice analysis points to a similar role for coercion. Where players hold interests in common but also interests which conflict, cooperation may offer the prospects of joint gains; but non-cooperative strategies may offer better prospects of immediate advantage. And the actors may therefore be unable to organize so as to secure their common interests. But by introducing the element of force into social life – by employing force to extract penalties from those who fail to cooperate – people may be able to form sanctionable agreements which insure the execution of common, cooperative strategies.

As seen in the analysis of the behavior of the settler farmers in Kenya, it was in this way that the state was pressed into the service of agents in the market; it was used by similarly situated agents to police their own behavior, thereby organizing collusively and rendering the market a means of redistributing income. Similarly in South Africa: appreciating the power of the incentives to compete and, recognizing the level of competition recorded by Palmer and Parsons, it becomes obvious that the *economic* history of that region must be written in terms of *political* economy. The political arrangements worked out between the active agents of the industrial economy – the mines, the manufacturers, the railways and the government – are absolutely central to the analysis of the triumph of the capitalist sector. The ways in which political instruments were developed by these competing actors to compel concessions from each of their immediate short-run interests so as to reap the common benefits to be extracted from the indigenous economy: this political story is central to the economic history of that troubled portion of the continent.

In either form of political economy – social choice or Marxist – the state thus becomes a critical variable. By allocating power, the state allocates the capacity to organize; through access to means of coercion, individual agents acquire the capacity to engage in collective action. The emergence of organized economic interests and the introduction of patterns of bias resulting from the onslaught of concerted self-interested behavior thus follow from the introduction of power into economic life.

THE ROLE OF POLITICS IN POLITICAL ECONOMY

Thus far I have concentrated on the commonalities and complementarities between the approach taken in these essays and that of its major alternative. It may well be useful, however, to push farther and to focus on the issues that divide the two forms of political economy. For ultimately the collective-choice and Marxist approaches fundamentally disagree; and an issue that clearly divides them is the autonomy of politics.

In recent years Marxist scholars have developed a more fully elaborated *political* economy. They have done so by focusing on the state. Some have imparted new vigor to the classic position that the state is an agent of the interests of dominant classes. In the African context, this point unites those who otherwise stand as contestants: the dependency theorists and the more classical Marxists.[26] As exemplified by Leys in his 1975 study of Kenya, dependency theorists view the state as an agent of international capital: the state assists in extracting surplus from peripheral societies and transferring it to the core, thereby leading to a failure of local capital accumulation and to the 'underdevelopment' of African societies.[27] Against this position stand the works of Warren, Sklar, and the later Leys. These scholars argue that the state has been used to promote local capital formation and to advance the interests of a nascent indigenous bourgeoisie *even at the expense* of international capitalists.[28] The difference is clear; it centers on the nature of the class interests advanced by the state. Where the positions concur is in their portrayal of the state as an agency of class interests.

Other scholars impute a more independent role for the state. Rather than acting as the passive agency of particular interests, they argue, the state stands relatively independent of such interests and thereby facilitates the attainment of otherwise unattainable objectives. Some theorists thereby complement the class-based theory of the state; in the spirit of Poulantzas, they argue that the state provides a means whereby the short-run interests which divide members of the dominant class can be overcome so as to secure the interests which they hold in common. Standing independent of the pre-eminent class, the state can coerce its members and thereby assist them in consolidating their position of social domination.[29] Others view the role of the relatively autonomous state as serving not class interests but the interests of the dominant mode of production. Capitalism, they stress, contains an inherent contradiction; it requires accumulation for its reproduction, but accumulation generates class antagonism. The state, acting out of the interests of capitalism, must therefore stand apart from the dominant class and compel it to lower its rate of accumulation; only by exacting such concessions can it placate the lower classes, secure the reproduction of labor power, and thereby guarantee the reproduction of the capitalist order.[30]

In these essays, I have presented evidence to support such views; I have also presented evidence which requires their modification. Clearly, the states examined in this volume do serve the interests of dominant classes. In the analysis of traditional kingdoms, for example, indicators of state formation strongly correlated with marks of class formation: patterns of financial privilege, social privilege, and involuntary economic redistribution. In the colonial and post-colonial periods, too, states were employed to channel resources out of the peasant sector and into the hands of mercantile and industrial classes. Moreover, the states played the role portrayed by those who insist upon their relative autonomy. As argued above, a critical role for the state in Africa has been to provide the means whereby dominant groups can organize. And, as noted in the essay on pre-colonial states in Africa, while facilitating the rise of economic privilege, states also promote economic prosperity, thereby providing legitimacy through the generation of common benefits.

Where, then, do I take issue with the Marxist interpretations? The point of divergence is my insistence upon the necessity of according fully autonomous status to politics. This necessity arises at two levels: at the level of logic and at the level of evidence.

For all the theorists we have encountered, the state ultimately stands in the service of the economy. Politically, the state may oppose the interests of dominant classes; it may even lower the level of capital accumulation. But, in each case the end result is the same: the enhancement of underlying productive forces.

One obvious problem with this position is that it is non-refutable. Where the state acts against the interests of basic economic forces, these forces can be reinterpreted as not being all that basic; alternatively, the state may be viewed as acting in their 'deeper' interests. Where the actions of the state harm short-run interests, these actions can be seen as enhancing interests in the longer run. 'Short steps back' can be viewed as preludes to 'long steps forward'. In these and other ways, the necessary relationship between politics and economics can be preserved; but the relationship is then preserved only by placing the argument beyond the reach of refutation.

An alternative would be to accord the political realm independent standing in the arguments. To *reduce* the political to the economic is to evade logical derivation and to shelter arguments, as in the ways above, from empirical analysis.[31] But by separating the political from the economic, the causal impact of economic factors upon politics can be derived and tested.

Not only the canons of rational discourse but also the simple power of experience suggest the importance of according autonomy to politics. For not only have we seen how economic forces affect politics, but we have also seen that political institutions can affect economic forces. The nature of colonial institutions, for example, led to highly contrasting outcomes of the process of the commercialization of agriculture, with producer interests subject to expropriation in one case and the beneficiaries of such expropriations in the other. And politicians, we have seen, select economic policies not out of a regard for their economic merits but out of a regard for their political utility; economic inefficiency, we saw, can be politically useful. The political is not merely reducible to the economic; rather, it stands apart from it and can act upon it, often in a manner that is costly in economic terms.

The approach taken in these essays thus breaks with the Marxist position by asserting the independent status and determining power of politics. States have their own objectives. They want taxes and revenues and intervene actively in their economic environments to secure them. Politi-

146

cians want power. And they use the instruments of the state to secure and retain it by manipulating the economy to political advantage. In Africa, as we have seen, political elites have rendered economic markets instruments of political organization.

In Marxist thought, as recently argued by G. A. Cohen, the state can be explained as a structure that promotes the full realization of the economic possibilities associated with the prevailing modes of production.[32] In Africa, however, the state has historically been both more and less than that. As we have seen, in the pre-colonial, the colonial, and the post-colonial period, it is the state that is pressed into service in efforts to revolutionize economic forms. Instead of simply reflecting the dominant mode of production, it can also seek to transform it. In addition, rather than securing the fullest realization of the productive potentialities at society's command, the state can in fact both fetter and undermine them. The African case thus compels recognition of the possibility that political forces may be fully autonomous and, as a consequence, may act at the cost of economic rationality and solely in service of themselves.[33]

Notes

1 The preservation of order in stateless societies

1 E. E. Evans-Pritchard, *The Nuer* (Oxford: The Clarendon Press, 1940), pp. 175–6.
2 *ibid.*, p. 16.
3 *ibid.*, p. 36.
4 *ibid.*
5 *ibid.*, p. 16, italics mine.
6 *ibid.*, p. 49. Several readers have in effect argued at this point: 'You don't convince me. Maybe the Nuer are not like us. Maybe they find it unthinkable to steal cattle from other Nuer. Maybe they would experience great shame if they did so, and so not enjoy the cattle they stole. For such reasons, maybe there isn't much of a problem of order among the Nuer, and thus no reason to pursue the topic of this paper.'

I have several counter-arguments. First, my basic one is that Evans-Pritchard delimits the boundary of the society in terms of the area within which disputes can be peacefully resolved; the group is thus distinguished by the existence of mechanisms for the peaceful resolution of conflict rather than by the absence of conflict, as the commentators would have it. Second, any reading of the material on the Nuer reveals them to be as contentious and greedy as the rest of us; it was in part because this was the case that Evans-Pritchard was motivated to study how they managed to avoid social chaos. Third, in so far as the readers argue that the existence of a moral community weakens the incentives to harm others, as opposed to eradicating them entirely, I would agree with their point; in fact, I develop it in the last portion of the paper.
7 P. P. Howell, *A Manual of Nuer Law* (London: Oxford University Press for the International African Institute, 1954), pp. 200–1.
8 See ch. 1 of Max Gluckman, *Custom and Conflict in Africa* (Oxford: Basil Blackwell, 1960).
9 For other efforts to apply game theory to anthropology, see Frederik Barth, 'Segmentary Opposition and the Theory of Games: A Study of Pathan Organization', *Journal of the Royal Anthropological Society*, 89 (1959): 5–22; and Martin Southwold, 'A Games Model of African Tribal Politics', in Ira R. Buchler and Hugo G. Nutini, eds., *Game Theory in the Behavioral Sciences* (Pittsburgh: University of Pittsburgh Press, 1969). For reviews, see the contribution in Buchler and Nutini, eds., *Game Theory* and also the articles by Anthony P. Glascock, 'Optimization Theory and the Analysis of Political Behavior', *Political Anthropology*, 1 (1975): 136–54; and Douglas R. White, 'Mathematical Anthropology', in John J. Honigman, ed., *Handbook of Social and Cultural Anthropology* (Chicago: Rand-McNally, 1979). For formulations which have strongly influenced the development of this essay, see also Frederick G. Bailey, *Stratagems and Spoils: A Social Anthropology of Politics* (New York: Schocken, 1969) and Charles R. Plott and Robert A. Meyer, 'The

Technology of Public Goods, Externalities, and the Exclusion Principle', in Edwin S. Mills, ed., *Economic Analysis of Environmental Problems* (New York: National Bureau of Economic Research, 1975). The *locus classicus* for the introduction to game theory for the social sciences is Duncan R. Luce and Howard Raiffa, *Games and Decisions* (New York: John Wiley and Sons, 1957).

10 It should be noted that, by all accounts, the Nuer do translate physical pain and suffering and even death into cattle equivalents. See Evans-Pritchard, *The Nuer*, p. 127 and Howell, *A Manual of Nuer Law*, pp. 25–48.

11 A keen-eyed reader will no doubt discern a moral hazard in this system of compensation. See the discussion in note 19.

12 Evans-Pritchard, *The Nuer*, pp. 121ff.

13 Peter J. Greuel, 'The Leopard-Skin Chief: An Examination of Political Power Among the Nuer', *American Anthropologist*, 73 (1971): 1115–20.

14 Bruce Haight, 'A Note on the Leopard-Skin Chief', *American Anthropologist*, 74 (1972): 1316.

15 Evans-Pritchard, *The Nuer*, p. 173.

16 *ibid.*, p. 174. For further discussions, see E. E. Evans-Pritchard, *Nuer Religion* (Oxford: The Clarendon Press, 1956), pp. 109–10, 290ff, and 300. See also Howell, *A Manual of Nuer Law*, pp. 43–4.

17 John W. Burton, 'Some Nuer Notions of Purity and Danger: Dedicated to the Memory of E. E. Evans-Pritchard (1902–1973)', *Anthropos*, 69, 3–4 (1974): 517–36; John W. Burton, 'Living with the Dead: Aspects of the Afterlife in Nuer and Dinka Cosmology (Sudan)', *Anthropos*, 73, 1–2 (1978): 141–60; T. O. Beidelman, 'Nuer Priests and Prophets: Charisma, Authority and Power among the Nuer', in T. O. Beidelman, ed., *The Translation of Culture* (London: Tavistock, 1971), pp. 375–415.

18 See the display of threatening behavior that takes place during the period of arbitration as recorded in Evans-Pritchard, *The Nuer*, p. 153.

19 Several other properties of this process warrant comment. First, as much as possible, the Nuer render the leopard-skin chief an 'impartial' arbiter. Thus, he is a relatively poor person with no large cattle holdings; he is therefore less likely to be a party to disputes or to have a stake in their outcomes. This argument has been contested by Greuel ('The Leopard-Skin Chief') who contended that the leopard-skin chief amassed large cattle holdings. I must agree with Haight ('A Note on the Leopard-Skin Chief'), however, that Greuel's contention finds little support in Evans-Pritchard's data. Second, it is clear that the limits of the bargain should insure that neither party does better after violence than before. In particular, family II should not be allowed to gain more than ten cattle; for then it will have an incentive to entice family I to aggress and then to assess damages.

In the jargon of political economy, the creation of such an incentive would represent a 'moral hazard'. Moral hazards arise when arrangements which are designed to correct social problems in fact create incentives which exacerbate them; insuring against the risks of automobile accidents, for example, may lead to less careful driving and thus to a higher frequency of accidents. It is interesting to note that the Nuer appear to be aware of this class of problems. For example, the ethnographic accounts suggest that they take great pains to insure that the families of women do not benefit substantially from cattle paid in damages for adultery or premarital impregnations; they do so by placing restrictions on the use that can be made of such cattle (see Evans-Pritchard, *Nuer Religion*, pp. 186–7). See also the discussion in Howell, *A Manual of Nuer Law*, p. vii.

20 Evans-Pritchard, *The Nuer*, pp. 174ff.

21 *ibid.*, pp. 170–1. See also Howell, *A Manual of Nuer Law*, pp. 23ff, 39.

22 Evans-Pritchard, *The Nuer*, pp. 150ff; also Howell, *A Manual of Nuer Law*, pp. 24, 41.

23 The essay appears in Max Gluckman, *Custom and Conflict in Africa* (Oxford: Basil Blackwell, 1960).

24 See the essay by Elizabeth Colson entitled 'Social Control and Vengeance in Plateau Tonga Society' which appears in her book *The Plateau Tonga of Northern Rhodesia (Zambia): Social and Religious Studies* (Manchester: The Institute for Social Research, University of Zambia, 1970).

25 *ibid.*, pp. 102–21.

26 See Gluckman, *Custom and Conflict*, pp. 11–12. Gluckman's conjecture is supported by the evidence of ritual avoidance between Nuer families involved in a dispute, particularly a homicide. Evans-Pritchard comments, for example: 'Until the blood-feud is closed . . . the kin of the slayer and the slain may not eat or drink from vessels from which the other has eaten or drunk . . . Even to use the same vessels at the home of a third party who is in no way connected with the feud may entail the most serious consequences. A third party may cause death to one side or the other by eating or drinking with both' (*Nuer Religion*, p. 179; see also p. 294 and Howell, *A Manual of Nuer Law*, p. 220). Given the necessity for such a high degree of avoidance, the disruptions of neighborhood life occasioned by disputes must have been extremely high, and so too the incentives for their resolution.

27 Gluckman, *Custom and Conflict*, p. 13.

28 Evans-Pritchard, *Nuer Religion*; Beidelman, 'Nuer Priests and Prophets'; and Burton, 'Some Nuer Notions of Purity and Danger'.

29 Gluckman, *Custom and Conflict*, p. 94.

30 Evans-Pritchard, *Nuer Religion*, p. 170.

31 Gluckman, *Custom and Conflict*, p. 94.

32 Evans-Pritchard, *Nuer Religion*, p. 297.

33 *ibid.*, pp. 173, 174–5.

34 Burton, 'Living with the Dead', p. 145.

35 Walter Goldschmidt, *Sebei Law* (Berkeley and Los Angeles: University of California Press, 1967), pp. 83–7.

36 Again, it is critical to emphasize that these beliefs are apparently not strong enough to eradicate self-interested behavior or the tendency to violate the property rights of others; rather, they appear to weaken the incentives for such violations, thus making them less frequent and facilitating their control through the mechanisms outlined above.

37 T. M. S. Evans, 'Leopard Skins and Paper Tigers: "Choice" and "Social Structure" in *The Nuer*', *Man*, 13 (1978): 100–15.

38 Beidelman, 'Nuer Priests and Prophets'.

2 The centralization of African societies

1 Lucy Mair, *Primitive Government* (Baltimore: Penguin Books, 1962), p. 160.

2 See, for example, the discussions in Robin Horton, 'Stateless Societies in the History of West Africa', in J. F. A. Ajayi and Michael Crowder, eds., *The History of West Africa*, 1 (London: Longman, 1971); Gwilym Iwan Jones, *The Trading States of the Oil Rivers* (London: Oxford University Press for the International African Institute, 1963); and Robert F. Stevenson, *Population and Political Systems in Tropical Africa* (New York: Columbia University Press, 1968).

3 The sample set of societies and the magnitude of the documentation which my researchers covered for each is indicated in Table 21, p. 57.

4 See Henri Pirenne, *Medieval Cities* (Princeton: Princeton University Press, 1925) and *Mohammed and Charlemagne* (London: Allen and Unwin, 1939). See also Immanuel Wallerstein, *The Modern World System* (New York: Academic Press, 1974), as well as Jeremy A. Sabloff and C. C. Lamberg Karlovsky, *Ancient Civilization and Trade* (Albuquerque, New Mexico: University of New Mexico Press, 1975). Note also the following quote: 'What was "peace" for the author of *Beowolf* but the prospect of exchanging gifts between peoples!' From George Duby, *The Early Growth of the European*

Economy: Warriors and Peasants from the Seventh to the Twelfth Century (London: Weidenfeld and Nicolson, 1974), quoted in George Dalton, 'The Impact of Colonization on Aboriginal Economies in Stateless Societies', in George Dalton, ed., *Research in Economic Anthropology*, 1 (Greenwich, Conn.: JAI Press, 1978), p. 131.

In the contemporary period, what is here being called the 'Smithian' argument is being advanced by such 'neo-classical' economists as North and Thomas: see Douglass C. North and Robert Paul Thomas, *The Rise of the Western World* (Cambridge: Cambridge University Press, 1973); the Marxist variant is being advanced by G. A. Cohen, *Karl Marx's Theory of History: A Defense* (Princeton, New Jersey: Princeton University Press, 1978). The parallel thesis of the two – that political institutions exist to secure property rights which will enable the realization of efficiency gains – is striking.

See also Robert Brenner, 'The Origins of Capitalist Development: A Critique of Neo-Smithian Marxism', *New Left Review*, 104 (1977): 25–92.

5 See, for example, Catherine Coquéry-Vidrovitch, 'The Political Economy of the African Peasantry and Modes of Production', in Peter C. W. Gutkind and Immanuel Wallerstein, eds., *The Political Economy of Contemporary Africa* (Beverly Hills: Sage Publications, 1976); see also Claude Meillassoux, ed., *The Development of Indigenous Trade and Markets in West Africa* (London: Oxford University Press for the International African Institute, 1971).

6 Elizabeth Colson, 'Trade and Wealth Among the Tonga', in Paul Bohannan and George Dalton, eds., *Markets in Africa* (Evanston: Northwestern University Press, 1962), p. 606.

7 *ibid.*

8 *ibid.*

9 *ibid.*

10 I. M. Lewis, 'Lineage Continuity and Modern Commerce in Northern Somaliland', in Bohannan and Dalton, *Markets in Africa*, pp. 369–70.

11 Colson, 'Trade and Wealth', p. 607.

12 Mair, *Primitive Government*, p. 58.

13 Aidan William Southall, *Alur Society* (Cambridge: W. Heffer and Sons, 1956), pp. 80ff.

14 For the Sukuma, see J. Gus Liebenow, 'Responses to Planned Political Change in a Tanganyika Tribal Group', *American Political Science Review*, 50, 2 (June 1956): 422–61. For the Anuak, see Max Gluckman, *Politics, Law and Ritual in Tribal Society* (Oxford: Basil Blackwell, 1965), pp. 125–6. For the Tio, see Jan Vansina, *The Tio Kingdom of the Middle Congo 1880–1892* (London: Oxford University Press for the International African Institute, 1973), p. 319. For the societies of southeastern Nigeria, see David Northrup, *Trade Without Rulers: Pre-Colonial Economic Development in South-Eastern Nigeria* (Oxford: The Clarendon Press, 1978) and Malcolm Ruel, *Leopards and Leaders: Constitutional Politics Among a Cross River People* (London: Tavistock Publications, 1974). For the kingdoms of Ruanda and Burundi, note Maquet, who states: 'The Watutsi used several strategies but rarely, it seems, direct military conquest. The ascendancy which the invaders gained from their war-like reputation and the prestige of their wealth enabled them to arbitrate disputes between peasants.' Jacques J. Maquet, *Power and Society in Africa* (New York: McGraw-Hill, 1971).

15 Northrup, *Trade Without Rulers*; K. Onwuka Dike, *Trade and Politics in the Niger Delta, 1830–1885* (Oxford: The Clarendon Press, 1956); and Simon Ottenberg, 'Ibo Oracles and Intergroup Relations', *Southwestern Journal of Anthropology*, 14, 3 (1958): 295–317.

16 Northrup, *Trade Without Rulers*, p. 127.

17 For a related study, see Ruel, *Leopards and Leaders*.

18 Jack Goody, 'The Over-Kingdom of Gonja', in Daryll Forde and P. M. Kaberry, eds., *West African Kingdoms in the Nineteenth Century* (London: Oxford University Press, 1967), p. 184.

19 See, for example, Peter C. Lloyd, 'The Political Structure of African Kingdoms: An Explanatory Model', in Michael Banton, ed., *Political Systems and the Distribution of Power* (London: Tavistock Publications, 1965) and 'The Political Development of West African Kingdoms'. *The Journal of African History*, 9, 2 (1968): 319–29; Aidan William Southall, 'A Critique of the Typology of States and Political Systems', in Michael Banton, ed., *Political Systems*; J. H. M. Beattie, 'Checks on the Abuse of Political Power in Some African States: A Preliminary Framework for Analysis', *Sociologus*, 9 (1959): 97–115; and Lucy Mair, 'How Far Have We Got in the Study of Politics?', in Meyer Fortes and Sheila Patterson, eds., *Studies in African Social Anthropology* (London: Academic Press, 1975).

20 I did not do the coding myself, and purposely so. I first wrote a long paper in which I summarized the arguments concerning the economic basis for state formation in pre-colonial Africa. I developed a code book to collect information from the Human Relations Area Files which would allow me to test these arguments. I then had the data collected 'blind', i.e. by coders who had not read my paper or discussed the ideas in it with me. My research assistants knew I was looking for relationships between economic and political factors in African tribal societies, but they had no knowledge of the exact arguments I was trying to test nor of the particular relationships that would have serve as tests of them. By keeping them 'blind' I thereby attempted to shield against bias in my research procedures.

21 It should be noted that I reassessed these relationships while controlling for the factor of ecological variation. While the small number of cases made difficult the use of such procedures, the results suggest that 'economic' factors – the possession of markets, caravans and long-distance trade – continue to affect the level of political centralization, even when ecological factors are controlled.

22 For a general analysis of the public-goods problem, see Mancur Olson, *The Logic of Collective Action* (Cambridge, Mass.: Harvard University Press, 1971); see also William H. Riker and Peter C. Ordeshook, *An Introduction to Positive Political Theory* (Englewood Cliffs, N. J.: Prentice Hall, 1973). For an application of economic analysis to the problem of institutional change, see Lance E. Davis and Douglass C. North, *Institutional Change and American Economic Growth* (Cambridge: Cambridge University Press, 1971) and North and Thomas, *The Rise of the Western World*. For an interesting application to African materials, see Richard A. Posner, 'A Theory of Primitive Society, With Special Reference to Law', *The Journal of Law and Economics*, 23 (1980): 1–53. For a telling critique of institutional arguments which fail to take account of the public-goods problem, see Samuel L. Popkin, *The Rational Peasant: The Political Economy of Rural Society in Vietnam* (Berkeley and Los Angeles: University of California Press, 1979).

23 One form of investment which correlated strongly with political centralization was investment in irrigation and water storage. The number of cases was far too small to yield a significant relationship. None the less, the parallel with Wittfogel's analysis of non-African cases is intriguing. See Karl A. Wittfogel, *Oriental Despotism* (New Haven and London: Yale University Press, 1957).

24 See, for example, Jan Vansina, 'Long-Distance Trade Routes in Central Africa', *The Journal of African History*, 3, 3 (1962): 375–90 and Jan Vansina, 'Trade and Markets Among the Kuba', in Bohannan and Dalton, *Markets in Africa*. See also Catherine Coquéry-Vidrovitch, 'The Political Economy of the African Peasantry and Modes of Production'.

25 Andrew D. Roberts, 'Nyamwezi Trade', in Richard Gray and David Birmingham, eds., *Pre-colonial African Trade* (London: Oxford University Press, 1970), p. 52.

26 Vansina, *The Tio Kingdom*, pp. 8, 258.

27 Kwamina B. Dickson, *A Historical Geography of Ghana* (Cambridge: Cambridge University Press, 1969).

28 Indicative of the importance of the costs of security is the magnitude of the change in the behavior of the long-distance traders when they were provided with protection by central states. Hopkins notes that, in the nineteenth century, Hausa caravans of 1,000 to 2,000 people were common. But he argues: 'There were diseconomies of scale which became apparent during the colonial period. With greater freedom of movement and more secure markets, long-distance traders began to travel in small groups, an arrangement which gave them flexibility in timing departures and arrivals, offered them a wider choice of routes, and reduced their overheads, since it was no longer necessary to contribute towards the cost of guards and guides.' Anthony G. Hopkins, *An Economic History of West Africa* (New York: Columbia University Press, 1973), p. 63.

By transferring the provision of security outside their firms, the organizers of caravans were then able to operate at a lower scale and thus, given the nature of their enterprise, to conduct their business more efficiently and so earn higher profits. These gains in efficiency represented benefits from the existence of states, and so constituted material incentives for their formation. For an excellent review of the literature on long-distance trade, see William O. Jones, 'Agricultural Trade Within Tropical Africa: Historical Background', in Robert H. Bates and Michael F. Lofchie, eds., *Agricultural Development in Africa: Issues of Public Policy* (New York: Praeger Publishers, 1980). It should be noted that Jones, in a personal communication, vigorously dissents from this portion of my analysis.

29 Philip Bonner, 'Early State Formation among the Nguni: The Relevance of the Swazi Case'. Paper prepared for African History Seminar, University of London, School of Oriental and African Studies, 1978, p. 7.

30 *ibid.*

31 Stevenson, *Population and Political Systems*, p. 220.

32 Northrup, *Trade Without Rulers*.

33 *ibid.*, p. 87.

34 *ibid.*, pp. 86–7.

35 Robin Law, 'Slaves, Trade and Taxes: The Material Basis of Political Power in Precolonial West Africa', in George Dalton, ed., *Research in Economic Anthropology*, 1 (Greenwich, Conn.: JAI Press, 1978).

36 Coquéry-Vidrovitch, 'The Political Economy of African Peasantry and Modes of Production'.

37 I. A. Akinjogbin, *Dahomey and Its Neighbours, 1708–1818* (Cambridge: Cambridge University Press, 1967).

38 See, for example, the discussion in David Kimble, *A Political History of Ghana* (Oxford: The Clarendon Press, 1963).

39 Gabriel Kolko, *Railroads and Regulation* (New York: Norton, 1970).

40 Guillermo A. O'Donnell, *Modernization and Bureaucratic Authoritarianism* (Berkeley: Institute of International Studies, University of California, 1973).

41 It should also be noted that the source of the relationship between craft specialization and political centralization does *not* result from the government's purchase of crafts; hence the data in Table 22.

42 Ivor Wilks, *Asante in the Nineteenth Century: The Structure and Evolution of a Political Order* (Cambridge: Cambridge University Press, 1975).

43 See the discussions in J. A. Atanda, 'The Changing Status of the Alafin of Oyo Under Colonial Rule and Independence', in Michael Crowder and Obaro Ikime, eds., *West African Chiefs* (New York: Africana, 1970); Peter Morton-Williams, 'The Yoruba Kingdom of Oyo', in Forde and Kaberry, eds., *West African Kingdoms*; and Robin Law, *The Oyo Empire c. 1600 – c. 1836* (Oxford: The Clarendon Press, 1977). See also David D. Laitin, 'The International Economy and State Formation Among the Yoruba in the Nineteenth Century'. Paper prepared for delivery at the 1981 Annual Meeting of the American Political Science Association, New York, 3–6 September 1981.

44 See, for example, the discussion in Donal B. Cruise O'Brien, *The Mourides of Senegal* (Oxford: The Clarendon Press, 1971).

45 Elizabeth Colson, 'African Society at the Time of the Scramble', in Lewis H. Gann and Peter Duignan, eds., *Colonialism in Africa, 1870–1960* (Cambridge: Cambridge University Press, 1969), p. 41.

46 Gluckman, *Politics, Law and Ritual*, p. 161.

47 Bonner, 'Early State Formation Among the Nguni', and J. D. Omer-Cooper, *The Zulu Aftermath: A Nineteenth-Century Revolution in Bantu Africa* (Evanston, Ill.: Northwestern University Press, 1969).

48 Frederick Engels, *The Origin of the Family, Private Property and the State* (New York: International Publishers, 1972); Harold Demsetz, 'Toward a Theory of Property Rights', *American Economic Review*, 52, 2 (May 1967): 347–56. Lance E. Davis and Douglass C. North, *Institutional Change and American Economic Growth* (Cambridge: Cambridge University Press, 1971); Douglass C. North and Robert Paul Thomas, *The Rise of the Western World* (Cambridge: Cambridge University Press, 1973); and Douglass C. North, *Structure and Change in Economic History* (New York: W. W. Norton, 1981).

49 Robert L. Carneiro, 'A Theory of the Origin of the State', *Science*, 169, 3946 (1970): 733–8.

50 See, for example, M. M. Postan, 'Medieval Agriculture in its Prime: England', in M. M. Postan, ed., *The Cambridge Economic History of Europe*, 1 (Cambridge: Cambridge University Press, 1966) and Emmanuel Le Roy Ladurie, *The Peasants of Languedoc* (Urbana, Ill.: University of Illinois Press, 1974). See also Robert Brenner, 'Agrarian Class Structure and Economic Development', *Past and Present*, 70 (1976): 30–75. For an interpretation that closely parallels my own, see Michael Hechter and William Brustein, 'Regional Modes of Production and Patterns of State Formation in Western Europe', *American Journal of Sociology*, 85, 5 (1980): 1061–94; also, Albert O. Hirschman, 'Exit, Voice and the State', *World Politics*, 31 (October 1978): 90–107.

51 Stevenson, *Population and Political Systems*; Richard Vengroff, 'Population Density and State Formation in Africa', *African Studies Review*, 19 (1976): 67–74.

52 Vansina, *The Tio Kingdom*, p. 82.

53 *ibid.*

54 *ibid.*, pp. 82–3.

55 Andrew D. Roberts, 'Nyamwezi Trade', in Gray and Birmingham, *Pre-Colonial African Trade*, p. 42; see also Hopkins, *An Economic History of West Africa*, p. 38.

56 I also tested the relationship using analysis of variance. The relationships were not significant. However, as noted earlier, analysis of variance assumes a normal sampling distribution, which we lack here; not much significance should therefore be attributed to this result.

57 David Birmingham, 'Early African Trade in Angola and its Hinterland', in Gray and Birmingham, p. 167.

58 *ibid.*, p. 166.

59 See also the discussions in Brian Fagan, 'Early Trade and Raw Materials in South Central Africa', in Gray and Birmingham, *Pre-Colonial African Trade*; Nicola Sutherland-Harris, 'Trade and the Rozvi-Mambo', in Gray and Birmingham, *Pre-Colonial African Trade*; Hopkins, *An Economic History of West Africa*, pp. 47ff; and the discussion in Wilks, *Asante in the Nineteenth Century*.

60 As Wilks states: 'The imposition of tolls and market dues was ... a widespread means of raising revenues and being ... relatively simple and virtually riskless, it may well have been preferred ... to direct trading' (*Asante in the Nineteenth Century*, p. 62).

61 For a further discussion, see J. D. Fage, *States and Subjects in Sub-Saharan African History* (Johannesburg: Witwatersrand University Press, 1974).

62 Jan Vansina, *Kingdoms of the Savanna* (Madison, Wis.: University of Wisconsin Press, 1968), p. 150.

63 Andrew D. Roberts, *A History of the Bemba: Political Growth and Change in Northeastern Zambia before 1900* (Madison, Wis.: University of Wisconsin Press, 1973), p. 182.
64 See, for example, Fage, *States and Subjects*; Law, *The Oyo Empire*; and Laitin, 'The International Economy and State Formation Among the Yoruba'.
65 Wilks, *Asante in the Nineteenth Century*, p. 681.
66 *ibid.*, p. 680.
67 E. Phillip LeVeen, 'The African Slave Trade Response', *African Studies Review*, 18 (1975): 9–28 and Henry A. Gemery and Jan S. Hogendorn, 'The Atlantic Slave Trade: A Tentative Model', *Journal of African History*, 15 (1974): 223–46.
68 Much of this research is summarized in Roland Oliver, 'The East African Interior', in Roland Oliver, ed., *The Cambridge History of Africa*, 3 (Cambridge: Cambridge University Press, 1977).
69 See, for example, Patricia Mercer, 'Shilluk Trade and Politics from the Mid-Seventeenth Century to 1861', *The Journal of African History*, 12, 3 (1971): 407–26; S. I. Mudenge, 'The Role of Foreign Trade in the Rozvi Empire: A Reappraisal', *Journal of African History*, 15, 3 (1974): 373–91; and Max Gluckman, 'The Kingdom of the Zulu of South Africa', in Meyer Fortes and Evans-Pritchard, eds., *African Political Systems* (London: Oxford University Press for the International African Institute, 1970) and 'The Rise of the Zulu Empire', *Scientific American*, 202, 4 (April 1960): 157–68.
70 Franz Oppenheimer, *The State: Its History and Development Viewed Sociologically* (New York: Vanguard Press, 1926).
71 Karl Polanyi, *Dahomey and the Slave Trade: An Analysis of an Archaic Economy* (Seattle: University of Washington Press, 1966).
72 Claudine Tardits and Claude Tardits, 'Traditional Market Economy in South Dahomey', in Bohannan and Dalton, eds., *Markets in Africa*, pp. 101–2.
73 Elman R. Service, *Origins of the State and Civilization* (New York: W. W. Norton, 1975).
74 Morton H. Fried, *The Evolution of Political Society* (New York: Random House, 1967).
75 For a discussion of these dynamics, see Margaret Levi, 'The Predatory Theory of Rule', *Politics and Society*, 10, 4 (1981): 431–65 and Douglass C. North, *Structure and Change in Economic History* (New York: W. W. Norton, 1981).
76 Colson, 'African Society at the Time of the Scramble', p. 44.
77 See the discussion in Morton-Williams, 'The Yoruba Kingdom of Oyo'; Law, *The Oyo Empire*; and Atanda, 'The Changing Status of the Alafin of Oyo Under Colonial Rule and Independence'.
78 A good discussion is contained in Martin Southwold, *Bureaucracy and Chiefship in Buganda: The Development of Appointive Office in the History of Buganda* (Kampala, Uganda: East African Institute of Social Research, 1961).
79 For a general discussion of the limits to power, see Beattie, 'Checks on the Abuse of Political Power in Some African States'.
80 Max Gluckman, *Custom and Conflict in Africa* (Oxford: Basil Blackwell, 1959), p. 46.
   In Benin, primogeniture determined succession to office. None the less, competition prevailed; conflict simply centered on who was first born. See the discussion in Michael Crowder and Obaro Ikime, 'Introduction' in Michael Crowder and Obaro Ikime, eds., *West African Chiefs*, p. xi.
   In a passage typical of much recent work on oral traditions, Jan Vansina discredits the myth of dynastic harmony and continuity among the Bushoong; his comments are highly relevant here: 'A re-examination of the data leads to the startling conclusion that many successions were in fact disputed, thus giving substance to the Bushoong feeling that parties to most struggles were made up of the king and his followers on the one hand, and his heir apparent and his followers on the other. In almost every generation a struggle took place' *The Children of Woot: A History of the Kuba* (Madison, Wis.: University of Wisconsin Press, 1978), p. 156.

155

81 The case of Rwanda and Burundi forms a constant counterpoint to this argument, simply because the relationship between the Watutsi and the Bahutu appears to have been among the most exploitative in the traditional societies of Africa. None the less, within that society, competition within the Watutsi ruling class clearly existed; it appeared to curtail the degree to which the rulers were able to exact resources from their followers; and it led to positive benefits for followers. Thus, Gravel documents the 'play for power' within the ruling stratum and the promotion of even Hutu lineages into the ruling 'caste' that resulted; see Pierre Bettez Gravel, *Remera: A Community in Eastern Ruanda* (The Hague and Paris: Mouton, 1968), and René Lemarchand, 'Power and Stratification in Rwanda: A Reconsideration', *Cahiers d'Etudes Africaines*, 4 (1966): 592–610. The institution of clientship, and the competitive search among the ruling elite for clients, also placed limits on the degree to which the rulers could demand resources and services from their followers; as Maquet states: 'When a lord appeared to be too demanding of his clients, he no longer found new ones, and those he had would try to leave him', Jacques J. Maquet, 'The Problem of Tutsi Domination', in George Dalton, ed., *Tribal and Peasant Economies* (Garden City, New York: The Natural History Press for the American Museum of Natural History, 1967), p. 85.

 None the less, there can be little doubt but that the position of the Hutu followers was far more unfavorable than that of their counterparts in other African societies. I would attribute this to the relatively high ratio of men to land in this kingdom – something that allowed the rulers to set a relatively high price on access to land. I would also argue that most commentators overestimate the degree of exploitation that existed in the pre-colonial era, an error that arises from extrapolating present information into the past. In the post-colonial era, the growth of population promoted and enabled even greater exactions by the rulers as the price of Hutu access to land. In addition, the colonial rulers curtailed the level of competition within the Watutsi elite; this enabled the elite to cohere in opposition to the Hutu to a degree that hitherto had been impossible. Lemarchand's argument supports this theory when he states: 'The impact of indirect rule has been, first of all, to destroy the old balance of forces between cattle chiefs, land chiefs and army chiefs, which in previous times had served to protect the Hutu peasantry against undue exactions … Not only did [the concentration of power] deprive the Hutu of opportunities to play one chief off against another, but it also eliminated the channels of appeal offered by the previous arrangement.' René Lemarchand, *Rwanda and Burundi* (London: Pall Mall Press, 1970), pp. 119–20. Lemarchand goes on to document the extent to which the rulers' levies increased under colonial rule and concludes by noting that the exploitative aspect of the relationship between the Watutsi and the Bahutu was 'unquestionably worse' under colonial rule (*ibid.*, p. 123).

82 Ronald Cohen, 'The Kingship in Bornu', in Michael Crowder and Obaro Ikime, eds., *West African Chiefs*, p. 192.

3 Pressure groups, public policy and agricultural development

1 I omit from this discussion the subject of agricultural research. What little I know about it suggests that the pattern I observe in the markets for other inputs would obtain here as well.

2 Richard D. Wolff, *The Economics of Colonialism: Britain and Kenya, 1870–1930* (New Haven and London: Yale University Press, 1974), p. 98.

3 Roger van Zwanenberg, 'The Development of Peasant Commodity Production in Kenya, 1920–1940', *The Economic History Review*, 2nd ser., 27, 3 (August 1974): 445.

4 Wolff, *The Economics of Colonialism*, p. 99.

5 See the discussion of Labour Circular No. 1 of October 1919 in W. McGregor Ross, *Kenya From Within: A Short Political History* (London: George Allen and Unwin, 1927) and in Norman Leys, *Kenya* (London: Hogarth Press, 1924).

6 A detailed discussion is provided in P. S. Hammond, 'Cocoa [A. Agronomy]', in J. Brian

Wills, ed., *Agriculture and Land Use in Ghana* (London: Oxford University Press for the Ghana Ministry of Food and Agriculture, 1962), pp. 252–6.

7 M. P. K. Sorrenson, *The Origins of European Settlement in Kenya* (Nairobi: Oxford University Press, 1968), p. 141.

8 Supportive of this interpretation was the fact that the state later sought to recapture the land rents through a land tax; the introduction of this tax was successfully resisted by the large-scale producers.

9 Wolff, *The Economics of Colonialism*, p. 60; Norman Leys, *Kenya*, p. 279.

10 As Casely Hayford states with pardonable pride: 'As a matter of fact, the "lazy Fanti" is capable of putting forth effort amidst his own surroundings which men of no other race on earth can. Who, in truth, have been the pioneers and developers of the mahogany, gold, and rubber industries of the Gold Coast but the "lazy Fanti"?' Casely Hayford, *Gold Coast Native Institutions* (London: Sweet and Maxwell, 1893), p. 75.

11 For a charmingly old-fashioned account of the contributions of some of these gentlemen to public life, see Magnus J. Sampson, *Gold Coast Men of Affairs (Past and Present)* (London: Dawsons of Pall Mall, 1969).

12 The best accounts are contained in the works of Polly Hill. See Polly Hill, *The Gold Coast Farmer: A Preliminary Survey* (London: Oxford University Press, 1956) and Polly Hill, *The Migrant Cocoa Farmers of Southern Ghana: A Study in Rural Capitalism* (Cambridge: Cambridge University Press, 1963).

13 Quoted in W. K. Hancock, *Survey of British Commonwealth Affairs Volume II: Problems of Economic Policy, 1918–1939* (London: Oxford University Press, 1942), p. 185.

14 See the discussion in David Kimble, *A Political History of Ghana: The Rise of Gold Coast Nationalism, 1850–1928* (Oxford: The Clarendon Press, 1963).

15 Evidence of this is contained in the land prices published by Polly Hill; they tended to uniformity across a fairly large region of the interior and to respond 'correctly' to changes in the prices of the cash crops grown on them. (Hill, *The Migrant Cocoa Farmers*, p. 50.)

16 Elspeth Huxley, *White Man's Country*, II, 2nd edn (London: Chatto and Windus, 1953), pp. 95ff.

17 Ross, *Kenya From Within*, ch. 14.

18 E. A. Brett, *Colonialism and Underdevelopment in East Africa: The Politics of Economic Change, 1919–1939* (New York: NOK Publishers, 1973); see also M. F. Hill, *Permanent Way: The Story of the Kenya and Uganda Railway*, 2nd edn (Nairobi: East African Railways and Harbours, 1961) and Roger Gibb, *Report by Mr Roger Gibb on Railway Rates and Finance in Kenya, Uganda, and Tanganyika Territory: September 1931* (Cmd 4235) (London: His Majesty's Stationery Office, 1933).

19 Ronald James Church, 'The Railways of West Africa – A Geographical and Historical Analysis', Ph.D. Dissertation, University of London, 1936, pp. 129ff. An interesting reason for the subsequent concentration of railway extensions in the western region was the willingness of the mining companies to contribute directly to the costs of construction, either by providing written guarantees of traffic levels or by direct payment. See Church, 'The Railways of West Africa', pp. 133ff. The cocoa farmers, being smaller and more numerous, would find it more difficult to organize financing in this way.

20 See, the discussion in G. B. Kay, *The Political Economy of Colonialism in Ghana: A Collection of Documents and Statistics 1900–1960* (Cambridge: Cambridge University Press, 1972).

21 See, the discussion in Church, 'The Railways of West Africa', pp. 147ff and Kay, *The Political Economy of Colonialism*, pp. 137ff.

22 Gibb, *Report by Mr Roger Gibb*; Brett, *Colonialism and Underdevelopment*; and S. N. Hinga and Judith Heyer, 'The Development of Large Farms', in Judith Heyer, J. K. Maitha, and W. M. Senga, eds., *Agricultural Development in Kenya: An Economic Assessment* (Nairobi: Oxford University Press, 1976), pp. 222–64. It should also be noted that during the depression railway charges were rebated to producers.

23 It should be noted that two early investigations of the railways do in fact argue that cocoa was charged an excessively high rate – i.e., a rate that lay above the marginal costs of transporting it. Thus Hammond viewed the rate on cocoa as being set in a way that extracted the natural rent that accrued to cocoa growing in Ghana; he thus posited a monopoly premium on the price charged for the transport of cocoa; see Frederick Dawson Hammond, *Report on the Railway System of the Gold Coast* (London: the Crown Agents for the Colonies, 1922), pp. 66–7. Ormsby-Gore's famous dictum that 'cocoa and cocoa alone at present enables the railway to pay its way' only makes sense if cocoa were charged at a rate above the cost of transport, while other goods were charged at a rate that imposed losses on the railway; unfortunately, his report does not inspire confidence in his ability to draw a valid inference on the point; see W. G. A. Ormsby-Gore, *Report by the Hon. W. G. A. Ormsby-Gore, M.P., on his Visit to West Africa During the Year 1926* (Cmd 1744) (London: His Majesty's Stationery Office, 1926), p. 53.

24 See the discussion in Church, 'The Railways of West Africa', pp. 149ff; Kwamina Basumafi Dickson, *A Historical Geography of Ghana* (Cambridge: Cambridge University Press, 1969), p. 233; and Kay, *The Political Economy of Colonialism*, p. 194.

25 Discussions are contained in United Kingdom Government, *Report of the Commission on the Marketing of West African Cocoa* (Cmd 5845) (London: His Majesty's Stationery Office, 1938); and in Polly Hill's works, *The Gold Coast Farmer* and *The Migrant Cocoa Farmers*.

26 Hill, *The Gold Coast Farmer*, p. 56.

27 *ibid.*, p. 52.

28 Indeed, it was precisely such a reduction in the effective rate of interest that drove the local purchasers to turn against the export houses when they formed a cartel to purchase the 1937–8 cocoa crop. The local purchasers joined, and in many localities led, the efforts by the farmers to withhold the crop from the market, thereby driving the price back up – and the rate of interest as well (see United Kingdom, *Report of the Commission on the Marketing*).

29 Up to 50 per cent of the farmers in the same districts reputedly sold forward (United Kingdom, *Report of the Commission on the Marketing*, p. 31).

30 Elspeth Huxley, *No Easy Way: A History of the Kenya Farmers' Association and Unga Limited* (Nairobi: Private Printing, 1957), p. 74.

31 *ibid.*, p. 4.

32 *ibid.*, p. 116. This policy was technically difficult to implement. Many are skeptical of the impact on African maize production. But even those who are most skeptical, such as Munro, often conclude that the restrictions on maize marketing had a major, negative impact on the growth of commerce in the African reserves. If this is true, as Munro and others contend, then the restrictions on maize marketing must have been effective. See Winthrup Harold Munro, 'An Economic Study of Maize Marketing in Kenya, 1952–1966', Ph.D. Dissertation, Department of Economics, University of Michigan, 1973.

33 Huxley, *No Easy Way*, p. 137.

34 *ibid.*

35 The source of this information is A. A. Haller, 'Kenya's Maize Control: A Rejoinder to Mr Miracle's Article', *East African Economic Review*, 6, 2 (1959): 125–7.

36 The best information on the structure of markets in Kenya is contained in van Zwanenberg, *The Agricultural History of Kenya*; Brett, *Colonialism and Underdevelopment*; and Huxley, *No Easy Way*. See also L. Winston Cone and J. F. Lipscomb, *The History of Kenya Agriculture* (Nairobi: University Press of Africa, 1972) and William O. Jones, 'Agricultural Trade Within Tropical Africa: Historical Background', in Robert H. Bates and Michael F. Lofchie, eds., *Agricultural Development in Africa* (New York: Praeger Publishers, 1980), pp. 10–45.

37 As an example of the way in which the formation of shipping cartels furnished an incentive for the merchant houses to combine, we can note the following 'Report of the Commercial Bills Committee' of the Birmingham Chamber of Commerce of 10 April 1895; it was written

after E. L. Jones negotiated a rate agreement with a competing German line, Woermann Line, for the provision of services to West Africa. 'I understand that a settlement between the shipowners has now been arrived at which included the ... German lines ... The settlement is unfortunate inasmuch as it has taken the direction of leveling up the rates instead of leveling down as was hoped would have been the result of this foreign competition ... It is much to be regretted that in these matters merchants do not hold and work together with anything like the same amity as the shipowners so that although the merchants are numerically stronger and although their custom is indispensable to the shipowners they constantly allow themselves to be worsted in negotiations of this character ... Until therefore the merchants learn from experience a sensitivity of common purpose [in] any joint action it is perhaps only fair that they should meanwhile be subject to ... hiring conditions less advantageous than they would otherwise enjoy.' (From the files of Lance Davis and Robert Huttenback.)

38 See the discussion in United Kingdom, *Report of the Commission on the Marketing.*
39 Hancock, *Survey of British Commonwealth Affairs*, p. 207.
40 Merril Joseph Bateman, 'Cocoa in the Ghanaian Economy', Ph.D. Dissertation, Massachusetts Institute of Technology, 1965, p. 178.
41 See the discussion in Charlotte Leubuscher, *The West African Shipping Trade, 1909–1959* (Leyden: Sythoff-Leyden, 1963); P. N. Davies, *The Trade Makers: Elder Dempster in West Africa, 1852–1972* (London: Allen and Unwin, 1973); and Charles Wilson, *The History of Unilever*, I, II and III (New York: Frederick A. Praeger, 1968).
42 Allan McPhee, *The Economic Revolution in British West Africa* (London: G. Routledge and Sons, 1926), pp. 91ff.
43 Davies, *The Trade Makers*, pp. 186ff; see also Wilson, *The History of Unilever*, ch. 17.
44 During the attempted boycott of the farmers during the 1937–8 crop year, a sharp fall in the graded quality of the cocoa that was marketed was noted by the authorities. By June 1938, the proportion of grade I had fallen to 40 per cent from a level of 75 per cent in November of the previous year. The authorities attributed this decline in quality to deterioration from prolonged storage (see United Kingdom, *Report of the Commission on the Marketing*, p. 65).
45 Brett, *Colonialism and Underdevelopment*, p. 75.
46 Norman Leys, *Kenya*, p. 119.
47 Roger van Zwanenberg, with Anne King, *An Economic History of Kenya and Uganda: 1800–1970* (London: Macmillan, 1975), p. 37.
48 United Kingdom, *Report of the Commission on the Marketing*, pp. 17–18.
49 W. H. Beckett, *Akokoaso: A Survey of a Gold Coast Village* (London: Percy Lind for the London School of Economics and Political Science, 1944).
50 Hill, *The Gold Coast Farmer*, p. 87.
51 Huxley, *No Easy Way*, p. 14.
52 William Tordoff, *Ashanti Under the Prempehs: 1885–1935* (London: Oxford University Press, 1965), pp. 271ff.
53 Huxley, *White Man's Country.*
54 Sam Rhodie, 'The Gold Coast Cocoa Hold-up of 1930–31', *Transactions of the Historical Society of Ghana*, 9 (1968): 105–27.
55 *ibid.*, p. 115.
56 Hill, *The Migrant Cocoa Farmers*, p. 148.
57 Bateman, 'Cocoa in the Ghanaian Economy', p. 7.
58 Dickson, *A Historical Geography*, p. 147.
59 There was another important forest crop: rubber. We do know that the price per ton of rubber compared very favorably with the price for cocoa (Bateman, 'Cocoa in the Ghanaian Economy', p. 7). But we know a lot less about the costs of production of this crop, and so we cannot readily explain why people left it for the production of cocoa. One major reason may

have been the property rights over rubber trees. The literature suggests that the destructive management of the rubber trees increased the costs of production to the point where cocoa became the more attractive crop. And without some explanation based on property rights, it is difficult to explain why techniques of production were used that led to the destruction of the trees.

60 The Nowell Commission wrote: United Kingdom, *Report of the Commission on the Marketing*.

61 Materials on this subject may be gleaned from Martin Wight, *Studies in Colonial Legislatures, vol. II, The Gold Coast Legislative Council* (London: Faber and Faber, 1946); David Kimble, *A Political History of Ghana* (Oxford: The Clarendon Press, 1963); Marjorie Ruth Dilley, *British Policy in Kenya Colony* (New York: Thomas Nelson and Sons, 1937); and George Bennett, 'The Development of Political Organizations in Kenya', *Political Studies*, 5, 2 (1957): 113–30; *Kenya: A Political History* (London: Oxford University Press, 1963); and 'Settlers and Politics in Kenya', in Vincent Harlow *et al.*, eds., *History of East Africa*, II (Oxford: The Clarendon Press, 1965), pp. 263–332.

62 Brett, *Colonialism and Underdevelopment*, p. 194.

63 Dilley, *British Policy in Kenya Colony*, p. 89.

64 Wight, *Studies in Colonial Legislatures*, p. 158.

65 Huxley, *White Man's Country*, II, p. 88.

66 Wight, *Studies in Colonial Legislatures*, p. 92. The government pledged, however, never to use its official majority to override the unanimous opposition of the unofficial representatives of African and European interests. This pledge was nugatory, however, as Wight's analysis of the voting of African and European members of the Legislative Council reveals that they never voted as a bloc (*ibid.*, pp. 89–95).

67 *ibid.*, pp. 136–7.

68 Bennett, *Kenya: A Political History*, pp. 39–40.

69 Wight, *Studies in Colonial Legislatures*, p. 134.

70 This is supported by materials contained in the notes taken from the Minute Books of the various chambers of commerce by Lance Davis and Robert Huttenback.

71 Report on Delegation to Lord Kimberley at the Colonial Office, 28 May 1873; Minutes of the Manchester Chamber of Commerce, from the files of Lance Davis and Robert Huttenback.

72 Wight, *Studies in Colonial Legislatures*, p. 75.

73 United Kingdom, *Report of the Commission on the Marketing*, p. 52.

74 *ibid.*, p. 53.

75 *ibid.* See also Josephine Milburn, 'The 1938 Gold Coast Cocoa Crisis: British Business and the Colonial Office', *African Historical Studies*, 3, 1 (1970): 57–74.

76 M. P. K. Sorrenson, *The Origins of European Settlement in Kenya* (Nairobi: Oxford University Press, 1968), p. 87.

77 Bennett, 'Settlers and Politics in Kenya', p. 278.

78 Brett, *Colonialism and Underdevelopment*, p. 201.

79 Gibb, *Report by Mr Roger Gibb*, p. 8.

80 *ibid.*, p. 15.

81 Huxley, *No Easy Way*, p. 45.

82 C. C. Wrigley, 'Kenya: The Pattern of Economic Life', in Vincent Harlow and E. M. Chilver, eds., *History of Africa* (Oxford: The Clarendon Press, 1965), p. 236.

4 The commercial rise of agriculture and the rise of rural political protest

1 For discussions of the history of the commercialization of African agriculture, see Jan S. Hogendorn, 'Economic Initiative and African Cash Farming: Pre-Colonial Origins and Early Colonial Development', in Peter Duignan and L. H. Gann, eds., *Colonialism in*

Africa 1870–1960, vol. 4, The Economics of Colonialism (Cambridge: Cambridge University Press, 1975), pp. 283–328; Anthony G. Hopkins, *An Economic History of West Africa* (New York: Columbia University Press, 1973); Bruce F. Johnston, 'Changes in Agricultural Productivity', in Melville J. Herskovits and Mitchell Horwitz, eds., *Economic Transition in Africa* (Evanston: Northwestern University Press, 1964), pp. 151–78; Allan McPhee, *The Economic Revolution in British West Africa* (London: G. Routledge and Sons, 1926); Charles Wilson, *The History of Unilever*, I, II, and III (New York: Frederick A. Praeger, 1968); and Richard D. Wolff, *The Economics of Colonialism: Britain and Kenya* (New Haven and London: Yale University Press, 1974). See also such government reports as Board of Trade, *Memorandum on Transport Development and Cotton Growing in East Africa* (Cmd 2463) (London: His Majesty's Stationery Office, 1925).

2 See the discussion in P. T. Bauer, *West African Trade: A Study of Competition, Oligopoly and Monopoly in a Changing Economy* (London: Routledge and Kegan Paul, 1963); Josephine Milburn, 'The 1938 Gold Coast Crisis: British Business and the Colonial Office', *African Historical Studies, 3*, 1 (1970): 57–74; and United Kingdom Government, *Report of the Commission on the Marketing of West African Cocoa* (Cmd 5845) (London: His Majesty's Stationery Office, 1938).

3 The magnitude of the monopsony rents is suggested in the rapidly rising price of options to purchase licensed gins. See G. Andrew Maguire, *Toward 'Uhuru' in Tanzania* (Cambridge: Cambridge University Press, 1969), p. 86.

4 Cyril Ehrlich, 'The Ugandan Economy: 1903–1945', in Vincent Harlow and E. M. Chilver, eds., *History of East Africa*, II (Oxford: The Clarendon Press, 1965), p. 466.

5 See the discussion in Maguire, *Toward 'Uhuru' in Tanzania*.

6 See Uganda Protectorate, *Report of the Commission of Inquiry into the Disturbances in Uganda During April, 1949* (Entebbe: Government Printer, 1950). It should also be noted that the cooperative unions in fact bought into the cartel. Rather than breaking up the monopsony and securing a competitive market, they simply secured ginning capacity within the structure of the market as mandated by colonial law. The result was that the cooperative societies ended up accumulating monopsony profits on their milling operations from their own cotton-growing members. See the discussion in Lionel Cliffe and J. S. Saul, 'The District Development Front in Tanzania', in Lionel Cliffe and John S. Saul, eds., *Socialism in Tanzania*, 1 (Nairobi: East African Publishing House, 1972), pp. 302–28; and John S. Saul, 'Marketing Cooperatives in a Developing Country: The Tanzanian Case', in Lionel Cliffe and John S. Saul, eds., *Socialism in Tanzania*, 2 (Nairobi: East African Publishing House, 1973), pp. 141–52.

7 See the discussion in Roland Young and Henry Fosbrooke, *Smoke in the Hills* (Evanston: Northwestern University Press, 1960).

8 An excellent review is contained in Lionel Cliffe, 'Nationalism and the Reaction to Enforced Agricultural Change in Tanganyika During the Colonial Period', *Taamuli*, 1 (July 1970): 1–15.

9 See the discussion contained in J. Brian Wills, ed., *Agriculture and Land Use in Ghana* (London: Oxford University Press, 1962).

10 Christopher Beer, *The Politics of Peasant Groups in Western Nigeria* (Ibadan: Ibadan University Press, 1976), p. 55.

11 *ibid.*, p. 60.

12 Kwamina Basumafi Dickson, 'Cocoa in Ghana', Ph.D. Dissertation, University of London, 1960, p. 275.

13 See the discussion in United Kingdom, *Report of the Commission of Inquiry into Disturbances in the Gold Coast, 1948* (Colonial No. 321) (London: His Majesty's Stationery Office, 1948).

14 Cliffe, 'Nationalism and the Reaction to Enforced Agricultural Change'; Maguire, *Toward 'Uhuru' in Tanzania*; and Peter F. M. McLoughlin, 'Agricultural Development in

Sukumaland', in John C. deWilde, ed., *Experiences With Agricultural Development in Tropical Africa*, 2 (Baltimore: Johns Hopkins University Press, 1967).

15 Robert H. Bates, *Rural Responses to Industrialization: A Study of Village Zambia* (New Haven and London: Yale University Press, 1978).

16 See the discussion in P. T. Bauer and B. S. Yamey, 'The Economics of Marketing Reform', *Journal of Political Economy*, 62 (1954): 210–35. They argue that there is in fact no problem here, save that of the stupidity of the government; for if there were a demand for a high-quality product, they argue, then the purchasers would offer a premium for it. They are both right and wrong. They are right, in this instance, concerning the acuity of the governments; they are wrong in thinking that the purchaser would offer an appropriate spectrum of prices. For, over the period in which the issue of quality control was most prominent, it was in fact the governments themselves who were buying the output of the cash-crop producers. This period was the 1940s and, in some instances, the early 1950s, when the colonial governments purchased the full national output under terms of bulk-buying agreements. Presumably, following the termination of these agreements, the market established price gradations reflecting the relative value of different qualities of output, and the need for public controls to secure high quality declined. This may account for the apparent reduction in the significance of this issue in the rural politics of Africa. It should also be stressed, however, that the governmental emphasis on quality standards both ante-dates and post-dates the period of the bulk-buying agreements.

17 Factors other than externalities made the imposition of regulations a political issue. The people did not like being coerced, plain and simple. They did not like the fact that the regulations were often imposed upon them without prior consulation and without soliciting the input of producers in the planning process. Moreover, the regulations were often poorly designed. They were developed on the basis of the average producer and thus often made little sense. For example, imposing the same percentage reduction in herd size on farmers in the lushest grazing areas, as on the farmers in arid zones, had little justification. The regulations were often insensitive to the interdependence of the production process. Building up herds served as a hedge on the production of food crops, which were periodically threatened by drought, for example; and limiting the production of cattle without adjusting for the increased risks to the farmer lowered his welfare. Lastly, some of the measures were simply destructive; digging bench terracing often brought to the surface sterile soils, and so reduced the productivity of gardens. For all these reasons, in addition to the problems arising from externalities, the regulations were unpopular.

18 See M. P. K. Sorrenson, *Land Reform in Kikuyu Country: A Study in Government Policy* (Nairobi: Oxford University Press, 1967) and *Origins of European Settlement in Kenya* (Nairobi: Oxford University Press, 1968). See also Carl G. Rosberg, Jr, and John Nottingham, *The Myth of 'Mau Mau'* (New York: Frederick A. Praeger, 1966).

19 See the discussion in David Kimble, *A Political History of Ghana: The Rise of Gold Coast Nationalism, 1850–1928* (Oxford: The Clarendon Press, 1963).

20 See, for example, Jean Stengers, 'The Congo Free State and the Belgian Congo Before 1914', in Peter Duignan and L. H. Gann, eds., *Colonialism in Africa 1870–1960, vol. 1, The History and Politics of Colonialism 1870–1914* (Cambridge: Cambridge University Press, 1969), pp. 261–92.

21 The best discussions are contained in Terrence J. Johnson, 'An Analysis of Southern Gold Coast Riots 1890–1920', *Economy and Society*, 1, 2 (1972): 164–93; Martin L. Kilson, 'Nationalism and Social Classes in British West Africa', *The Journal of Politics*, 20, 2 (1958): 368–87; Dennis Austin, *Politics in Ghana, 1946–1960* (London: Oxford University Press, 1970); K. A. Busia, *The Position of the Chief in the Modern Political System of Ashanti* (London: Oxford University Press, 1951); and Jarle Simensen, 'Rural Mass Action in the Context of Anti-Colonial Protest', *The Canadian Journal of African Studies*, 8, 1 (1974): 25–41.

22 See R. C. Pratt, 'Administration and Politics in Uganda, 1919–1945', in Vincent Harlow and E. M. Chilver, eds., *History of East Africa*, 2 (Oxford: The Clarendon Press, 1965); and Ehrlich, 'The Ugandan Economy'.

23 One example of this is the struggle between the outlying cocoa districts and the Ashanti Confederacy Council, which sought to extend its fiscal jurisdiction over these areas and so centralize the revenues derived from the commercial utilization of land. See John Dunn and A. F. Robertson, *Dependence and Opportunity: Political Change in Ahafo* (Cambridge: Cambridge University Press, 1973). Another example would be Nana Ofori Atta's attempt to expand the power of the Omanhene of Akim Abuakwa, and thereby lay hold of the revenues being generated by the richest cocoa lands of his time. See Hill, *The Migrant Cocoa Farmers*, p. 148.

24 See the materials in United Kingdom, *Report on the Legislation Governing the Alienation of Native Lands in the Gold Coast Colony and Ashanti* (Cd 6278) (London: His Majesty's Stationery Office, 1912) and United Kingdom, *Report of the Commission of Inquiry into Disturbances in the Gold Coast, 1948* (Colonial no. 321) (London: His Majesty's Stationery Office, 1948). See also the materials in Polly Hill, *The Migrant Cocoa-Farmers of Southern Ghana: A Study in Rural Capitalism* (Cambridge: Cambridge University Press, 1963). As Busia has noted 'The earlier land disputes settled by Government clearly show the relation between litigation about land and the new industries which enhanced its economic value. Earlier settlements of boundary disputes are tabulated below. [They] indicate . . . that most litigation took place in the mining and cocoa areas in South Ashanti' (*The Position of the Chief*, p. 205).

25 See Pratt, 'Administration and Politics'.

26 See the discussion in Greta Kershaw, 'The Land is the People: A Study of Kikuyu Social Organization in Historical Perspective', Ph.D. Dissertation, University of Chicago, 1972; and in Sorrenson, *Land Reform in Kikuyu Country*.

27 See the discussion in Lionel Cliffe, 'The Policy of Ujamaa Vijijini and the Class Struggle in Tanzania', in Lionel Cliffe and John S. Saul, eds., *Socialism in Tanzania*, 2 (Nairobi: East African Publishing House, 1973) pp. 141–52; John S. Saul, 'Marketing Cooperatives in A Developing Country: The Tanzanian Case', in Lionel Cliffe and John S. Saul, eds., *Socialism in Tanzania*, 1 (Nairobi: East African Publishing House, 1973), pp. 141–52; Michaela von Freyhold, *Ujamaa Villages in Tanzania* (New York and London: Monthly Review Press, 1979).

28 Kimble, *A Political History of Ghana*, p. 182.

29 *ibid.*, p. 190.

30 Martin L. Kilson, 'Nationalism and Social Classes in British West Africa', *The Journal of Politics*, 20, 2 (1958): 368–87; 'Grass-Roots Politics in Africa: Local Government in Sierra Leone', *Political Studies*, 12 (1964): 47–66; and *Political Change in a West African State: A Study of the Modernization Process in Sierra Leone* (Cambridge, Mass.: Harvard University Press, 1966).

31 William Tordoff, *Ashanti Under the Prempehs: 1885–1935* (London: Oxford University Press, 1965), p. 192.

32 Busia, *The Position of the Chief*, p. 165.

33 See also Simensen, 'Rural Mass Action in the Context of Anti-Colonial Protest'.

34 W. McGregor Ross, *Kenya From Within* (London: George Allen and Unwin, 1927), p. 153.

35 *ibid.*, p. 154.

36 Kimble, *A Political History of Ghana*, p. 182.

37 United Kingdom, *Report on the Legislation Governing the Alienation of Native Lands in the Gold Coast Colony and Ashanti* (Cmd 6278) (London: His Majesty's Stationery Office, 1938) and *Report of the Commission of Inquiry into Expenses Incurred by Litigants in the Courts of the Gold Coast and Indebtedness Caused Thereby* (Accra: Government Printing Department, 1945). Several institutional changes were innovated in an attempt to

ameliorate this crisis. One was the selection of wealthy persons as chiefs, the winning candidate being one who would pay off the public debt. Another was making the undertaking of a law suit contingent under the plaintiff's willingness then to assume the stool and to retire the debt it had incurred in clarifying its jurisdiction over his lands.

5 The nature and origins of agricultural policies in Africa

1 Frantz Fanon, *The Wretched of the Earth* (New York: Grove Press, 1965), p. 95.
2 *ibid.*, p. 97.
3 *ibid.*, p. 102.
4 Peter E. Temu, 'Marketing Board Pricing and Storage Policy with Particular Reference to Maize in Tanzania', Ph.D. Dissertation, Stanford University, 1975, p. 12.
5 For an important discussion, see William O. Jones, 'Agricultural Trade Within Tropical Africa: Historical Background', in Robert H. Bates and Michael F. Lofchie, eds., *Agricultural Development in Africa: Issues of Public Policy* (New York: Praeger Publishers, 1980), pp. 10–45.
6 See the data contained in Robert H. Bates, *Markets and States in Tropical Africa: The Political Basis of Agricultural Policies* (Berkeley and Los Angeles: University of California Press, 1981).
7 See, for example, Western Nigeria, Ministry of Trade and Industry, *Report of the Commission of Inquiry into the Alleged Failure or Miscarriage of Plans to Effect a Revision of the Producer Price of Cocoa in January 1961* (Ibadan: Ministry of Trade and Industry, 1962).
8 See Bjorn Beckman, *Organizing the Farmers: Cocoa Politics and National Development in Ghana* (New York: Holmes and Meier, 1976), p. 199 and G. M. Helleiner, *Peasant Agriculture, Government and Economic Growth in Nigeria* (Homewood, Ill.: Richard D. Irwin, 1966), p. 171.
9 See H. M. A. Onitiri and Dupe Olatunbosun, *The Marketing Board System* (Ibadan: Nigerian Institute of Social and Economic Research, 1974).
10 See, for example, David Walker and Cyril Ehrlich, 'Stabilization and Development Policy in Uganda: An Appraisal', *Kyklos*, 12 (1959): 341–53.
11 See, for example, the discussions in Kodwo Ewusi, *Economic Inequality in Ghana* (Legon, Ghana: Institute of Statistical, Social and Economic Research, University of Ghana, 1977); W. Edmund Clark, *Socialist Development and Public Investment in Tanzania, 1964–1973* (Toronto: University of Toronto Press, 1978); and Robert H. Bates, *Rural Responses to Industrialization: A Study of Village Zambia* (New Haven and London: Yale University Press, 1976).
12 Tanzania, 'Price Policy Recommendations for the 1978/79 Agricultural Price Review', Annex 9, Sisal (mimeographed, 1977) and 'Price Policy Recommendations for the 1978/79 Agricultural Price Review', Annex 10, Coffee (mimeographed, 1977).
13 See the discussion in Leslie E. Grayson, *Managing the Economic Development of Ghana* (Charlottesville: Printing Services of the University of Virginia, 1979) and Tony Killick, *Development Economics in Action* (New York: St Martin's Press, 1978).
14 Sayre P. Schatz, *Nigerian Capitalism* (Berkeley and Los Angeles: University of California Press, 1977).
15 Nicola Swainson, *Development of Corporate Capitalism in Kenya 1918–1977* (Berkeley and Los Angeles: University of California Press, 1980) and Carolyn Baylies, 'The State and Class Formation in Zambia', 2 vols., Ph.D. Dissertation, University of Michigan, 1978.
16 *Africa Business*, February 1980.
17 See the evidence in Federation of Nigeria, *Report of the Coker Commission of Enquiry into the Affairs of Certain Statutory Corporations in Western Nigeria* (Lagos: Government Printer, 1962).

18 For Kenya, see Clive S. Gray, 'Costs, Prices and Market Structure in Kenya' (mimeographed, 1977) and Jennifer Sharpley, 'Intersectoral Capital Flows and Economic Development in Kenya', Ph.D. Dissertation, Northwestern University, 1976; for Ghana, Beckman, *Organizing the Farmers*; for Nigeria, Jerome C. Wells, *Agricultural Policy and Economic Growth in Nigeria, 1962–68* (Ibadan: Oxford University Press for the Nigerian Institute of Social and Economic Research, 1974); for Tanzania, see Herbert C. Kriesel *et al.*, *Agricultural Marketing in Tanzania* (East Lansing, Michigan: Michigan State University, 1970) and Tanzania, 'Price Policy Recommendations for the 1978/79 Agricultural Price Review', 2, Review of the New Crop Buying Arrangements (mimeographed, 1977) and *Report of the Special Committee of Enquiry into Cooperative Movement and Marketing Boards* (Dar es Salaam: Government Printer, 1966).

19 Republic of Ghana, *Report of the Commission of Enquiry into the Local Purchasing of Cocoa* (Accra: Government Printer, 1967), p. 28.

20 *West Africa*, 27 November 1978: 2386.

21 *African Business*, January 1980.

22 The Maize and Produce Board of Kenya was in fact established to do the opposite: to control marketing so as to enable the local price to lie above the world price. But in recent years the Board has acted to restrain price increases. The adoption of hybrid seeds in the late 1970s led to rapid increases in maize supplies and to a fall in maize prices. With a glut market, the Board was both unable and unwilling to restrict the marketing of maize. Recent food shortages in Kenya have led to strong criticisms of maize exports and the Board is now being pressed to reduce exports and to expedite imports so as to lower the price of maize. Under conditions of rising prices, moreover, it is again attempting to regulate internal marketing. The Board has thus been recast as an instrument for lowering rather than increasing farm prices. For a summary of Parliamentary debates in Kenya concerning the role of the Board, see *The Weekly Review*, 4 July 1980.

23 Temu, 'Marketing Board Pricing and Storage Policy'; see also William O. Jones, *Marketing Staple Food Crops in Tropical Africa* (Ithaca and London: Cornell University Press, 1972).

24 Good discussions are contained in John Alfred Dadson, 'Socialized Agriculture in Ghana, 1962–1965', Ph.D. Dissertation, Department of Economics, Harvard University, 1970; J. Gordon, 'State Farms in Ghana', in A. H. Bunting, ed., *International Seminar on Change in Agriculture* (New York: Praeger Publishers, 1970); Frances Hill, 'Experiments with a Public Sector Peasantry', *African Studies Review*, 20, 3 (1977): 25–41; V. K. Nyanteng, 'Ghana: A Country Review Paper', Presented to the World Congress of Agrarian Reform and Rural Development (The Hague, Netherlands, 1979); Marvin P. Miracle and Ann Seidman, 'State Farms in Ghana', Paper no. 43 (Madison, Wis.: Land Tenure Center of the University of Wisconsin, 1968); Werner Roider, *Farm Settlements for Socio-Economic Development: The Western Nigerian Case* (München: Weltforum Verlag, 1971).

25 See Tony Killick, *Development Economics in Action* (New York: St Martin's Press, 1978); John C. deWilde, 'Price Incentives and African Agricultural Development', Paper presented to the Spring Seminar of the African Studies Program of the University of California at Los Angeles, 1977; and Doris Jansen Dodge, *Agricultural Policy and Performance in Zambia* (Berkeley, Calif.: Institute of International Studies, 1977).

26 Dodge, *Agricultural Policy*; Sharpley, 'Intersectoral Capital Flows'; and Tanzania, 'Price Policy Recommendations for the 1978/79 Agricultural Price Review', I, Summary and Price Proposals (mimeographed, 1977).

27 International Coffee Organization, *Coffee in Kenya, 1977* (London: International Coffee Organization, 1978).

28 See the data contained in Appendix B in Bates, *Markets and States*.

29 *ibid.*

30 *African Business*, May 1979.

31 C. K. Kline *et al.*, *Agricultural Mechanization in Equatorial Africa* (East Lansing: Michigan State University, 1969) and J. Dirck Stryker, 'Ghana Agriculture', Paper prepared for the West African Regional Project, 1975.

32 See, for example, David O. Ekhomu, 'National Food Policies and Bureaucracies in Nigeria', Paper presented at the African Studies Association Convention, Baltimore, Maryland, 1978.

33 *West Africa*, 3 April 1978; United States Agency for International Development, *Development Assistance Program FY 1976 – FY 1980, Ghana*, 4, Annex D – Agricultural Sector (Accra: USAID, 1975).

34 Ekhomu, 'National Food Policies'; also Janet Girdner and Victor Olorunsula, 'National Food Policies and Organizations in Ghana', Paper presented to the Annual Meeting of the American Political Science Association, New York, 1978.

35 Apollo I. Njonjo, 'The Africanization of the "White Highlands": A Study in Agrarian Class Struggles in Kenya, 1950–1974', Ph.D. Dissertation, Princeton University, 1977.

36 John Cohen and Dov Weintraub, *Land and Peasants in Imperial Ethiopia: The Social Background to Revolution* (Assen: Van Gorcum, 1975).

37 Donal B. Cruise O'Brien, *The Mourides of Senegal: The Political And Economic Organization of an Islamic Brotherhood* (Oxford: The Clarendon Press, 1971).

38 In many credit programs, the collection rate for large farmers is often lower than that for small-scale producers; the latter in effect subsidize the interest rate offered to the former. In Tanzania, the subsidy for fertilizer is paid from the earnings of the government monopsony; as the levies are raised from all farmers and fertilizer employed disproportionately by the more 'advanced', the subsidy program represents a transfer from small to large farmers. When cooperative societies serve as the marketing channels for produce and for inputs, studies have shown that, once again, it is the larger farmers who secure the bulk of the inputs distributed by the societies; but the deductions from crop sales that finance these services are imposed on all farmers. Once again the result is a redistribution of income.

39 See David Leonard, *Reaching the Peasant Farmer* (Chicago and London: University of Chicago Press, 1977) and H. U. E. Van Velzen, 'Staff, Kulaks and Peasants', in Lionel Cliffe and John Saul, *Socialism in Africa*, 2 (Dar es Salaam: East African Publishing House, 1973).

40 See Stryker, 'Ghana Agriculture'; Scott R. Pearson *et al.*, 'Incentives and Comparative Advantage in Ghanaian Industry and Agriculture', paper prepared for the West African Regional Project, 1976; International Bank for Reconstruction and Development, *Kenya: Into the Second Decade* (Baltimore: Johns Hopkins University Press, 1975) and *Ivory Coast: The Challenge of Success* (Baltimore: Johns Hopkins University Press, 1978); and International Labor Organization, 'Technical Paper No. 17 – Incentives for Resource Allocation', in *Growth, Employment and Equity: A Comprehensive Strategy for the Sudan*, II (Geneva: International Labor Organization, 1975).

41 This figure is offered for state enterprises in Ghana in 1966 by Tony Killick in *Development Economics in Action*, p. 171.

42 Quoted in *ibid.*, p. 185.

43 *West Africa*, 16 October 1978.

44 Relevant here are the analyses of the terms of trade between agriculture and industry. See the data in Dodge, *Agricultural Policy*; Sharpley, 'Intersectoral Capital Flows'; Killick, *Development Economics in Action*; and Fabian J. M. Maimbo and James Fry, 'An Investigation into the Changes in the Terms of Trade Between the Rural and Urban Sectors of Zambia', *African Social Research*, 12 (1971): 95–110.

45 Studies in other areas suggest that this configuration of decisions is common in the developing nations. See Raj Krishna, 'Agricultural Price Policy and Economic Development' in Herman M. Southworth and Bruce F. Johnston, eds., *Agricultural Development and Economic Growth* (Ithaca: Cornell University Press, 1967); United States General

Accounting Office, *Disincentives to Agricultural Production in Developing Countries* (Washington, D.C.: General Accounting Office, 1975); Keith Griffin, *The Green Revolution: An Economic Analysis* (Geneva: United Nations Research Institute, 1972); Carl Gotsch and Gilbert Brown, 'Prices, Taxes and Subsidies in Pakistan Agriculture, 1960–1976', World Bank Staff Working Paper no. 387 (Washington, D.C.: The World Bank, 1980); and Michael Lipton, *Why Poor People Stay Poor: Urban Bias in World Development* (Cambridge, Mass.: Harvard University Press, 1977). Indeed, it is argued by some that the principal problems bedeviling agriculture in the developing areas originate from 'bad' public policies. In the words of Schultz, given the right incentives, farmers in the developing world would 'turn sand into gold'. See Theodore W. Schultz, *Transforming Traditional Agriculture* (New York: Arno Press, 1976). Distortions introduced into agricultural markets by governments, he contends, furnish the most important reasons for their failure to do so. Theodore W. Schultz, ed., *Distortions of Agricultural Incentives* (Bloomington, Ind.: Indiana University Press, 1978). While Schultz's position is perhaps an extreme one, it none the less underscores the importance of understanding why third world governments, including African governments, select this characteristic pattern of agricultural policies.

46 Hiromitsu Kaneda and Bruce F. Johnston, 'Urban Food Expenditure Patterns in Tropical Africa', *Food Research Institute Studies*, 2, 3 (1961): 229–75.

47 See, for example, Federation of Nigeria, *Public Service Review Commission: Main Report (Udoji Report)* (Lagos: Government Printer, 1974); Federation of Nigeria, *Second and Final Report of the Wages and Salaries Review Commission, 1970–71 (Adebo Report)* (Lagos: Government Printer, 1975); and Federation of Nigeria, *The Attack on Inflation: Government Views on the First Report of the Anti-Inflation Task Force* (Lagos: Government Printer, 1975).

48 Robert H. Bates and William P. Rogerson, 'Agriculture in Development: A Coalitional Analysis', *Public Choice*, 35, 5 (1980): 513–28.

49 The assumption that people specialize in production and generalize in consumption generates one further assumption that is critical to the results of this model: that people petition for price rises in the goods they make but do not petition against the price rises demanded by others. Given our initial assumption, people will be more affected by a rise in the price of the commodity they make than by a change in the price of any commodity which they consume; and, given limited resources with which to lobby, they can better increase their real income by seeking increases in the price of their products than by opposing the price increases sought by others. That demands for, rather than against, price increases dominate lobbying efforts is well documented in Schattschneider's classic study of tariff making in the United States, E. E. Schattschneider, *Politics, Pressures and the Tariff* (New York: Arno Press, 1974). It was also confirmed in my interviews with members of the Price and Income Board in Ghana; they emphasized that 'opposition' to others' price increases took the form of demands for offsetting increases in the prices of their own commodities.

The critical role of the assumption that people lobby for but not against price increases can be seen in the fact that without it people outside the 'winning' coalition could 'vote' against the allocation proposed by that coalition; there would be no natural tendency for the 'least cost' coalition – the coalition of persons with the lowest 'αs' – to form. This possibility is in fact realized in many legislative settings. The American legislature, for example, is characterized by several basic institutions. One is a fiscal institution: projects which confer particular benefits are paid for by general taxation. Another is that all persons can vote and they can vote for or against any proposal. Particular-benefit, general-taxation fiscal policies generate political dynamics very similar to those analyzed in this model, where the rise in the price of one person's good imposes costs upon all other actors. But, because in legislatures persons can vote against as well as for proposed measures, those hurt by a proposal can defeat it by voting against it. The least-cost, minimal-winning coalition (which forms in our model) therefore tends, in legislative settings, not to form. Programs, in order to pass, can not be minimum-winning; instead they have to be 'log-rolled' and all-inclusive.

50 See Bates and Rogerson, 'Agriculture in Development'; Schultz, ed., *Distortion of Agricultural Incentives*; and Yujiro Hayami, 'Japan's Rice Policy in Historical Perspective', *Food Research Studies*, 14, 4 (1975): 359–80.

51 See, for example, Dadson, 'Socialized Agriculture in Ghana', and Wells, *Agricultural Policy and Economic Growth in Nigeria*.

52 Cruise O'Brien, *The Mourides*.

53 Ghana, *Report of the Commission of Enquiry into the Affairs of the Cocoa Purchasing Company* (Accra: Government Printer, 1956).

54 Anne O. Krueger, 'The Political Economy of the Rent-Seeking Society', *American Economic Review*, 64, 3 (1974): 291–301 and Richard A. Posner, 'The Social Costs of Monopoly and Regulation', *Journal of Political Economy*, 83, 4 (1975): 807–27.

55 Kenya, *Report of the Maize Commission of Inquiry, June 1966* (Nairobi: Government Printer, 1966).

56 In Zambia, one of the cooperative societies which I studied in Luapula purchased the subsidized fertilizers. It then reaped the rental premium associated with the subsidy by selling the fertilizer at market-clearing prices to the local commercial farmers.

57 Robert H. Bates, *Rural Responses to Industrialization: A Study of Village Zambia* (London and New Haven: Yale University Press, 1976).

58 Frantz Fanon, *The Wretched of the Earth* (New York: Grove Press, 1965).

Conclusion

1 For representative works, see William H. Riker, *The Theory of Political Coalitions* (New Haven and London: Yale University Press, 1962); Mancur Olson, *The Logic of Collective Action* (Cambridge, Mass.: Harvard University Press, 1965); Thomas C. Schelling, *The Strategy of Conflict* (New York: Oxford University Press, 1963); and *Micromotives and Macrobehavior* (New York: W. W. Norton, 1978); Anthony Downs, *An Economic Theory of Democracy* (New York: Harper and Row, 1957); James M. Buchanan and Gordon Tullock, *The Calculus of Consent* (Ann Arbor: University of Michigan Press, 1962). For a review of these and other contributions, see William H. Riker and Peter C. Ordeshook, *An Introduction to Positive Political Theory* (Englewood Cliffs, N. J.: Prentice Hall, 1973); for a critical review, see Brian M. Barry, *Sociologists, Economists, and Democracy* (London: Collier-Macmillan, 1970).

2 A highly accessible treatment of 'rational ignorance' is contained in Downs, *An Economic Theory*. For a somewhat more technical but still introductory treatment, see Herman Chernoff and Lincoln Moses, *Elementary Decision Theory* (New York: John Wiley and Sons, 1967).

3 An example is the so-called 'dominated winner paradox' offered by Peter Fishburn in his article 'Paradoxes of Voting', *American Political Science Review*, 68 (1974): 537–47 and discussed by Kenneth A. Shepsle and Barry R. Weingast in their paper, 'Rational Choice Explanations of Social Facts', Working Paper for the Center for the Study of American Business, Washington University, St Louis, May 1981. The procedure is based on majority rule and involves the sequential elimination of alternative resolutions. A vote is taken between the first two alternatives. The majority loser is eliminated and the winner paired against the next alternative. The process is continued until the last alternative enters the voting; the survivor is then declared the winner. Let the order of alternatives be x first, then a, then b, and then y. And consider the three voters with the following preferences:

voter 1: $x y b a$ (read: x is preferred to y which is preferred to b which is preferred to a.)
voter 2: $a x y b$
voter 3: $b a x y$

In the first vote, *a* beats *x* (since voters 2 and 3 prefer *a* to *x* and the majority rules); *a* then loses to *b* and *b* in turn loses to *y*. Thus, *y* is the winner. But *y* has the perverse property that *every* voter prefers *x* to *y*.

4 This is a statement of consistent rationality. As a condition on individual preference orderings, it merely requires that they be acyclic. See A. K. Sen, *Collective Choice and Social Welfare* (San Francisco: Holden-Day, 1970). Quasi-transitive and transitive rationality are more demanding; but, for many purposes, consistent rationality is all that is required.

5 See the expository treatment offered in James Quirk and Rubin Saposnik, *Introduction to General Equilibrium Theory and Welfare Economics* (Homewood, Ill.: Richard D. Irwin, 1969).

6 Michael P. Todaro, *Economic Development in the Third World* (London and New York: Longman, 1977), p. 9.

7 Kenneth Arrow, *Social Choice and Individual Values* (New York: John Wiley and Sons, 1963). See also the more accessible discussion in A. K. Sen, *Collective Choice and Social Welfare*, and the highly accessible 'Vickery Proof' outlined in Dennis Mueller, *Public Choice* (Cambridge: Cambridge University Press, 1979).

8 A useful review is Mueller, *Public Choice*.

9 See, for example, the so-called 'Clark tax' discussed in Nicholas Tideman, 'Introduction' in *Public Choice*, 29, 2 (1977): 1–14.

10 See the review contained in Riker and Ordeshook, *An Introduction to Positive Political Theory*. See also Cornelius Cotter *et al.*, eds., *Political Science Annual, V: Collective Decision Making* (Indianapolis: Bobbs-Merrill, 1973), and especially the chapter by Kenneth Shepsle entitled 'Theories of Collective Choice'. For more recent work on legislatures, see Morris P. Fiorina, *Congress: Keystone of the Washington Establishment* (New Haven and London: Yale University Press, 1977) and recent papers: Barry R. Weingast, Kenneth A. Shepsle and Christopher Johnsen, 'The Political Economy of Benefits and Costs', *Journal of Political Economy* (forthcoming); Randall L. Calvert and Barry Weingast, 'Congress, the Bureaucracy, and Regulatory Reform', Paper prepared for Delivery at the Second Annual Meeting of the Association for Public Policy Analysis and Management, Boston, 23–5 October 1980. See also Morris P. Fiorina and Roger G. Noll, 'Voters, Legislators, and Bureaucrats', *Journal of Public Economics*, 9 (1978): 239–54.

11 See, for example, Maurice Godelier, *Rationality and Irrationality in Economics* (London: New Left Books, 1972) and *Perspectives in Marxist Anthropology* (Cambridge: Cambridge University Press, 1977); Emmanuel Terray, *Marxism and 'Primitive' Societies* (New York: Monthly Review Press, 1972); Claude Meillassoux, *Femmes, greniers et capitaux* (Paris: Maspero, 1975) (translated as *Maidens, Meal and Money*, Cambridge: Cambridge University Press, 1981); and Pierre-Philippe Rey, 'The Lineage Mode of Production', *Critique of Anthropology*, 3 (1975): 27–79; *Colonialism, néo-colonialism et transition au capitalisme* (Paris: Maspero, 1971), and *Les Alliances des classes* (Paris: Maspero, 1973). Useful reviews are contained in David Seddon, ed., *Relations of Production: Marxist Approaches to Economic Anthropology* (London: Frank Cass, 1978); the special issue of *Critique of Anthropology*, 4, 13 and 14 (Summer 1979); and the review article by Keith Hart, 'The Contribution of Marxism to Economic Anthropology', Paper Presented at the Inaugural Conference of the Society for Economic Anthropology held in Bloomington, Ind. 17–19 April 1981. See also Maurice Bloch, ed., *Marxist Analysis and Social Anthropology* (London: Malaby Press, 1975).

12 For contrasting viewpoints, see, on the side of the substantivists, Karl Polanyi, ed., *Trade and Market in Early Empires* (New York: The Free Press, 1957); and on the side of the formalists, Edward E. LeClair, 'Economic Theory and Economic Anthropology', *American Anthropologist*, 64 (1962): 1179–1203. For an excellent overview and critique, see Scott Cook, 'The Obsolete "Anti-Market" Mentality: A Critique of the Substantive Approach to Economic Anthropology', *American Anthropologist*, 68 (1966): 323–45.

13 Godelier, *Rationality and Irrationality in Economics*, p. 253.

14 Maurice Godelier, *Perspectives in Marxist Anthropology* (Cambridge: Cambridge University Press, 1977), p. 45. For interesting examples of the application of formal reasoning to agrarian 'non-market' institutions, see such works as Dennis L. Chinn, 'Team Cohesion and Collective Labor Supply in Chinese Agriculture', *Journal of Comparative Economics*, 3 (1979): 375–94; Louis Putterman, 'Is Democratic Collective Agriculture Possible? Theoretical Considerations and Evidence from Tanzania', *Journal of Development Studies* (forthcoming); and Clive Bell and Pinhas Zusman, 'A Bargaining Theoretic Approach to Cropsharing Contracts', *American Economic Review*, 66 (September 1976): 578–87.

15 An excellent review of this literature is contained in Gary Fromm, ed., *Studies in Public Regulation* (Cambridge, Mass.: The MIT Press, 1981); see particularly the article by Paul Joskow and Roger Noll, 'Theory and Practice in Public Regulation: A Current Overview'.

16 Nikolai Bukharin, *The Economic Theory of the Leisure Class* (New York and London: Monthly Review Press, 1977), p. 36.

17 The theories of value are equivalent only in very special circumstances: with linear production sets, fixed coefficients, and labor as the only primary (i.e. non-produced) input, then prices are proportional to the value of labor inputs. For a preliminary statement of this result, see Robert Dorfman, Paul Samuelson, and Robert Solow, *Linear Programming and Economic Analysis* (New York: McGraw-Hill, 1958).

18 Bukharin, *The Economic Theory*, pp. 38–9.

19 One of the more engaging treatments of this position in Marx's work is offered by Raymond Firth, 'The Skeptical Anthropologist? Social Anthropology and Marxist Views on Society', in Maurice Bloch, ed., *Marxist Analyses and Social Anthropology* (London: Malaby Press, 1975), pp. 29–60. See also Jon Elster, 'Marxism, Functionalism and Game Theory', unpublished.

20 The list of contributions is too long to summarize. Perhaps the best review, however, is Aidan Foster-Carter, 'The Modes of Production Debate', *New Left Review*, 107 (1978): 47–77; see also John Law, 'In Search of a Marxist Perspective on Pre-Colonial Tropical Africa', *Journal of African History*, 21, 3 (1978): 441–52. Good bibliographies appear regularly in the *Review of African Political Economy*; another is contained in Peter C. W. Gutkind and Immanuel Wallerstein, eds., *The Political Economy of Contemporary Africa* (Beverly Hills, Calif.: Sage Publications, 1976).

21 Robin Palmer and Neil Parsons, eds., *The Roots of Rural Poverty in Central and Southern Africa* (Berkeley and Los Angeles: University of California Press, 1978).

22 Leroy Vail, 'Railway Development and Colonial Underdevelopment', in Palmer and Parsons, eds., *The Roots of Rural Poverty*, pp. 365–95.

23 Martin Legassick, 'Gold, Agriculture, and Secondary Industry in South Africa', in Palmer and Parsons, eds., *The Roots of Rural Poverty*, p. 178.

24 Bogumil Jewsiewicki, 'Unequal Development: Capitalism and the Katanga Economy', in Palmer and Parsons, eds., *The Roots of Rural Poverty*, pp. 317–44.

25 Nicos Poulantzas, *Political Power and Social Classes* (Atlantic Highlands: Humanities, 1975), p. 285, italics mine.

26 A good example of this argument is contained in the so-called 'Kenyan debates'; see, for example, the articles by Rafael Kaplinsky, J. S. Henley, and Colin Leys in *Review of African Political Economy*, 17 (1980).

27 Colin Leys, *Underdevelopment in Kenya* (Berkeley and Los Angeles: University of California Press, 1975).

28 Bill Warren, 'Imperialism and Capitalist Industrialization', *New Left Review*, 81 (1973): 3–44; Richard L. Sklar, 'The Nature of Class Domination in Africa', *The Journal of Modern African Studies*, 17, 4 (1979): 531–52; Colin Leys, 'Capital Accumulation, Class Formation and Dependency: The Significance of the Kenya Case', in Ralph Miliband and John Saville, eds., *The Socialist Register 1978* (New York: Humanities Press, 1978).

29 Poulantzas, *Political Power*. I also identify Anderson with this position, interpreting him as contending that the emerging relative autonomy of the state in the absolutist period in effect saved the aristocracy from itself. See Perry Anderson, *Passages from Antiquity to Feudalism* (London: New Left Books, 1974) and *Lineages of the Absolutist State* (London: New Left Books, 1974).

30 This 'capital logic' theory of Kenya's post-independence development is advanced in Bjorn Beckman, 'Imperialism and Capitalist Transformation: Critique of a Kenyan Debate', *Review of African Political Economy*, 19 (1980): 48–62. See also the position developed by John Lonsdale and Bruce Berman in their articles, 'Coping with the Contradictions: The Development of the Colonial State in Kenya, 1895–1914', *Journal of African History*, 20 (1979): 487–505 and 'Crises of Accumulation, Coercion and the Colonial State: The Development of the Labor Control System in Kenya, 1919–1929', *Canadian Journal of African Studies*, 14, 1 (1980): 37–54. See also James O'Conner, *The Fiscal Crisis of the State* (New York: St Martin's Press, 1973).

31 I use the term 'reduce' advisedly. Recent works by G. A. Cohen and Jon Elster have elaborated the non-reductionist elements in Marxist analysis. The causal elements implicit in Marxist political economy operate, they argue, through a (legitimate) species of functionalism or through intentionality (i.e. human design). Both forms of explanation are, of course, subject to refutation; they are therefore amenable to investigation. In the first, if the effect is present, then it must never be the case that the cause is absent. In Elster's language, functional arguments locate causes in effects; functionality implies necessity (but not sufficiency) in causation. In the second case, empirical tests, to be satisfactory, must generally follow fairly complete analysis and exposition. For the hypothesis of causal design is consistent with a large variety of outcomes, and the particular outcome can depend critically on accidental or institutional features. In the absence of detailed information about the context of choice making, then, non-correlation would appear to be the strongest test of such arguments. See Gerald Allan Cohen, *Karl Marx's Theory of History: A Defence* (London: Oxford University Press, 1978); Jon Elster, *Ulysses and the Sirens* (Cambridge: Cambridge University Press, 1979); and Jon Elster, *Logic and Society* (New York: John Wiley and Sons, 1978).

32 Cohen, *Karl Marx's Theory of History*.

33 My conclusion differs from the position of Theda Skocpol in that she tends to derive the autonomous status of the state from imperatives arising from the interplay of political forces operating at the level of the world system. See *States and Social Revolutions* (Cambridge: Cambridge University Press, 1978). I would not want to rest my argument on such narrow grounds. I diverge from Perry Anderson in that, while I see autonomous political transformations taking place which have decisive implications for underlying economic relationships, I do not necessarily see these political transformations as leading to 'progressive' transformations of the economy. Indeed, the African experience suggests that they can have a disastrous impact upon the development of the economy. See Perry Anderson, *Passages from Antiquity to Feudalism* (London: New Left Books, 1974) and *Lineages of the Absolutist State* (London: New Left Books, 1974).

Index

Index

economic interests, foreign: and colonial African commerce, 86–87, 90–91. *See also* merchant houses, British

Elder Dempster steamship line, 75

elections: colonial, 84; post-independence, 131–32

elites, political, 40, 42, 104, 130; and commoners, 42, 108, 156; and land rights, 65, 98; and nationalist movement, 99, 113. *See also* bureaucracy

Engel's law, 124

erosion, as production externality, 95

Ethiopia, 116

export crops: and taxation, 78; and subsidies, 78, 89, 115; and post-independence government, 112, 113, 118–19

export–import business, West African, 73–74

Fang, the, 57

Fanti, the, 103, 157

farmers, commercial

colonial period: Kenyan compared with Ghanaian cocoa producers, 61–91 passim; and competition for labor, 62–63; and land laws, 64–65; and railway, 66–68; and restraint of competition, 71–73, 158; and collusion, 77–80; and tax protests, 102–03; vs. other interest groups, 132–33

post-independence period: and government economic policy, 107–33 passim; government favoritism toward, 108, 114, 115–16; vs. subsistence farmers, 115–17, 166; vs. other interest groups, 132–33

farmers, settler: and market for labor, 61–62; vs. subsistence farmers, 62, 79, 98, 102–03; and lease of Crown lands, 64–65; distribution of, 78–80; organization of, 79–81, 83; and government representation of, 84–86

farmers, subsistence, 112, 122, 124, 125; colonial restrictions on, 62–63, 64–65, 72, 98, 100, 102, 158; vs. settler farmers, 62, 79, 98, 102–03; politicization of, 92–104 passim; vs. large-scale producers (post-independence), 115–16, 116–17, 127–28, 166

fertilizer, subsidies for, 115, 166

feuding: and political centralization, 14, 23–24, 26, 40, 45; and the slave trade, 37, 53

fisheries, Zambia, collective rights to, 97

food, post-independence, price of: and government subsidies, 114–15; and consumer protests, 121–22; and price-setting coalition, 122–23; compared with consumer goods, 122–23; and organized urban interest, 126. *See also* consumer goods, price of

food crops, 63, 78; and post-independence pricing policies, 107, 108, 111–15, 121–23

food supplies: and post-independence government policy, 112–13, 115; shortages of, 120; percentage of income spent on, 122, 124

'free-rider problem,' 82–83

Ganda, the, 25, 57

Ghana

colonial era: agricultural development in compared with Kenya, 61–90 passim; and market for labor, 62–63; transportation services in, 66, 68–69; and market for capital, 69–71; and export–import business, 73–74; and British economic interests, 86–87; taxpayers revolt in, 103

colonial government of: and land law, 65–66, 80, 99, 100, 101; and cocoa, 69, 75, 87–88, 95–96; and representation of local interests, 83–86; councils of, 83, 84–85, 87, 160; and centralization of power, 86–88; and seizure of 'waste' lands, 98

post-independence government of: and market intervention, 110, 129; political origins of, 113; and agricultural subsidies, 115, 116, 127; and consumer prices, 121–22

gins, cotton, 93–94, 161. *See also* cotton

Gold Coast. *See* Ghana

governments

colonial: structure and operation of re agriculture, 2, 76, 82–91, 93–97, 109, 162; and land laws, 64–65, 98; and producer vs. merchant interests, 82–87, 128, 132; elected vs. appointed representatives to, 84–85

post-independence: agricultural policies of, 107–33 passim; and patterns of market intervention, 108–14, 119, 122, 124–26, 127, 129–30; response of to private interests, 115, 121–26; export crop policy, 118–19; and social welfare, 118–21, 131; regulatory structure of and political power, 129–31

grain, 72, 113–14

grazing, collective, as production externality, 97

Great Britain, chambers of commerce in: and colonial African economic policy, 86–87, 160. *See also* economic interests, foreign; merchant houses, British

Griffith, Colonel, 73

6541 19 89